I0800251

IMAGES
of America

TANEY COUNTY MISSOURI

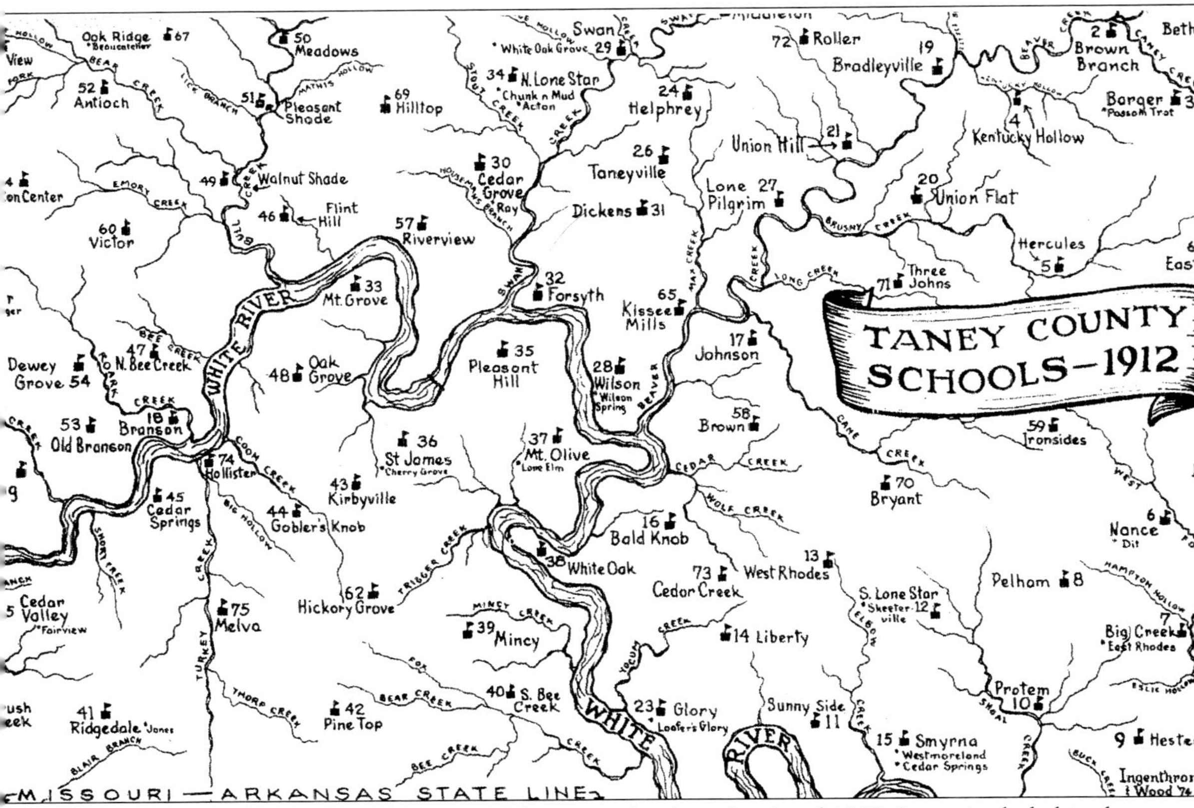

The above map is of Taney County, Missouri, schools and is dated 1912. It was included in the historical book written by Taney County native and author, Elmo Ingenthorn, entitled *The Land of Taney*, a history of an Ozark commonwealth, Ozark Regional History Series, Book II, published by The Ozarks Mountaineer regional magazine and bookstore in Kirbyville, Missouri. This shows the location of the numerous small community areas mentioned in *Images of America: Taney County*. This allows the reader a more comprehensive understanding of the geographic connection between schools and towns surrounding and centered along the White River, which was of major importance to the early Taney County pioneers during the mid-to-late 1800s and on into the 1900s.

IMAGES
of America

TANEY COUNTY MISSOURI

Vickie Layton Cobb

ARCADIA
PUBLISHING

ISBN 978-0-7385-1850-3

Published by Arcadia Publishing
Charleston, South Carolina

Printed in the United States of America

Library of Congress Catalog Card Number: 2001090052

For all general information contact Arcadia Publishing at:
Telephone 843-853-2070
Fax 843-853-0044
E-mail sales@arcadiapublishing.com
For customer service and orders:
Toll-Free 1-888-313-2665

Visit us on the Internet at www.arcadiapublishing.com

Contents

ACKNOWLEDGMENTS

The collection of historical information for the photographs and their captions came from the many people of Taney County and elsewhere. It would be impossible to list them all by name.

The author's grandparents, Randa and Ethel (Smith) Layton, both deceased, gave birth to the idea. Especially Randa, when he verbally shared his "recollections" of early Taney County, and told his granddaughter one morning at their breakfast table over biscuits with gravy and hot coffee prepared on grandma's old wood cook stove, "you ought to write some of this down." The seed was planted that winter morning in 1982, and from then on this collection grew. Not only did Randa and Ethel share memories and stories told to them by relatives who lived before them, but also photographs.

Like mining for precious jewels, other "old timers," also deceased, from Taney County began to do the same by sharing their historical as well as first-hand knowledge of the area and photographs that had been tucked away in boxes, old family albums, and trunks. It is to those who knew Taney County in the beginning, and those yet beyond the age of 70 at present, that gave life to this historical anthology.

INTRODUCTION

The history of Taney County, Missouri, is close to the lives and heritage of its people, who are direct descendants of the county's earliest pioneer families. Yet its history is a part of our American heritage, which makes our national and state history complete. Jackson Street in Forsyth, the county seat, was named after president Andrew Jackson. Taney County obtained its name from Roger B. Taney, who married Anne Key, the sister of Francis Scott Key, who wrote the words to our national anthem.

The White River was an important element, providing food, transportation, commerce, and the operation of numerous water-powered mills. These mills provided a steady flow of water with a vigorous current from its tributaries in pioneer times when corn was ground there.

Taney County was noteworthy for the abundance of honeybees making honey and beeswax from the honeycomb. Other agriculture products were tomatoes, with canning factories all along the White River. Mules, cattle, hogs, chickens, eggs, turkeys, corn, wheat, fruits, vegetables, timber, and hay created a vast industrial market for southwest Missouri as a whole.

Mining in Taney County centered on lead ore, which contains sulfur and often zinc, along with traces of silver. In 1890, members of the Turkey Creek Mining Company became a permanent organization, with J.E. Cobb as secretary. The Josie "B" Mine and the Silver Moon mine along Turkey Creek initiated the formation of the company.

Taney County and Branson are noted today for being among America's top tourist areas, with Silver Dollar City, the Shepherd of the Hills outdoor theme park based on Harold Bell Wright's novel, *The Shepherd of The Hills*. Table Rock Lake, Bull Shoals Lake, and the Buffalo River provide campgrounds and fishing. Branson is also home to many national entertainers, and is known as the Nashville of the Ozarks.

This book is a continuation of the author's contribution to the literary and historical collection from previously self-published books entitled *Fallen Leaves*, Volumes One and Two.

So embark on a journey with self-sufficient pioneers who traveled from different areas of America in the mid-1800s and homesteaded in the southwest part of Missouri, known as Taney County. Experience the love they had for each other and the new land upon which they built homes with determination to fulfill their dreams in Taney County, the land of their visions.

This book is dedicated to the author's family, those in the past who were the first to come and to those in the present and the future.

FALLEN LEAVES

Fallen leaves gently fall
from all of God's trees.
Their beauty and splendor disappear
but not even death can claim their memory.

Their lives resemble the passing of a quiet,
peaceful, flowing country stream.
Their spirits vanish into a hidden realm
the living know only in their dreams.

Although their earthly life has ended
another is born to take its place.
And that new life too, has its own
tears to cry and trials to face.

The ever changing cycle of life
is a deep spiritual mystery.
Every leaf that falleth from the tree of life
falls into the unknown hand of eternity.

Vickie Layton Cobb

One

EARLY PIONEERS

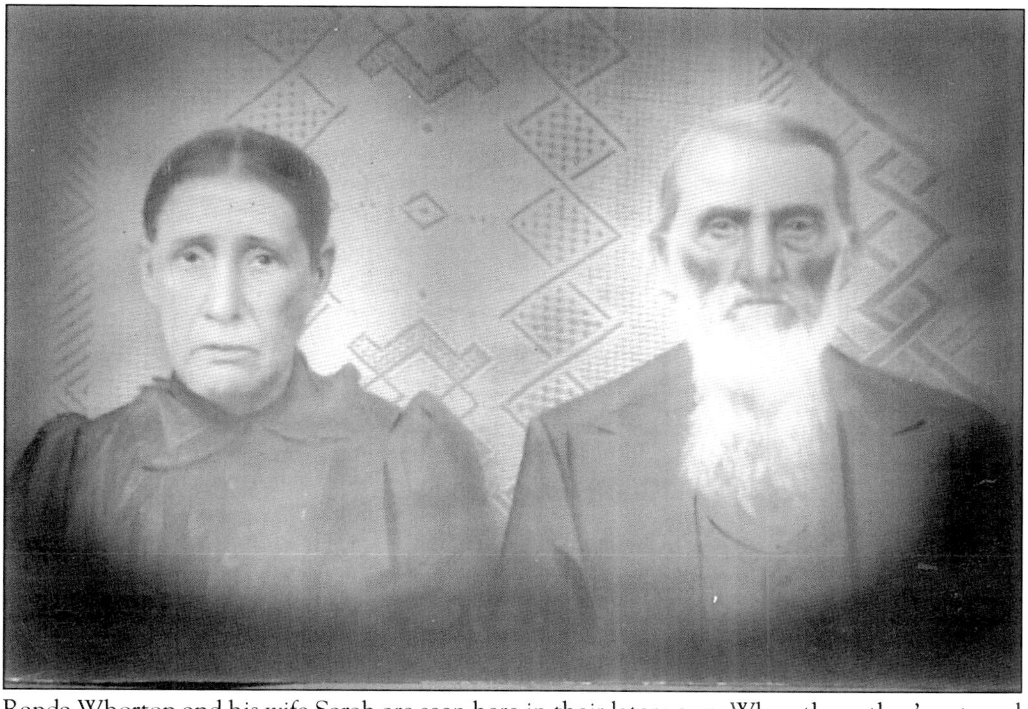

Randa Whorton and his wife Sarah are seen here in their later years. When the author's paternal grandfather, Randa Layton, was six years old, his father died of pneumonia. Randa's mother, Safronea, was the daughter of Randa and Sarah Whorton. Randa Layton's childhood was centered on the Whorton family. Randa Layton told the author stories he heard from his grandfather and grandmother Whorton about the Civil War, Indians, panthers, and pioneer wagon train journeys. Considerable amounts of historical data collected for this book were passed down by "word of mouth" from the author's great-great maternal grandparents, Randa and Sarah, through the author's grandfather, Randa Layton, and many more of the Ozark pioneers.

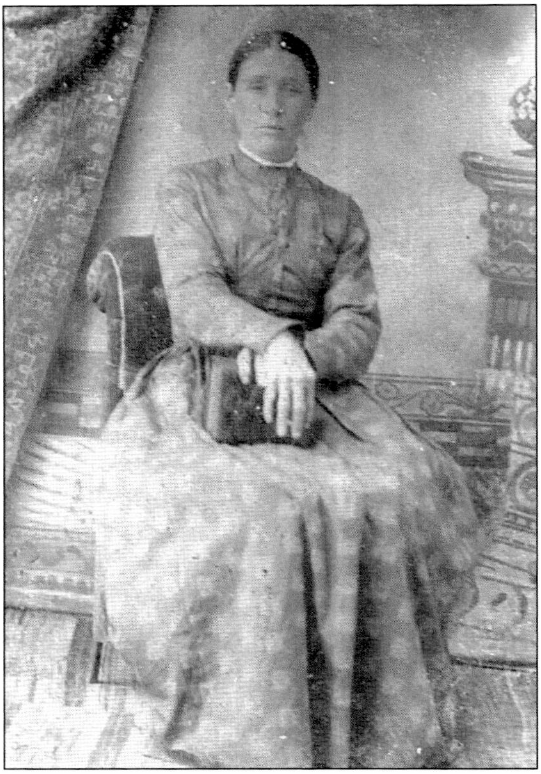

Sarah Catherine Bollinger-Whorton endured hardships unknown today. She was separated from her husband, Randa, who fought in the Civil War with no communication except an occasional letter. There was no Internet, e-mail, or www.whatever.com. There was only their faith in God. They lived one day at a time, hoping for the best until peace was finally declared. Her struggles during the Civil War included keeping the homestead and family members together safely. There were times when the enemy soldiers searched the cabin for food and other vital necessities. Once, they tied her hands together over the ceiling rafter, trying to force her to tell them where their money and food were hidden. But she did not give in to their demands. The soldiers poked their bayonets into the floorboards, searching for a clue of where things were hid. But she had hidden food, money, etc., inside barrels secured in the barn, and the soldiers never found them. When the war ended, she and Randa were reunited eye to eye, and returned home together hand in hand.

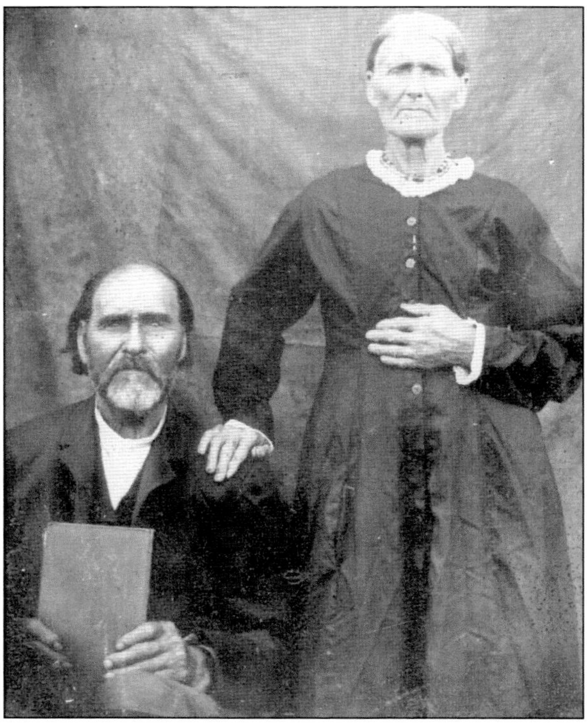

Randa Whorton's parents, Jepthah and Dollie Whorton, lived in Kingston, Arkansas, in Madison County during the 1840s, on the Whorton homestead by Whorton Creek. After the Civil War, former slaves once belonging to the Whorton family established the community of "Whorton." The slaves were considered like family and were buried in the Whorton family cemetery. In 1881, Dollie, now blind, journeyed with Randa and Sarah Whorton to Hollister, Missouri, and lived the remainder of her life on the first Taney County Whorton homestead. Upon her death, her body was hauled by wagon and team back to Kingston and laid to rest beside her husband Jepthah.

This photograph of Elizabeth (Lizzie) Whorton with her daughter and a pet fox was taken before the Civil War. Lizzie was one of Jepthah and Dollie Whorton's daughters. Toward the end of summer in the first year of the Civil War, Lizzie dreamed about her father Jepthah's death. She believed God was forewarning her in a dream that three men would approach the homestead on horseback, tie Jepthah's hands behind his back, order him to mount his horse, then follow him into a wooded area and shoot him. Lizzie begged him to ride to the Army Post and stay, but he refused to heed his daughter's warning. Then one day as he worked in the field hoeing corn, three men approached, and the gruesome dream became reality as the family followed them into the woods and watched as Jepthah was shot before their horrified eyes. The last words he spoke as he lay dying with his head cradled in Lizzie's lap were, "tell the boys to kill 'em!"

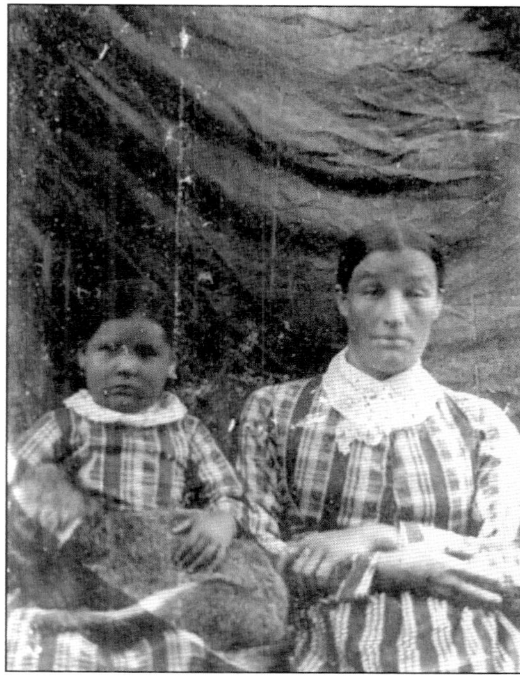

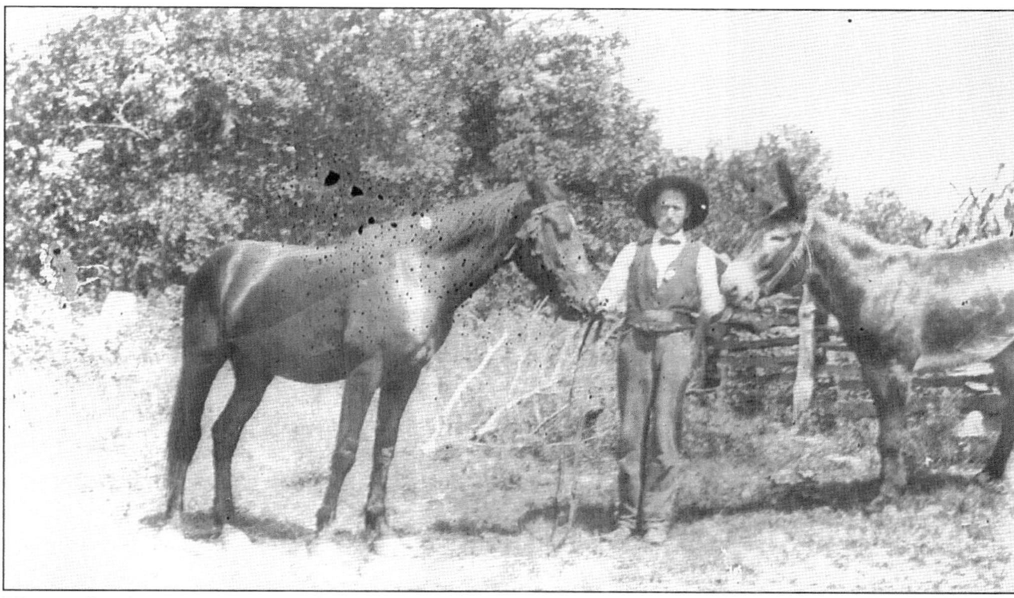

The author's great-great uncle, Jepp Whorton, was one of Randa and Sarah Whorton's sons. He was a horse and mule trader, and is shown here dressed up with a fine horse and mule in the latter 1880s. He was an expert rifleman, hunter, and trapper. When he was a little boy during the Civil War, he and his father Randa, along with some of his brothers and brothers-in-law, were away fighting. Jepp traveled by horseback with his mother to an Army refugee camp. It was in the cold of winter as they crossed partially frozen creeks, and his mother Sarah's shoes froze to the saddle stirrups. To free her from the ice-covered stirrups, he had to slide off the horse's back and take a stick or rock to break them loose.

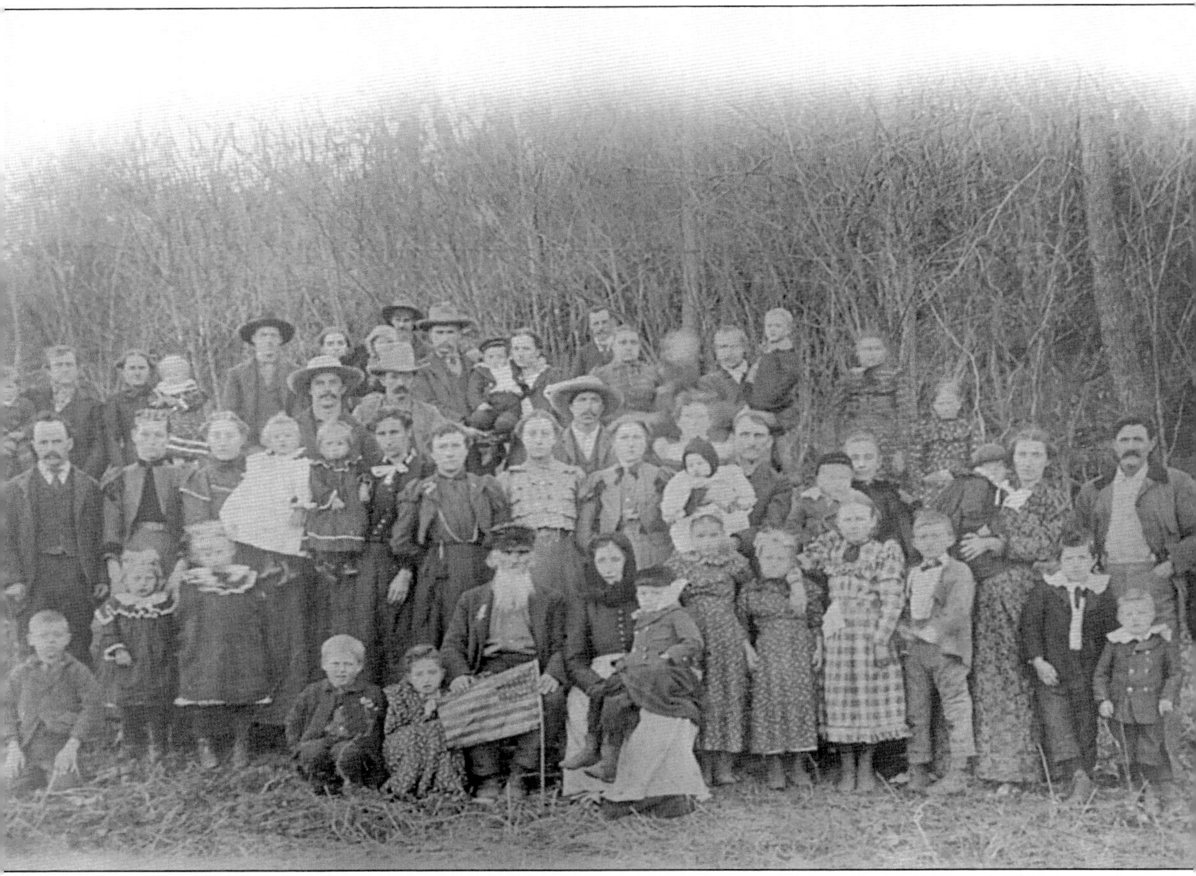

The "Whorton Reunion" photograph was taken in 1900, at Randa and Sarah Whorton's homestead on Turkey Creek in Hollister, Missouri. They are, from left to right: (front row) Tommy Strahan (boy kneeling), two girls are Annie and Emy Rittenhouse, boy and girl kneeling are Andy Whorton and Mattie Burks, Randa Whorton holds the flag, his wife Sarah holds Clem Whorton, three young girls are Maudie Burks, Tilda Burks, and Mollie Whorton, then Lester Breshears, Ben Layton, Randa Layton, and Walter Whorton; (second row) Isaac and Sinea Whorton Strahan, Mandy Whorton Rittenhouse, two babies are Alford Rittenhouse and Becky Burks, Mallie Whorton Burks, Martha Breshears, Ollie Whorton, Dollie Whorton, baby is Esby Whorton held by Newt Whorton, small boy is Clyde Whorton held by Lydia Rittenhouse Whorton, Edna Layton, baby with head on shoulder of her mother, Safronea Whorton Layton, then, her husband William David Layton; (third row) boy is Albert Whorton held by Gemes Whorton, Almede Whorton holds Margie Whorton, three men with hats and mustaches are Dave Rittenhouse, Jim Burks, and John Rittenhouse, then Maude Whorton Rittenhouse; (back row) man with hat is Dick Whorton, Millie Whorton holds Oscar Whorton, two men with hats and mustaches are George Breshears and Johnny Whorton, child is Paul Whorton held by Mrs. Johnny Whorton, Green Brantly, Kezia McGown Whorton, Les Whorton, Jepp Whorton holds Alvin Whorton, Rosa Swartz, and Nora Spruce. Identification to those in the photograph was obtained from the author's grandfather, Randa Layton, and his two sisters, Edna and Ollie, in an interview conducted in the early 1980s.

John Warmack and his wife are seen in this photograph taken in 1864. They were relatives of Randa and Sarah Whorton.

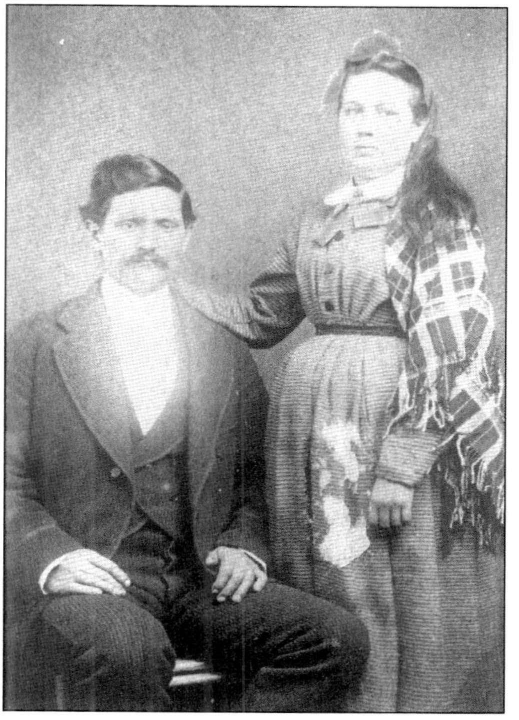

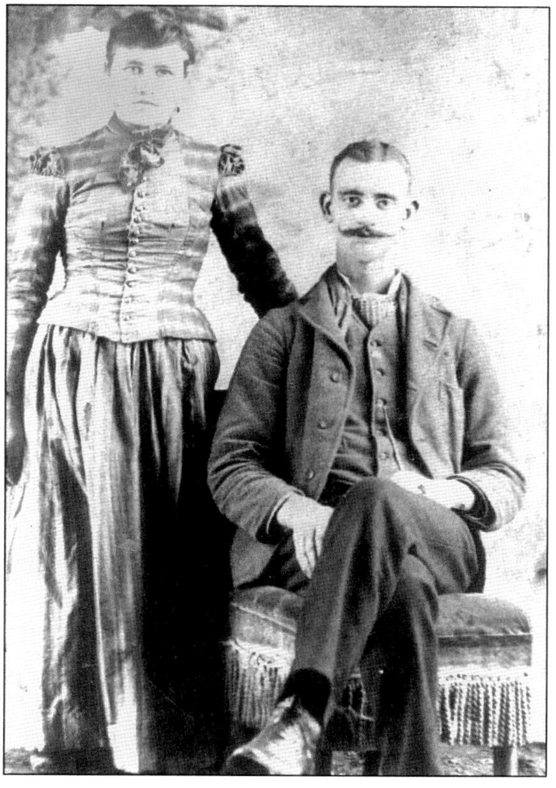

Martha Ann Tanner and Ugene Vanzandt from Kirbyville are seen here. They were friends of the author's great maternal grandmother, Safronea Whorton Layton. The Vanzandt Cemetery east of Branson in Kirbyville was named after the local Vanzandt family.

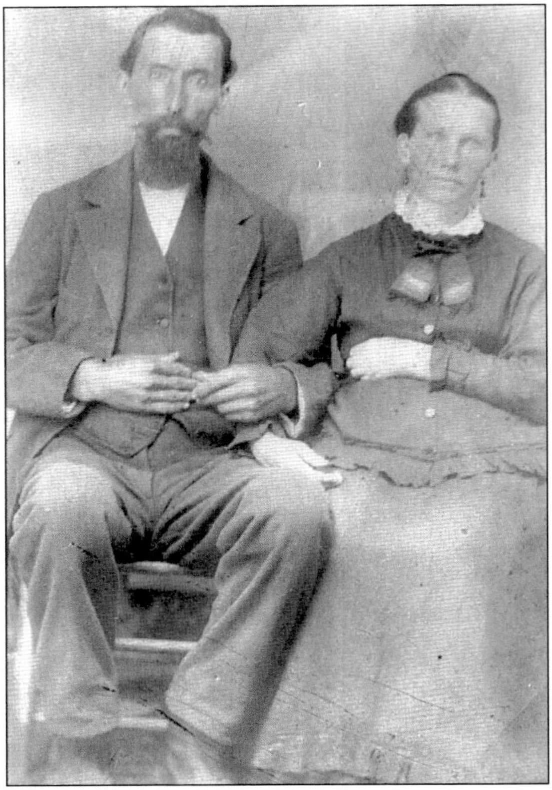

Photographed here are Jehew and Mollie Johnson. Mollie was Randa Whorton's sister Lavica's daughter, who was married to John Ralston. Lavica and John lived near the Whorton homestead on Turkey Creek. After Jehew and Mollie married, they left Turkey Creek and moved to Rogersville, Missouri. They had one son named Tom. After Jehew's death, Mollie lived to be in her mid-eighties, and often returned to visit the Whorton family in Taney County.

Pictured here is Safronea Whorton Layton's 160-acre homestead cabin in Oak Grove east of Branson. The cabin was built prior to the Civil War, and she purchased it from Douglas Mahnkey's grandfather, Alonzo S. Prather. Safronea stands near the fireplace as her son Lonnie and Margaret LeVey feed the chickens and turkeys. This photo was taken in the 1930s.

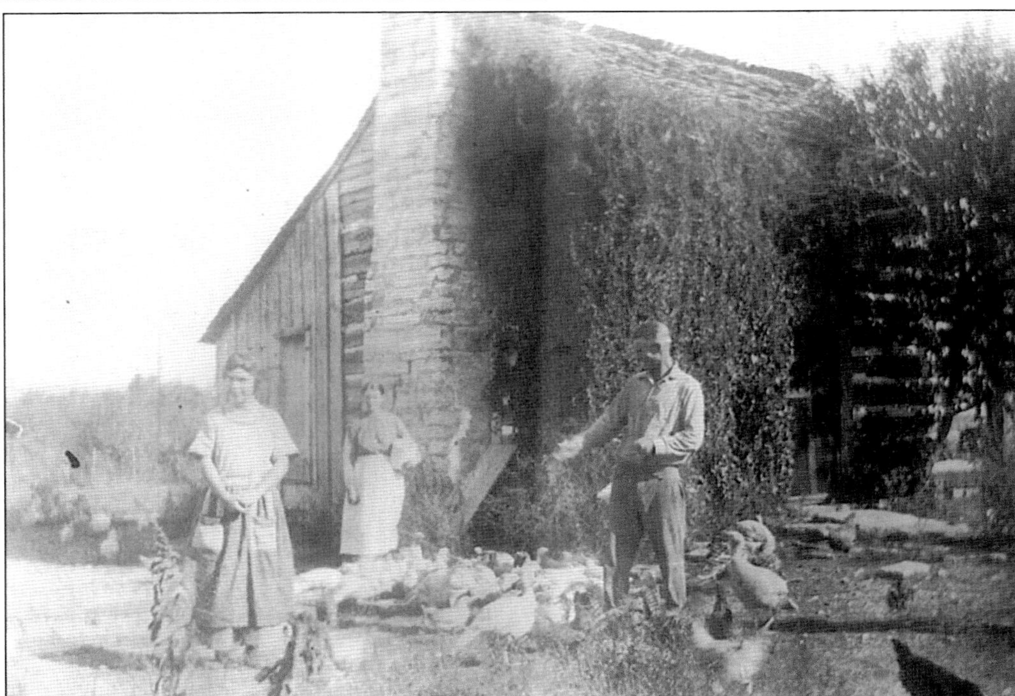

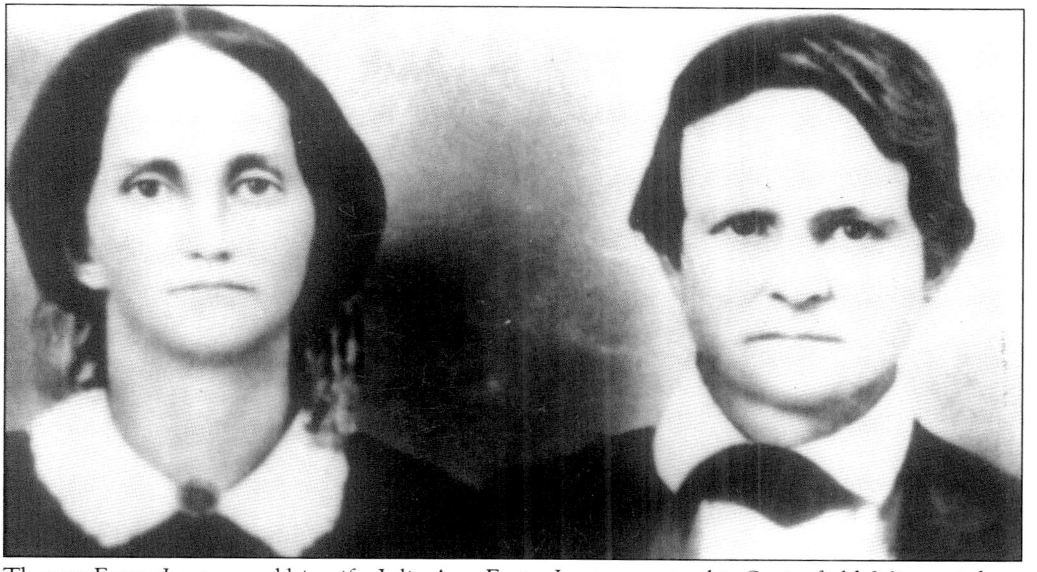

Thomas Foster Layton and his wife, Julia Ann Foster Layton, arrived in Springfield, Missouri, from Virginia, in the 1850s. Thomas opened the first mercantile store in Springfield, and was also a carpenter, building cabinets while Julia sewed for the wealthy Springfield men. Leaving Springfield, the Layton's homesteaded 160 acres south of Hollister, near Turkey Creek in the mid-1850s. Layton established "The Pinery" sawmill, including a general store and post office, and became known as the "Town of Layton." After the Civil War, Thomas became a politician and educator. It was quoted one time when Thomas was questioned about why he was misquoting some of the people on their taxes (supposedly, it was told they were Union sympathizers); his answer was "it was the only way we had to get even for loosing the war!" That was certainly a direct answer.

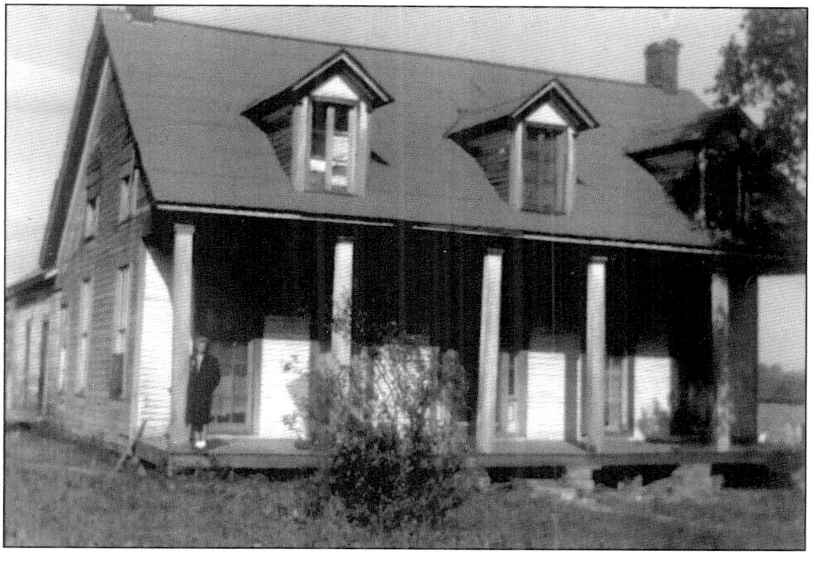

This is the house Tom and Julia Layton built when they homesteaded in Hollister. It took seven years to complete. The lumber used was sawed at Layton's sawmill. The hand rails to the stairway were hand carved by Jackie Breedon of Mildred. The author is a descendent of both men. The mansion was torn down in the 1960s, and Layton descendants, who still live on the original homestead, built another. Charlene Layton Rowland leans against the porch post on the far left of the old mansion. Legends passed down tell that the spirit of Julia haunted the old mansion after her death.

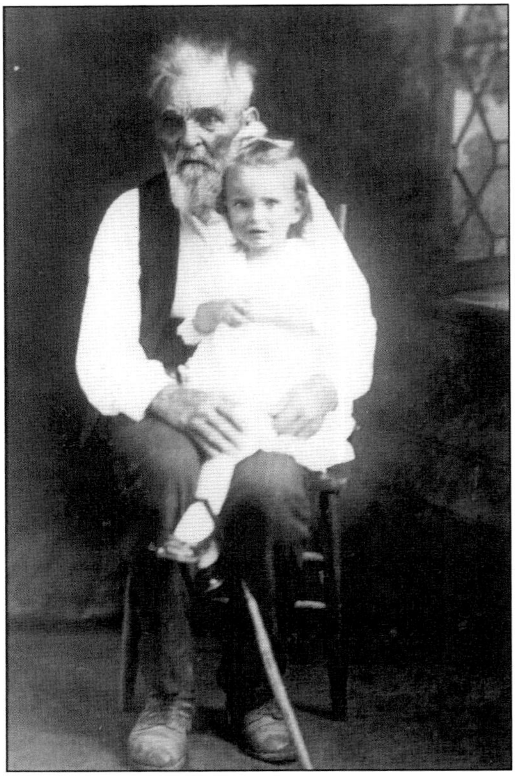

Jackie Breedon and his granddaughter, Ethel McCarty, are seen here. Jackie would hold Ethel in his lap, take out his billfold, open it, and say, "Ethel, take all the money you want." The Breedon family members were some of the first homesteaders to settle in the Mildred and Kirbyville area between Branson and Forsyth. Jackie is the author's great-great paternal grandfather. He was a carpenter and worked for Thomas Layton in the building of the "Layton Mansion."

The Breedon homestead is pictured here. Jackie Breedon is seated to the left of his wife. The home was built in the 1850s or '60s. It has since been remodeled and still stands today as of the year 2001.

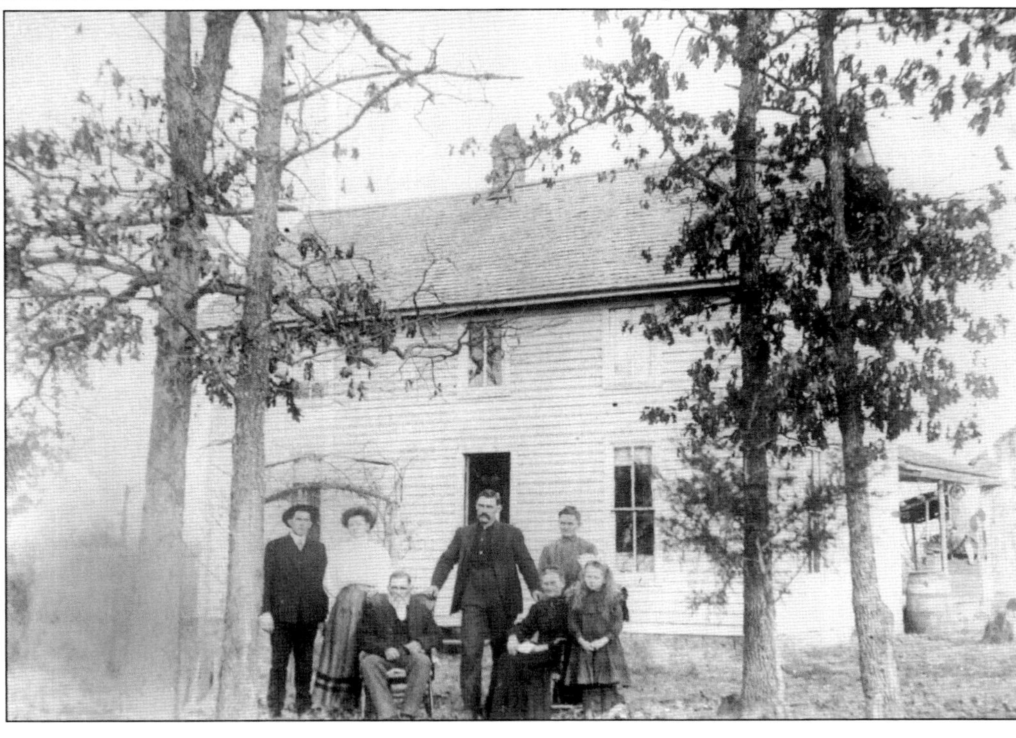

Jackie Breedon, or "Uncle Jackie" as he was known in his later days, is photographed here. He was the grandfather of the author's grandmother, Sallie Haworth Cobb.

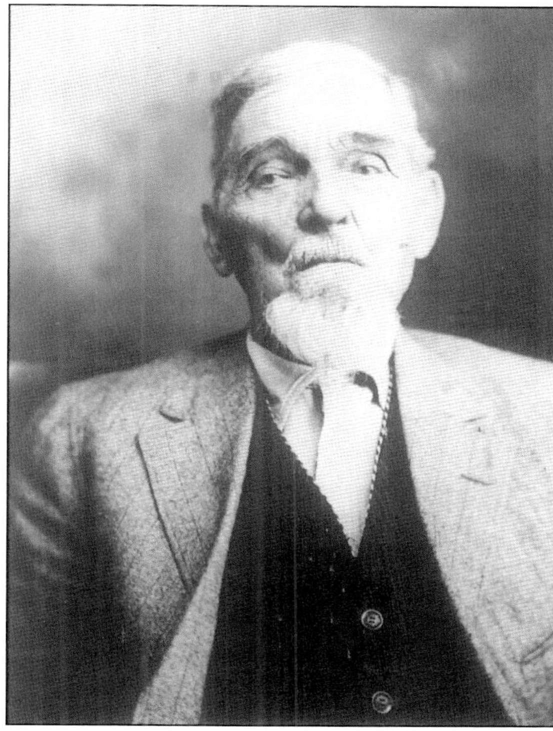

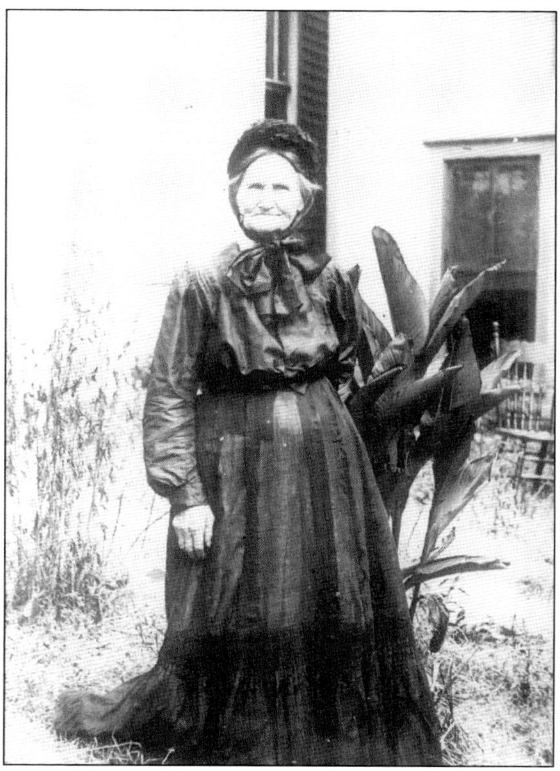

Pictured here is Jackie Breedon's wife. Her first name is not known. She is the great-great-grandmother of the author.

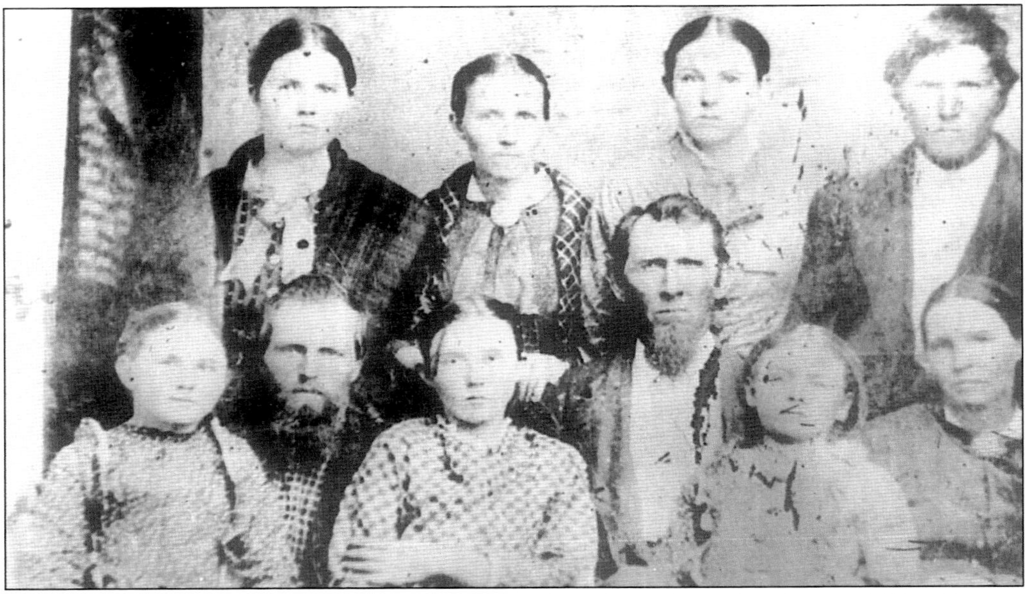

The John Byrd and Murana (Layton) Bedford family is shown here after the Civil War. Murana was Thomas Layton's sister. The second girl in the front row with her arm across her lap is the grandmother of Bobby Pruitt, photo contributor. Thomas Layton wrote letters to John Bedford in 1849, describing his journey to Sacramento, California, during the gold rush days when he guided an expedition driving 1,500 head of cattle to provide meat for the gold miners. While Murana was close to delivering Mary, John refused to leave for California with Thomas Layton until she gave birth and he knew all was well. This held up the California gold party's departure to Sacramento for three weeks. Layton guided this expedition in 1850. The Bedford's farm joined the Pruitt family's farm at the mouth of Mincy Creek. Bedford lived in Strafford, Missouri, in 1861, but moved his family to Taney County after the Civil War ended.

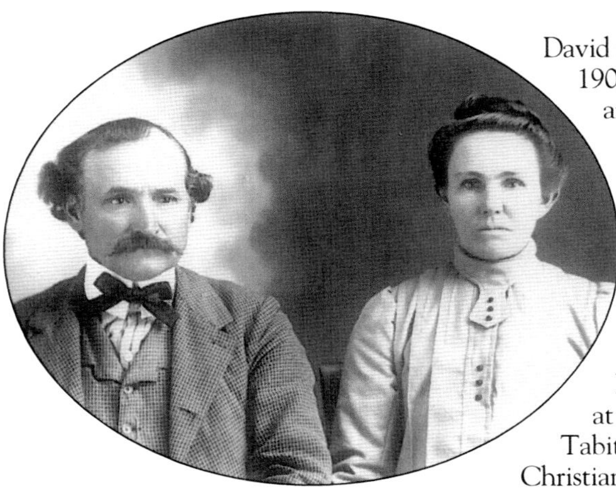

David and Tabitha Pruitt are shown here in 1900. David was the son of Andrew Jackson and Jane (Cameron) Pruitt. He was born in 1858, in Frankfort, Missouri, and died in 1945, in Grants Pass, Oregon. Tabitha's parents were John and Murana Bedford. Tabitha was born in Strafford, Missouri, in 1861. She died in 1940, in Grants Pass, Oregon. Their families moved to Taney County, Missouri, when David and Tabitha were small children. The Pruitt and Bedford families were neighbors at the mouth of Mincy Creek. David and Tabitha married in the Mincy Valley Baptist Christian Church, Easter Sunday in 1878. They left the church together on one horse. David had been secretary of the church at the age of 18, two years before their marriage. Their first two children, Sid and Cordelia, were born at Mincy; Robert at Kirbyville; Lula at Mincy; and Ben at Cedar Creek. From there, David and Tabitha with their wagon, along with 11 other families and wagons, headed to Oklahoma for the first land opening in 1889.

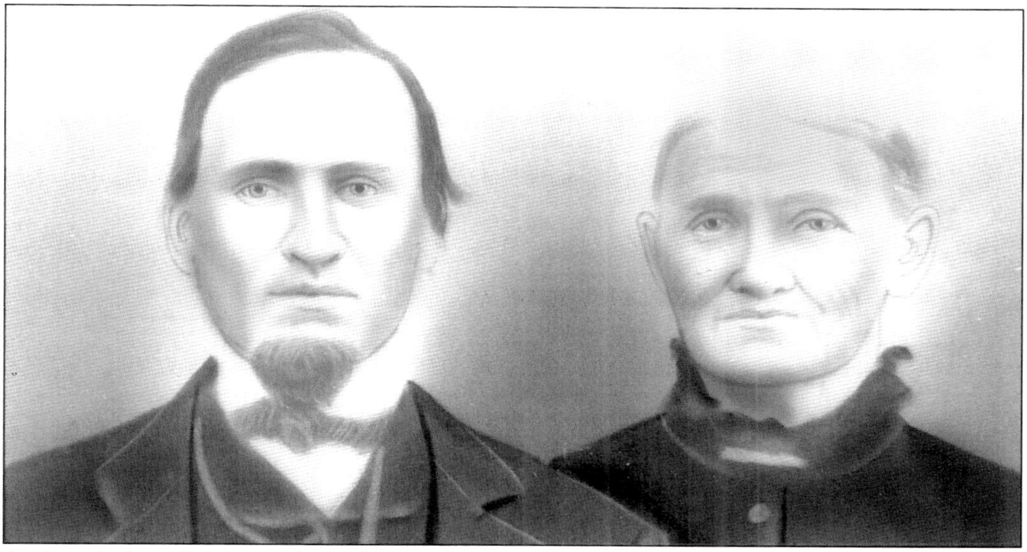

Andrew Jackson Pruitt and his wife Jane (Cameron) Pruitt are pictured here before 1879. Joseph Howard Cameron, Jane's father, came to Missouri from Tennessee, with Andrew and Jane, along with their two small boys in the mid-1850s. They settled in Frankfort, Missouri, of Saline County. Joseph, at the age of 100, drove the ox-drawn covered wagon, walking beside them carrying a staff to help support him as he walked. More children were born to Andrew and Jane while in Frankfort. They moved to Taney County and settled on the old Campbell place in Mincy, southeast of Branson. When Joseph was 107, he was thrown from a horse and lived three more years as an invalid. He died when he was 110, and is buried in Taney County.

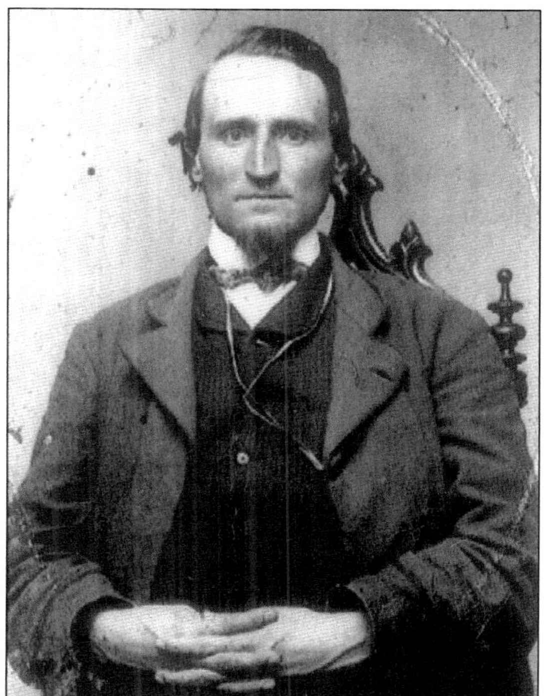

Andrew Pruitt taught school at Forsyth in Taney County. He was a lawyer specializing in pensions for Civil War widows. Andrew and his half brother, James Nathaniel Pruitt, fought together in the Civil War. Before the family moved from Frankfort, Missouri, a band of Union Soldiers rode their horses to the one-room schoolhouse where Andrew taught. He dismissed school. Not going home, he went with the soldiers on what must have been "urgent business," according to family history. He was captured three times during the Civil War, escaped twice barefooted, and was in a prisoner trade once. He died at age 49, in 1879, with pneumonia in Taney County.

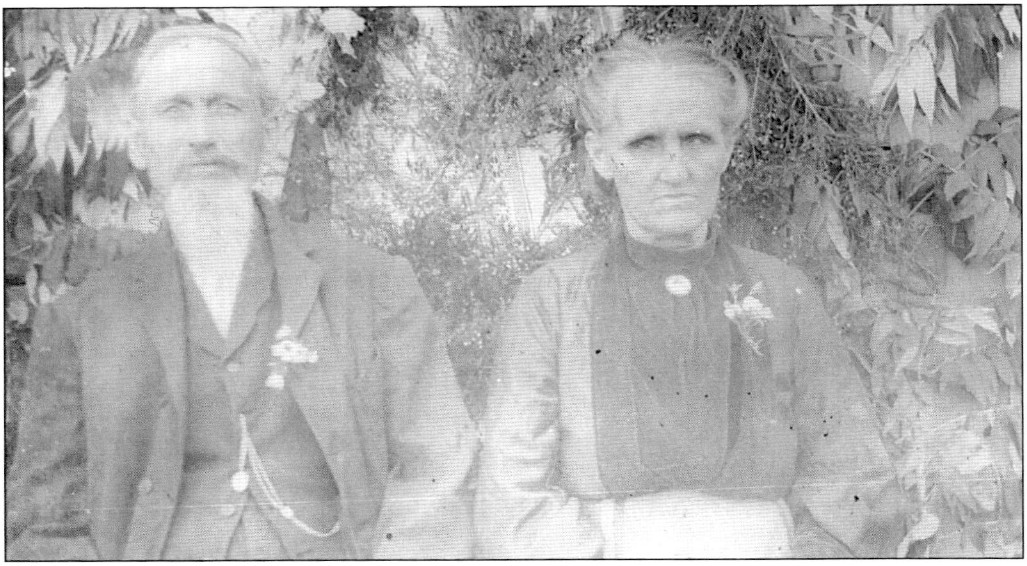

Charles H. and Laura Camille Jones Cobb left Vandalia, Illinois, with four children in 1879. He was 33, and she was 28. They homesteaded 160 acres, 1.5 miles east of the Highway 76 East and MM intersection south of Forsyth, east of where the Mildred store was located. They journeyed to Taney County in an ox-drawn wagon. Laura was part Cherokee Indian. She rode a high-spirited jet-black horse named Ebony. It was spoken of her that she "sat tall in the saddle and straight as an arrow" when Ebony walked on his hind feet. They are the author's great-great paternal grandparents.

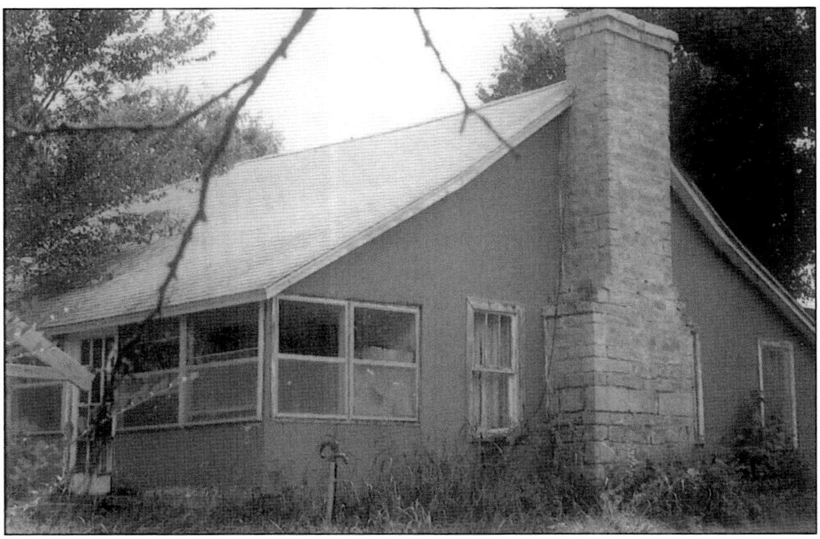

The Charles and Laura Cobb home is seen here as it appeared in 1990. The Cobbs built the log house when they first homesteaded. Later, the cabin was boxed in and the home remodeled. The chimney shown here is the one Charles built with his own hands. It was told that Charles concealed an ax in the old cellar part of the log house in case a tornado came through the area. He planned ahead in preparation to have the ax already there should he and his family have to take shelter during a storm, and the need might arise that he would have to hack their way out from debris above. Whether or not the old ax was ever discovered has always remained a mystery. At least none of the relatives who lived there following his death ever knew of its whereabouts.

Shown here are the author's paternal great-grandparents, James and Mary Francis Warner Cobb. They lived on the Blackwell Ferry Road in the Mildred community near Mt. Olives Church and schoolhouse. The school was previously named "Lone Elm." James and Mary were farmers. Today, the concrete foundation to the molasses mill once used to make their yearly supply of sorghum molasses from the cane crop is still visible from the road through the dense brush overgrowth. James was a son of Charles and Laura Cobb, the first Cobbs to settle in Taney County. One of Charles' brothers' daughters, Zeralda Cobb, married Jesse James, the famous outlaw from St. Joseph, Missouri.

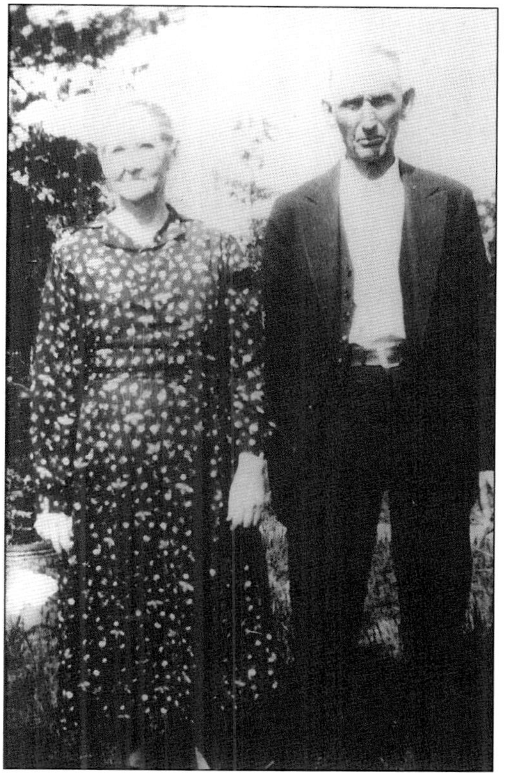

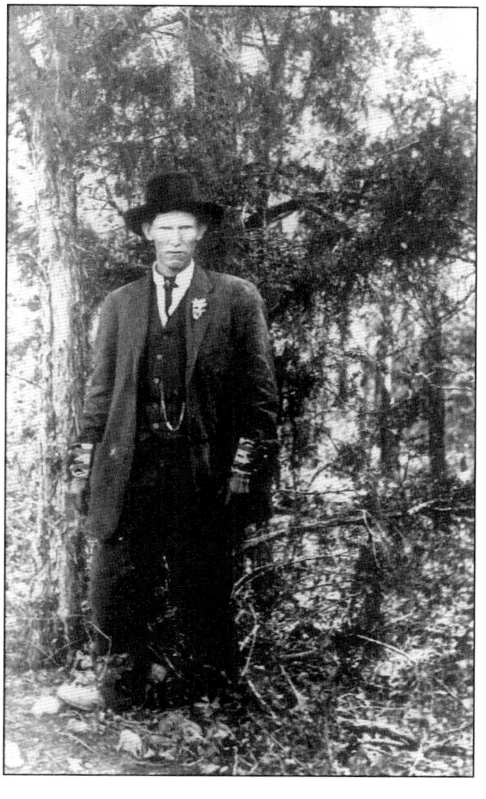

Jim Warner, who was Mary Warner Cobb's brother, was an ordained minister of the Baptist faith. He had sandy-red-colored hair. He worked for the Public Works in Oklahoma several years before he returned to Taney County in the early 1900s, and he lived in the Mildred and Mt. Olives area until his death. He married Melvina Edwards.

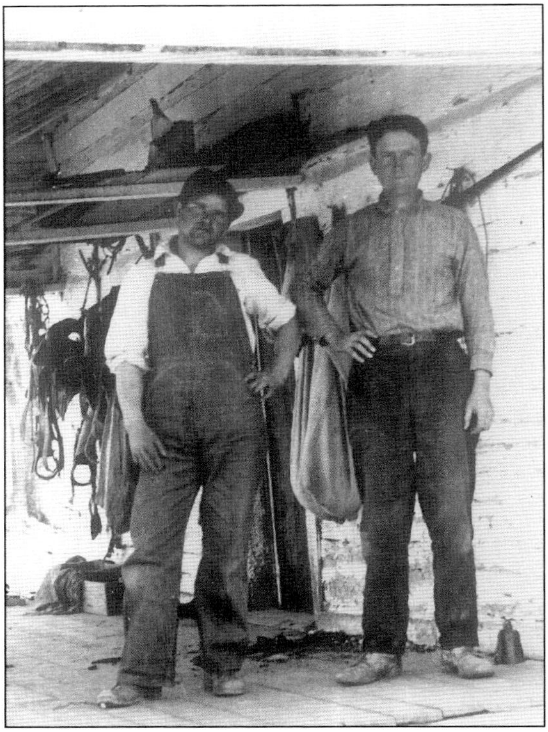

Sam Isum and Jess Cobb are photographed here. Sam was a preacher, and Jess was James Cobb's brother. Both men lived along the Blackwell Ferry Road in the Mildred community.

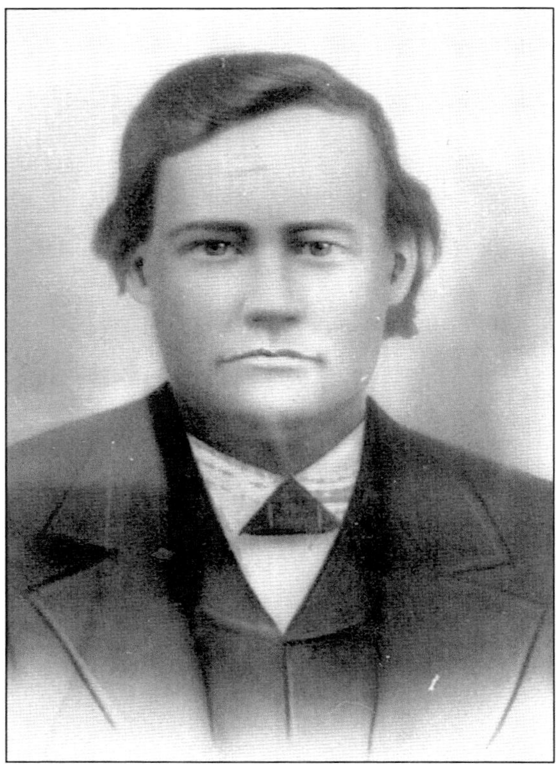

Edwin Harphan Warner was Mary Francis Warner Cobb's father. Edwin left Taney County in the 1890s for work in the Oklahoma hayfields. He died and was buried there.

Addie M. Crouch Warner was Edwin Warner's wife. She was a subscription schoolteacher in the 1890s, at a local Taney County school. A subscription school was where parents paid $1 or $2 per child per month. Addie died while in her forties, and is buried in Aurora, Missouri. She was Cherokee Indian.

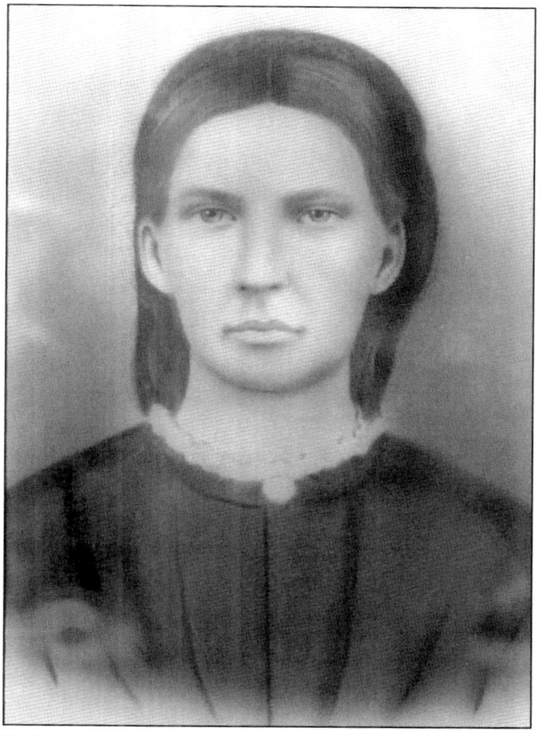

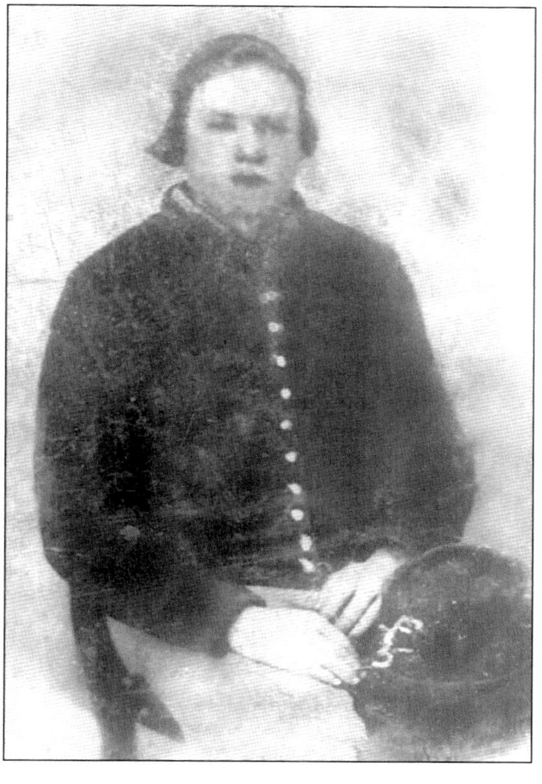

Edwin Harphan Warner is seen here in his Civil War uniform, while he was still a soldier. No information of his military record was available. This photo is courtesy of Dorothy West from Neodesha, Kansas. She found a tintype photograph of Edwin in her grandmother's belongings after her death. Written on the back of the piece of paper wrapped around the tintype were the words "this is my father Warner in Arme." The word "Army" was evidently misspelled.

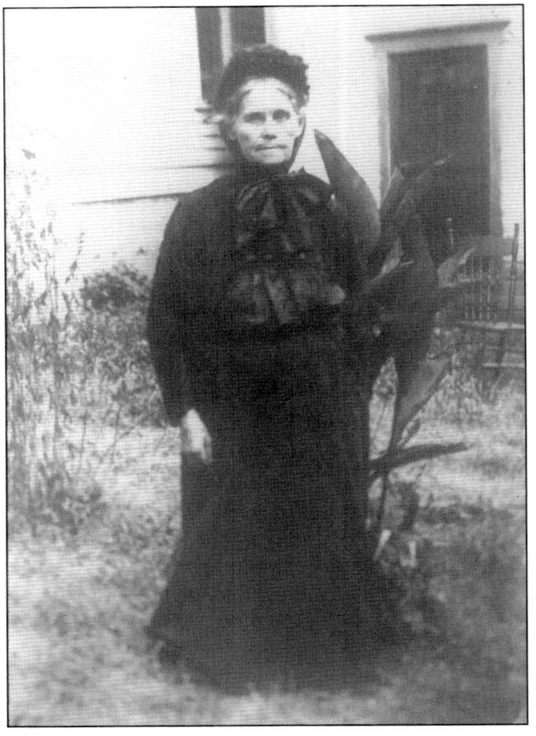

Sallie Haworth Cobb's aunt, Emily Halley, married a man by the name of Al Morris.

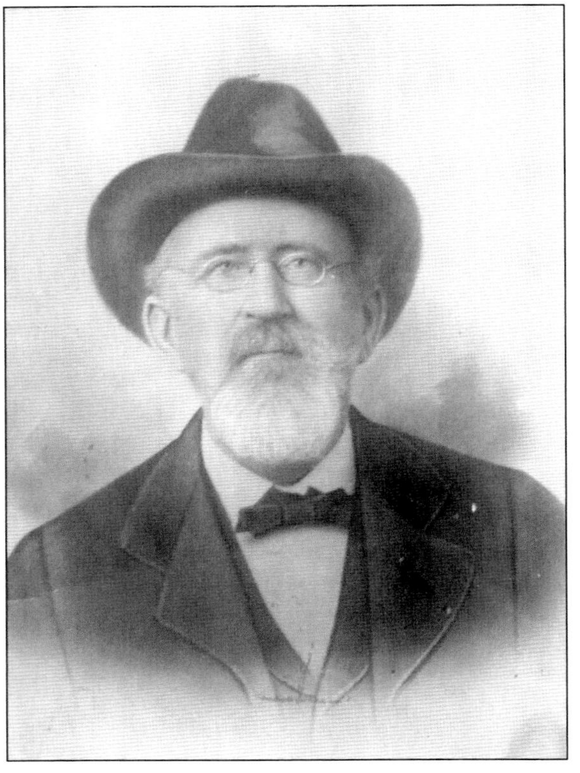

Jordan (Jurd) Haworth was John Haworth's uncle. He adopted John at 13, following his father's death. John's mother died when he was four. John was Sallie Haworth Cobb's father. Jurd was an old-time Baptist preacher who drove a horse and buggy.

This is Jordan Haworth's wife, Mary.

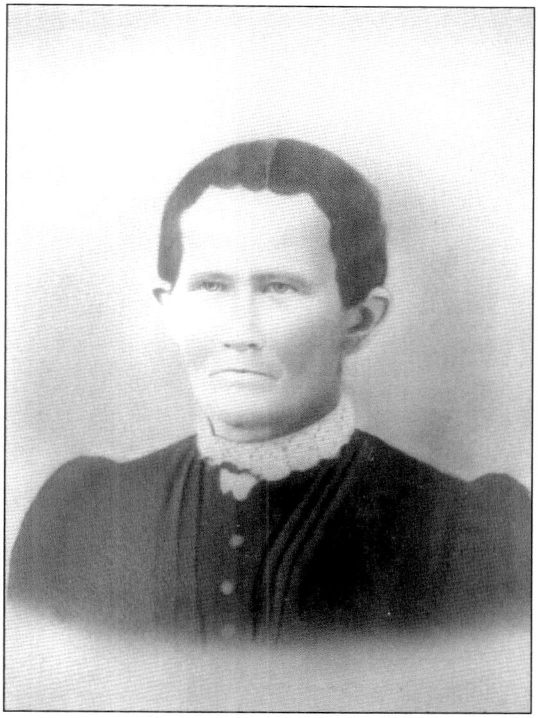

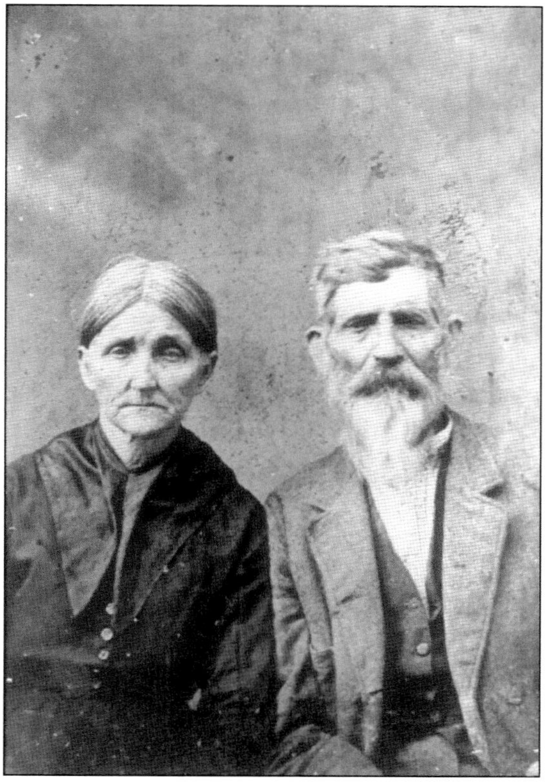

Peter and Nancy Cancada Ward Smith are shown here. He was born in 1828, and died in 1903. Nancy was born in 1831, and died in 1912. They left Georgia in 1870, in an ox-drawn wagon. It took them three months to reach Taney County. They homesteaded 160 acres in Kirbyville. Nancy was full-blooded Cherokee Indian. Their journey started out on the "Trail of Tears," en route to Oklahoma. Upon reaching Taney County, they settled east of Branson, instead of traveling on to Oklahoma. One year, Peter sold a yearling colt for $15. Back then, that was quite a sum of money. It was told that Peter said of the $15, "why that's more money than a family can spend in a year!"

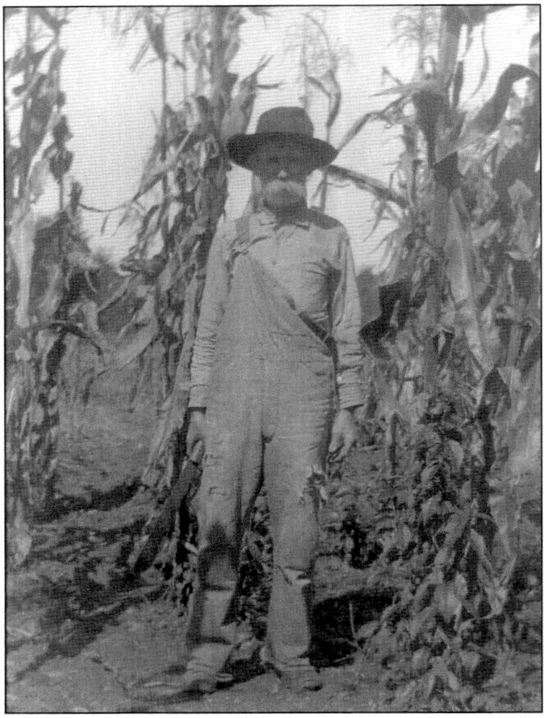

Tom Smith worked his cane corn crop on their Kirbyville farm about 1930 (note the machete in his right hand). Tom was born in 1859, and died in 1940. His wife Mary used lye from her ash hopper to make hominy from the cane corn kernels. An ash hopper was a wooden barrel with holes in the bottom and sat on boards with one side lower than the other. In the winter, ashes from the stove were put in the hopper. In the spring, Mary added water to the ashes. Underneath the barrel, a stone crock was placed. The reddish colored water that dripped into the crock was called lye.

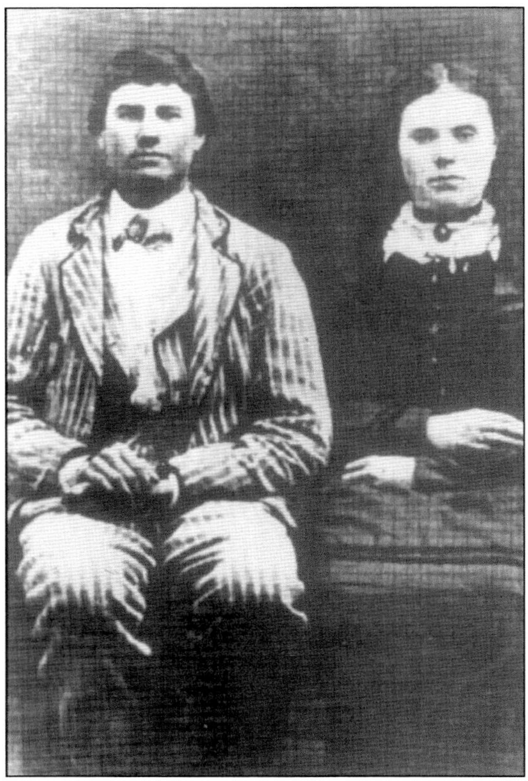

Samuel H. Snapp, born in 1854 in Forsyth, died May 9, 1886, in Kirbyville, when he was gunned down by Baldknobber member Wash Middleton. Snapp's wife, Sarah, was born in 1857, in Celina, Tennessee. She died in 1884. Samuel was the only anti-Baldknobber present at the Oak Grove schoolhouse in March of 1886, when Capt. Nat Kinney, leader of the Baldknobber's, shot Andrew Coggburn.

Andrew Coggburn was photographed at age 18, before his death in March of 1886. He was an anti-Baldknobber. Coggburn was shot in front of the Oak Grove General Baptist Church and schoolhouse by Nat N. Kinney, known as Captain Kinney. Coggburn's friend, Sam Snapp, was the only other anti-Baldknobber present. The Baldknobber's were a group of nightriders, organized to bring peace and order in Taney County and other local communities. They held their first meeting on a "bald knob" east of Branson in Oak Grove, and from then on were known as the "Baldknobbers." The bald knob where they first met was across the road from the log cabin where the author's great-grandmother, Safronea Layton, lived. She often told the younger family members that she watched as the hooded riders with lighted torches rode their horses past her home at night.

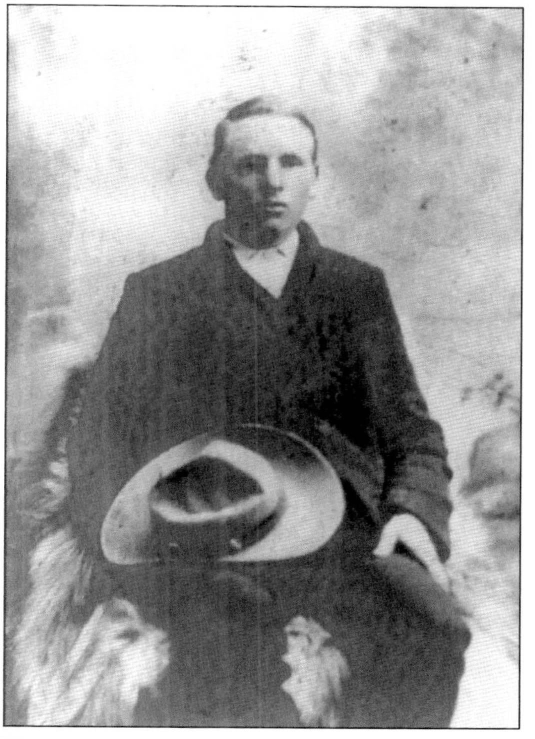

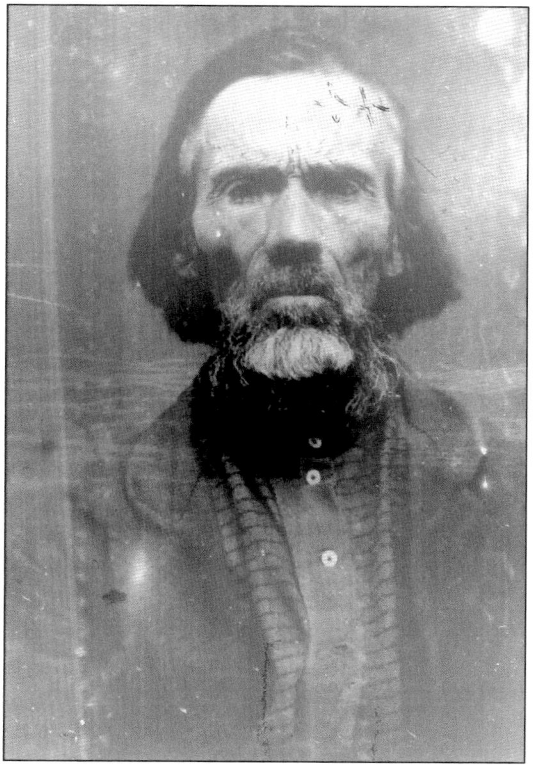

Wash Middleton is pictured here about 1886. He was the Baldknobber who killed Samuel Snapp in front of John Kintrea's store in Kirbyville on Main Street. After killing Snapp, Middleton realized Snapp was unarmed—except for the knife found in his overall pocket as he lay dead in the street. Middleton attempted to flee to his brother's home in Arkansas, 30 miles away, but was arrested en route. He stood trial, was convicted, and sentenced to 20 years. He was held in the Taney County jail that night after sentencing. As the story of old goes, he was deliberately allowed to escape. This time he made it to his brother's. Snapp's brothers offered a $1,000 reward for Middleton, dead or alive. He was later shot and killed by a detective in Arkansas at a picnic.

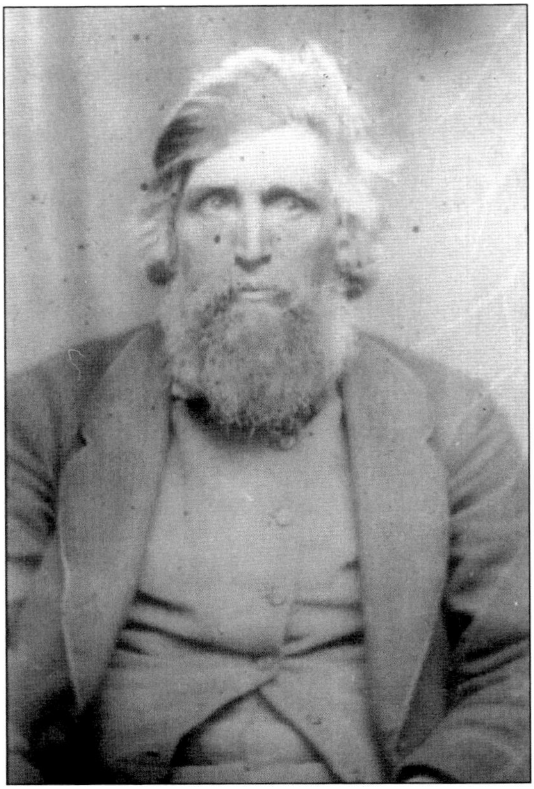

One of the old-time residents of Taney County, Preston Haggard, is pictured about the time of the Civil War. Several of the Haggard family members are buried at the Vanzandt Cemetery in Kirbyville. It has been told that these Haggards are some relation to the country music entertainer Merle Haggard.

This charcoal portrait of Thomas Franklin and Rachel Edminister Hall was drawn in the early 1900s. They lived in the Oak Grove community. Thomas was a Civil War soldier. He volunteered in 1861, in Buffalo, New York, and fought for the North. While held prisoner in Vicksburg, Mississippi, he contracted malaria, ague fever, diarrhea, and deafness. He was discharged in 1863. He also suffered a shattered elbow and a heart condition after the war, and was in poor health the remainder of his life. Thomas lived from 1843 to 1899. He and his wife, Rachel, met when he was in Maine. The Hall family was also among the early Taney County settlers.

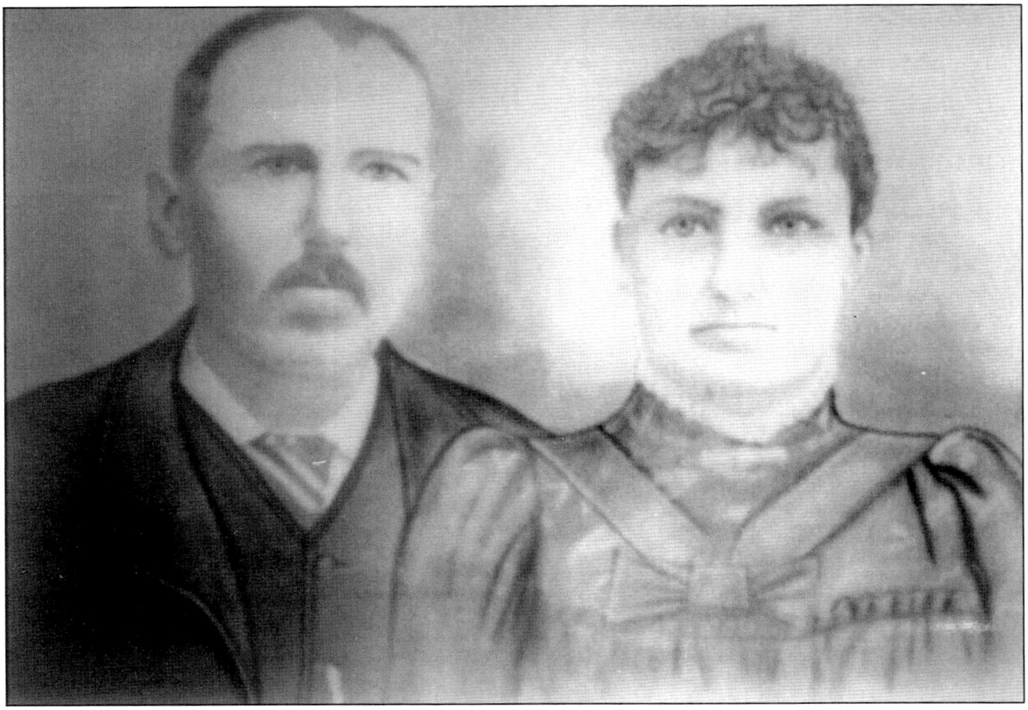

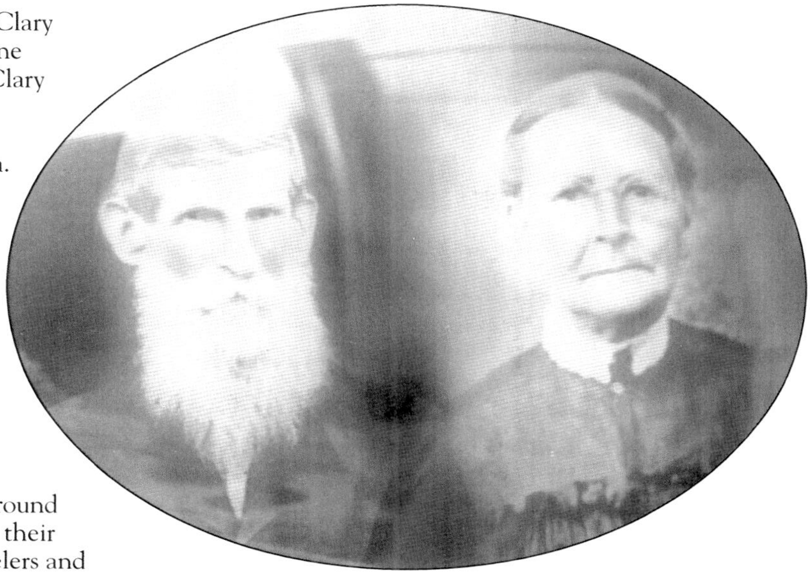

John Hannibal McClary and Emma Catherine (Stinchcomb) McClary were married in March of 1857, in Grandville, Indiana. John fought in the Civil War. The McClarys journeyed from Ohio with two other covered wagons of relatives and reached Taney County in October of 1868. John and Emma ran a campground and camp house on their homestead for travelers and freighters along the Springfield-Harrison Road east of Branson on what is now Highway 76 East. They sold provisions, such as a chicken for dinner, grain and hay for their horses, and mules or oxen to those who traveled by and to those who camped in their campground.

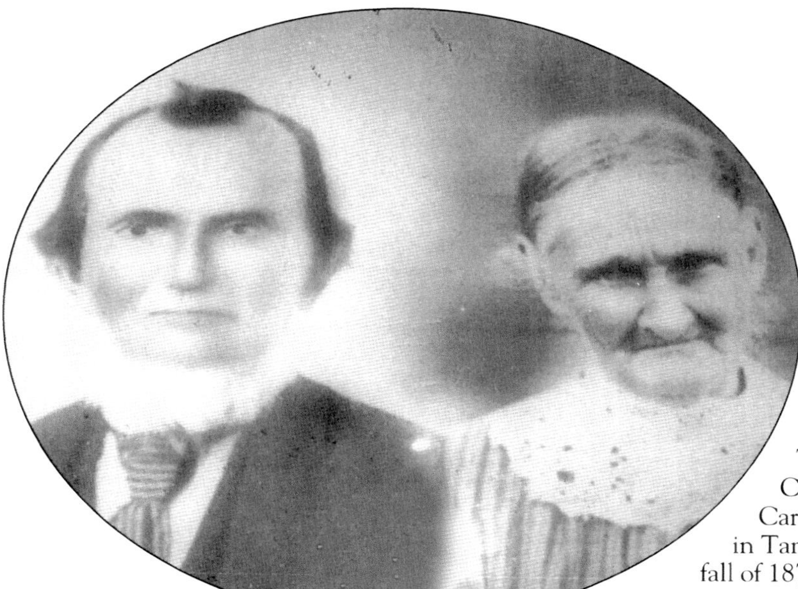

Pictured here are David Hadley Pickett and Catherine (Spoon) Pickett, whose nickname was "Corn Cob." They left Alamance County, North Carolina, and settled in Taney County in the fall of 1871. David paid a $14 government fee for their 160-acre homestead. They had $2 left, and with that he bought 50¢ of flour, 35¢ of pork, 50¢ of molasses, 50¢ of potatoes, and with the remaining 15¢ he bought an envelope, stamp, and paper to write his parents back east of their safe journey to Taney County. They lived in a cloth tent with their children until they built a log cabin from the timber on their homestead. David was an old-time Circuit Rider preacher.

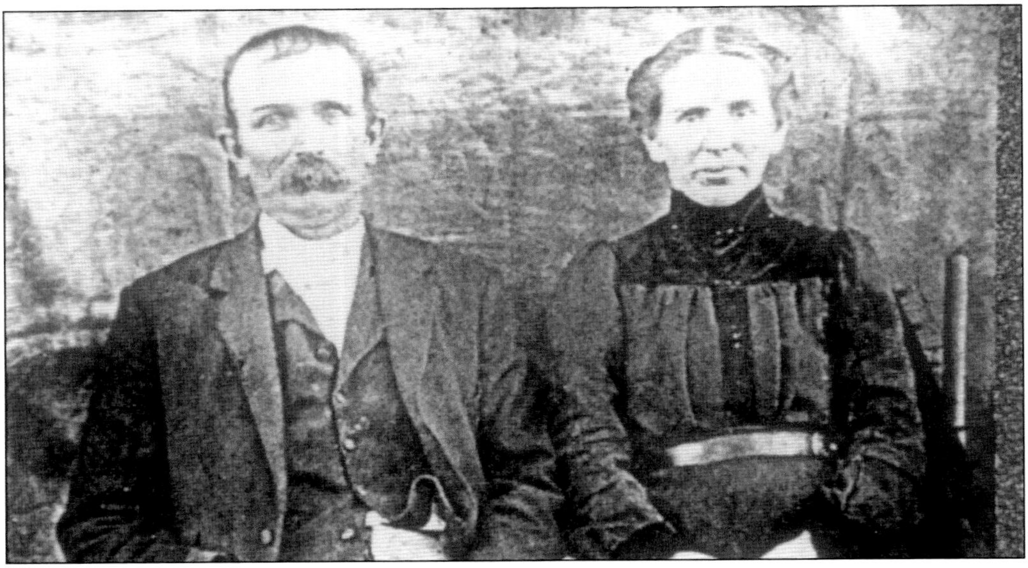

William D. Pickett and his second wife, Mary Edwards, were photographed here in 1885. He was the son of David and Elizabeth Pickett. William went to Kirbyville one day and asked a stranger what his name was. The stranger replied, "Cotton." He then asked William his name, and he answered, "Pickett." As the story goes, the stranger became angry, thinking William was making fun of his name "Cotton." He threw up his hands and dared Pickett to a fistfight. William covered his face and hollered, "My name is Pickett! William Daniel Pickett!" Then the fellow named Cotton said, "well, it'd better be, cause you dang well ain't gonna pick me!" The stranger apologized, and from then on the two men were friends.

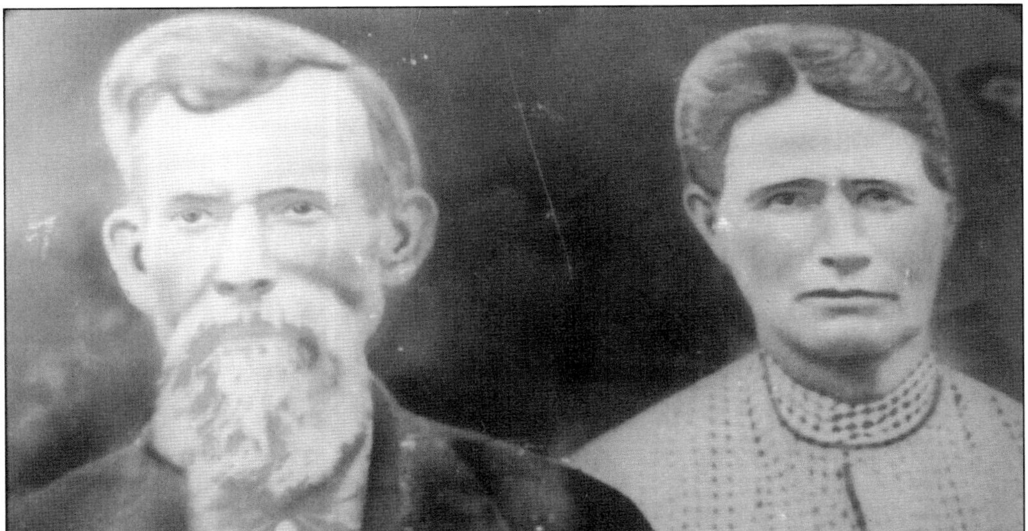

Pictured here are Albert and Mary Ann Edwards Pickett. They were Almeda Edwards Brittain's parents. Almeda was the pioneer preacher woman of the Ozarks. It was told that when Mary Ann worked in the fields hoeing corn or picking cotton, she'd lay her babies on a pallet nearby in the shade, close to where she worked. When a baby cried, she'd say, "hush up baby! This is the best part of your life—if you only knew it!"

Reuben S. Branson and his wife, Mary, known as Aunt Tommie, came to Taney County from Gasconade County, Missouri. They bought 7 acres of land from Thomas J. Berry. Rube moved his store there and sold merchandise to the pioneers. He was granted a postmaster's commission on June 13, 1882, and opened a post office in his store. He was also a druggist, carpenter, schoolteacher, and an excellent gardener who grew beautiful grapes and strawberries. Once, he had 70 beehives on his farm. At one time, they lived in Oak Grove near the Safronea Whorton Layton homestead, and were close friends of the Layton and Whorton families. The Bransons attended the Oak Grove General Baptist Church. It was from Reuben S. Branson that the town of Branson obtained its name.

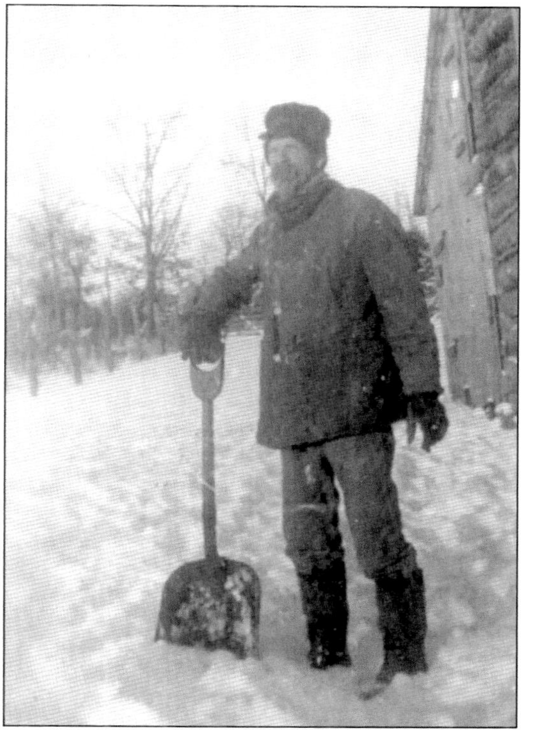

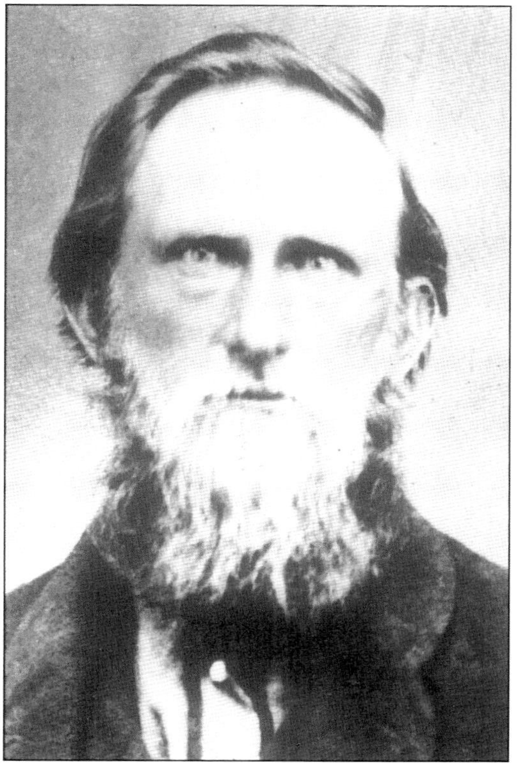

Samuel Allen was born in 1802, and died in 1867. He and his wife, Rebecca, left Monroe County, Kentucky, on February 9, 1842, for their journey to Missouri. They brought a team of mules, two cows, two mule colts, and various implements used in farming. Samuel made a new set of harnesses for the mule team that pulled the wagon. He had made a 4-foot overjet for the top of the wagon box. Slats were put across this for the bed tick and quilts Rebecca had made. This made a comfortable place for their 11-year-old daughter, Elizabeth Ann, to ride, while Samuel and Rebecca rode in the wagon seat. They traveled with three other families also moving to Missouri. Near the middle of May, the Allens reached Miller County, Missouri, where they homesteaded.

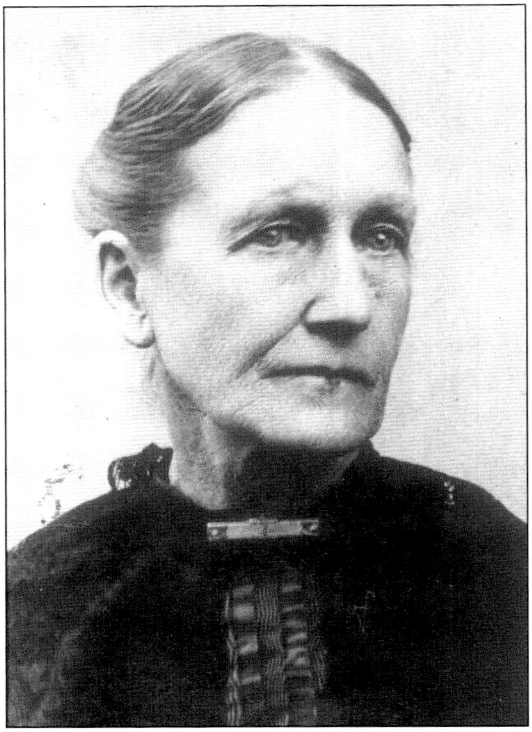

Rebecca Allen was struck by lightning in 1846, as she stood over the fireplace brewing soup for a sick child. Elizabeth, being the oldest child, helped raise the other children until Samuel remarried several years later. Rebecca was born in 1805. Samuel and Rebecca Allen are the author's maternal great-great-great-grandparents.

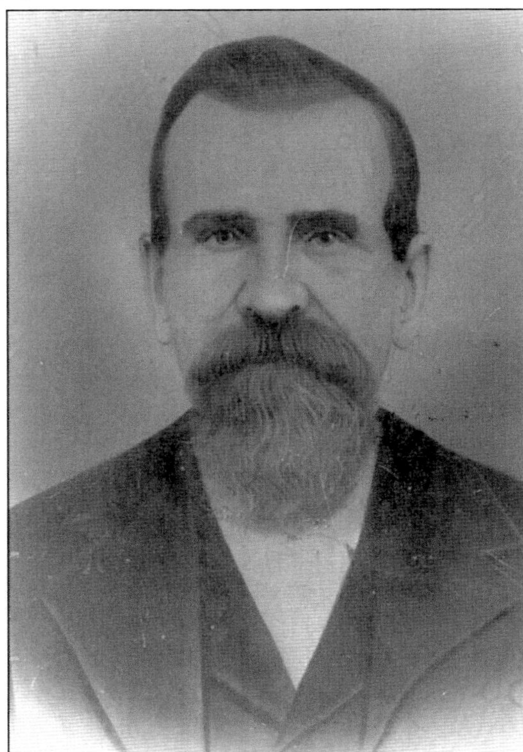

John Shell Coggburn was a son-in-law of Samuel and Rebecca Allen. He married their daughter, Elizabeth Ann Allen, on November 11, 1852, when she was 21 years old. After their marriage, they left Miller County and journeyed to Taney County, Missouri, and settled near Kirbyville, where they raised 11 children.

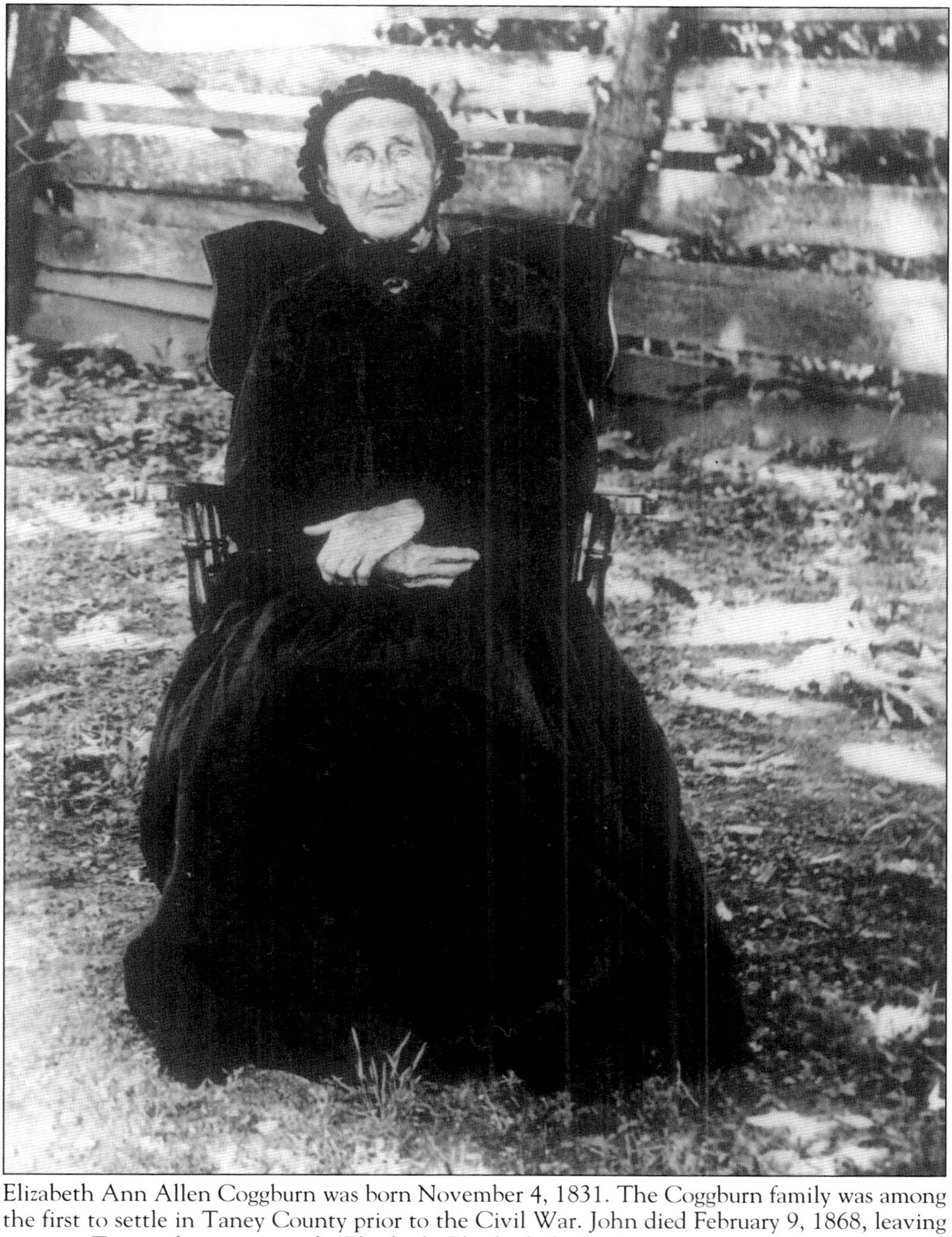

Elizabeth Ann Allen Coggburn was born November 4, 1831. The Coggburn family was among the first to settle in Taney County prior to the Civil War. John died February 9, 1868, leaving one son, Tom, at home to care for Elizabeth. Elizabeth died July 22, 1923, at the age of 91. Tom was born in 1875, and died March 10, 1912, at age 37. He poured kerosene on himself and then lit a match. Hearing his screams, Elizabeth took a bucket and busted the ice from a water barrel to douse the fire that engulfed him. He lay in bed, badly injured from his self-inflicted injury, and died in a few days. He was buried in the Vanzandt Cemetery, as were his parents. He never married. In this photograph, Elizabeth is 81 years old.

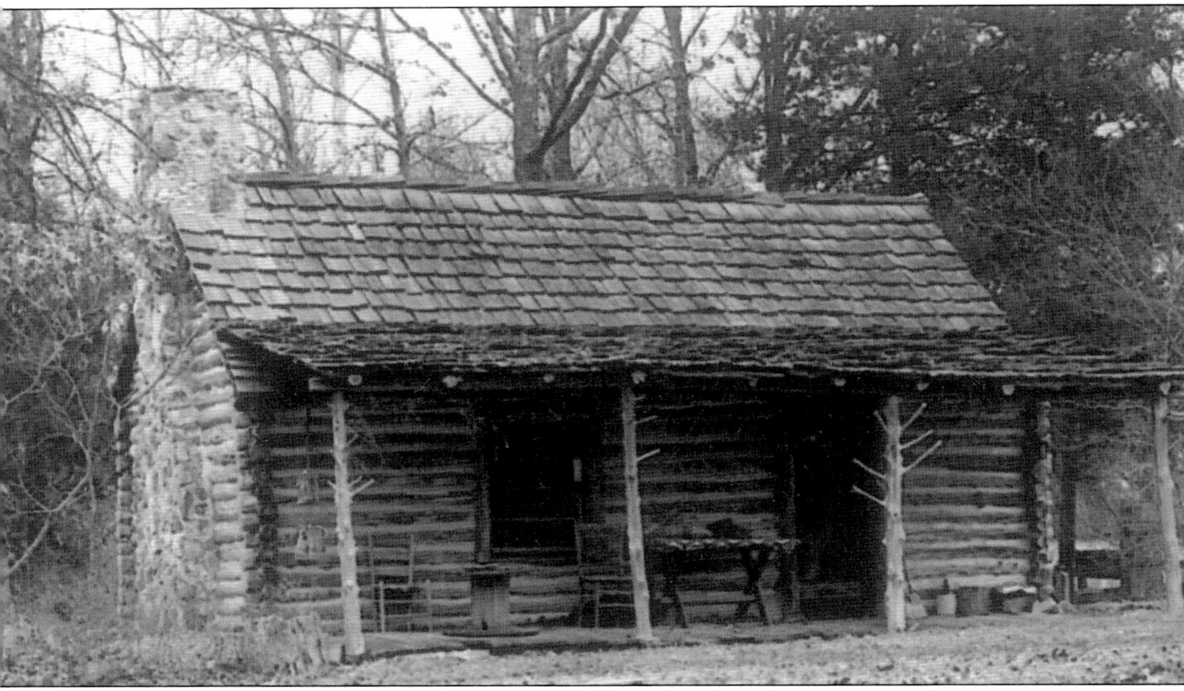

The pioneers with their broad axes hewed the logs tree by tree into proper size and shape for the construction of their log cabin homes. With their muscles and strength, combined with the cooperative help of another human being and often a well-trained mule, the logs were rolled or lifted into place, fitting into their proper notches. The shingles for the roof were "rifed" from cedar, and one by one hammered securely into their destined position with iron nails or wooden pegs. A "rife" tool was used for "rifing out the shingles" from a solid piece of cedar block. The fireplaces, built rock by rock with limestone mortar, were cemented into place, and the fireplace became not only the source for the cabin's heat but also cooking in cast iron pots that hung over the fire. The early pioneer cabins sprung up over the hills as newcomers settled in Taney County and called it home. Most of them are gone now, although signs of their existence still remain scattered over the land few and far between. Many fell to the hands of time, others to the hand of modern man clearing them from the land for modern day houses. This cabin sits near Kirbyville.

Two

Community Neighbors and Friends

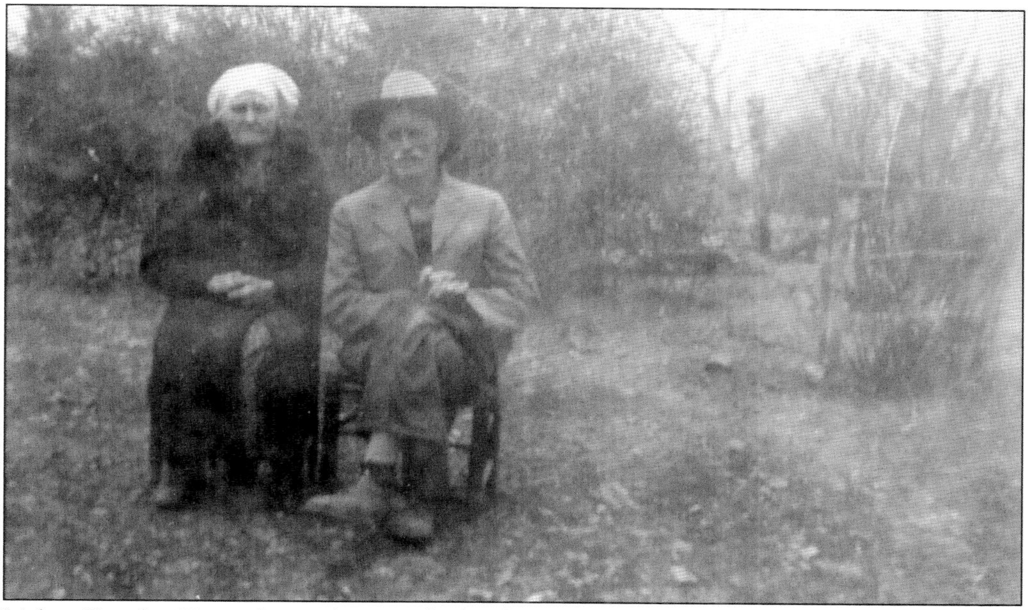

Melissa Breedon Haworth was photographed with her husband, Uncle John Haworth. Once, when John was a boy, one of the neighbor men, David Hadley Pickett, who lived nearby in Kirbyville, caught John peeking at his daughters through the cracks of his fence. Pickett got a switch and ran John off. It scared John so much that he didn't slow down until he got back to his home in Mildred. His adopted parents, Jurd Haworth and his wife Mary, asked why he was out of breath. John told them a varmint in the woods chased him home. His folks later found out the truth about the incident from Mr. Pickett, who told Jurd and his wife if he caught John peeking at his daughters again, he'd switch his butt for him. When John Haworth married and had a family of his own to raise, the Baldknobbers came to their home late one night to attempt to get John, who was an anti-Baldknobber, to join them. Unable to convince him, they had a shootout. The Baldknobbers had a saying, "either join the band, or leave the land!" Bullet holes filled the Haworth cabin, but no one was injured. Uncle John, along with other Taney County Anti-knobbers, stood their ground. Some survived, and others were laid to rest in local graveyards.

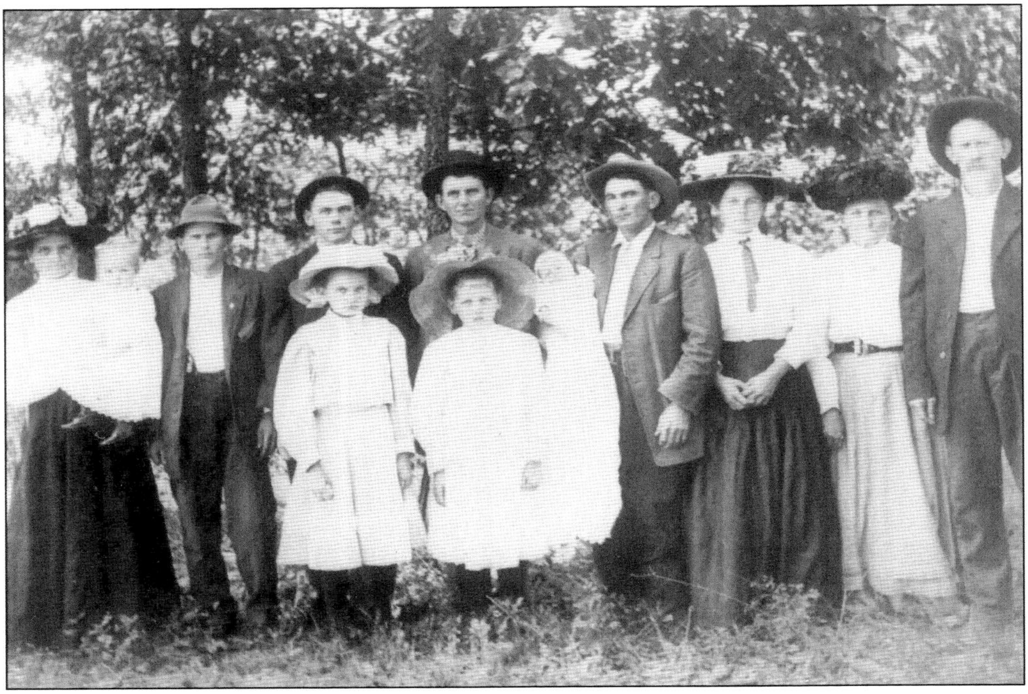

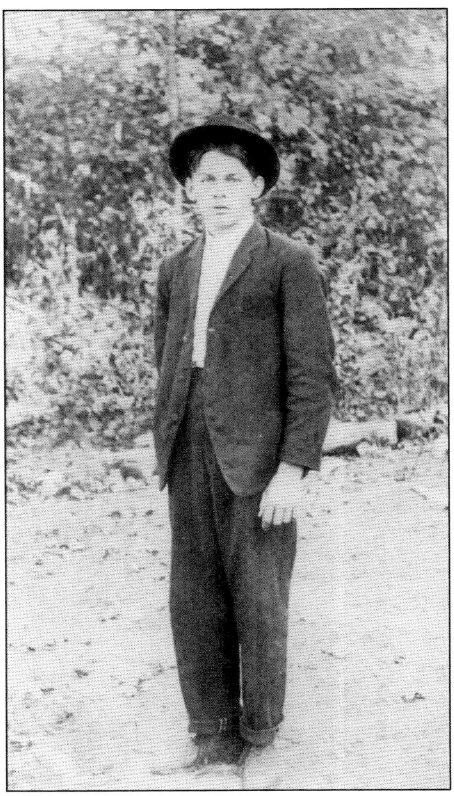

The John and Melissa Haworth family gathered for Sunday dinner after church services at Pleasant Hill (also known as Sardis) in Mildred, where Uncle John Haworth was the preacher. The church frequently had all day meetings with dinner on the ground, communion, and feet washing services. From left to right in the back row are: Maggie Haworth Stallcup, Hade Haworth, John Siah (Tater) Haworth, Mack Haworth, Evert Boyd, Sis Haworth Boyd, Melissa, and Uncle John Haworth. The girl on the left in the front is Sallie Haworth. The other girl's name is unknown. The two babies are Eva and Vernon Stallcup.

Haden (Hade) was John and Melissa Haworth's son. One time Hade and his brother-in-law, Charlie Cobb, rode their horses through the woods in search of homemade whiskey. The hill man who operated the still ran them off a jug of the fresh corn squeezins'. Hade became so intoxicated that Charlie tied his hands to the saddle horn and led the horse back to their homes in Mildred. Charlie untied Hade's hands, took him in the house, put his horse in the barn, and then rode on home himself.

Mack and Hattie Walker Haworth, originally from the Mildred community along the Blackwell Road, moved to Oklahoma and lived most their married life there. They had four daughters and one son. This photograph was taken by the bluff along the south side of the Powersite Dam in Forsyth in the early 1900s. On Sunday afternoons following church services, family and friends walked down the steep steps extending down the bluff's edge leading down to the dam. There were three wagons with John and Melissa's sons and their families leaving Taney County together en route to Oklahoma in the early 1900s.

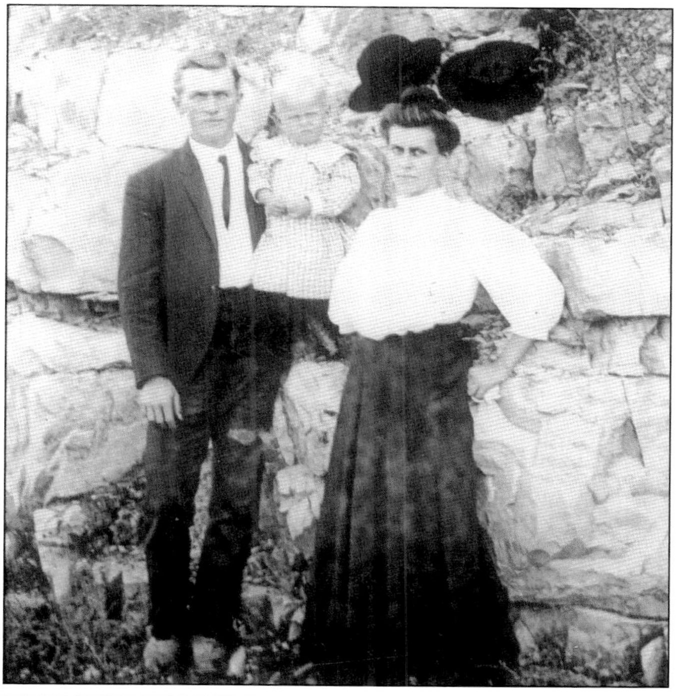

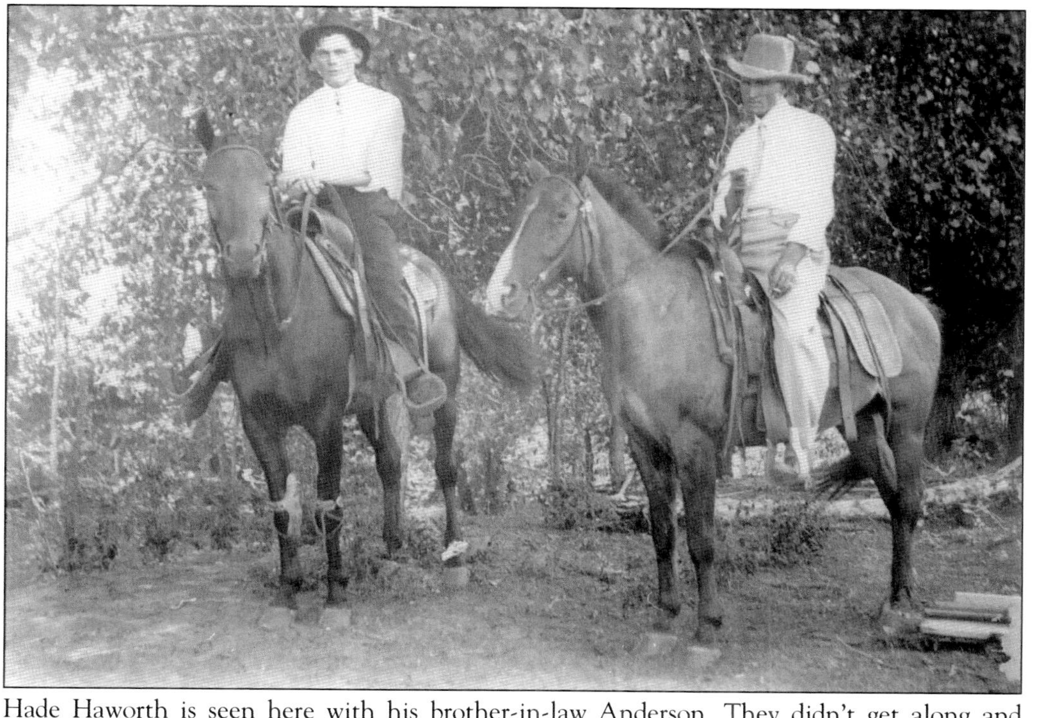

Hade Haworth is seen here with his brother-in-law Anderson. They didn't get along and generally fussed when they were together. In those days, the young men were proud of their horses. They often dressed up and groomed their horses to impress the girls they wanted to "spark." There was a saying in those days, "a good horse was sure to never tell on a fellar!"

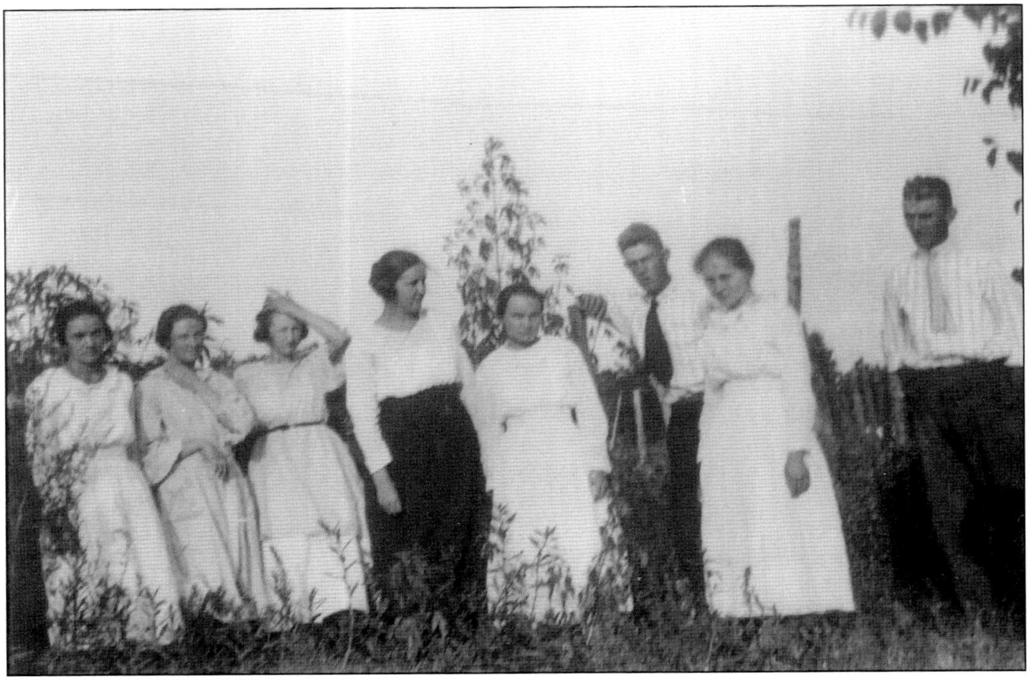

A group of young folks gather near Mt. Olives church and schoolhouse for a Saturday night pie supper. They are Thelma, Shirley, Eva Yandell, Sallie Haworth, and Frank Wade; the other three names are unknown. This photo was taken in 1920. Frank was sparkin' one of the Yandell sisters.

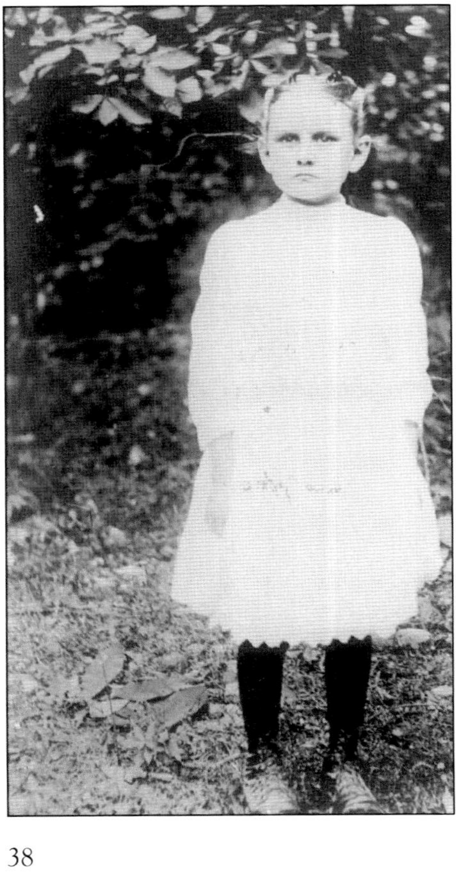

The author's paternal grandmother, Sallie Haworth Cobb, is shown here at age nine in the early 1900s. Sallie was playing at her grandfather, Uncle Jackie Breedon's, homestead one day when, for the first time, she met Almeda Edwards, a neighbor girl her age. Almeda rode in the back of her family's wagon to the Breedon homestead as they hauled a load of wheat to be threshed by a threshing machine. A threshing machine separates grain crops into grain or seeds and straw. The threshing machine owner, along with his hired harvest crew, traveled to one farm in each neighborhood at harvest time, and everyone in the community brought their wheat to be threshed before the crew traveled on to the next location. Sallie and Almeda played together for the first time that day. They became friends and spent most of their lives in Taney County.

One of Mack and Hattie Haworth's daughters, Anna, is pictured in her baby carriage at their home in Mildred.

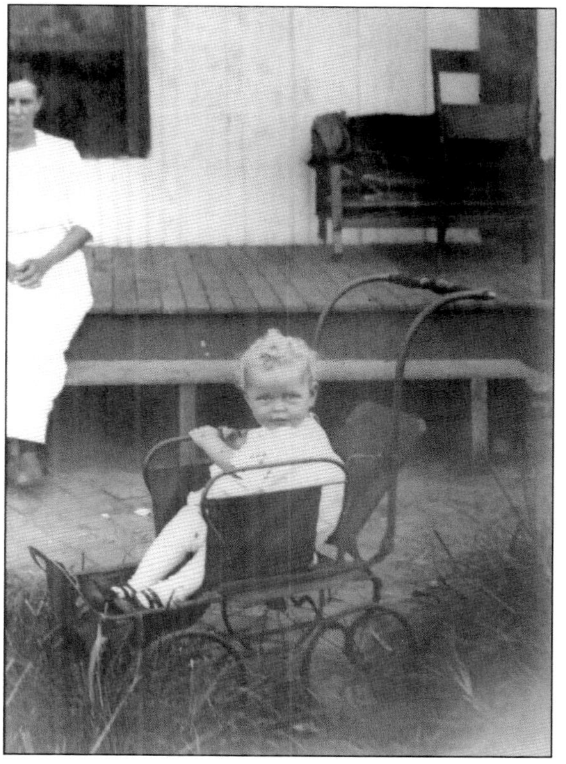

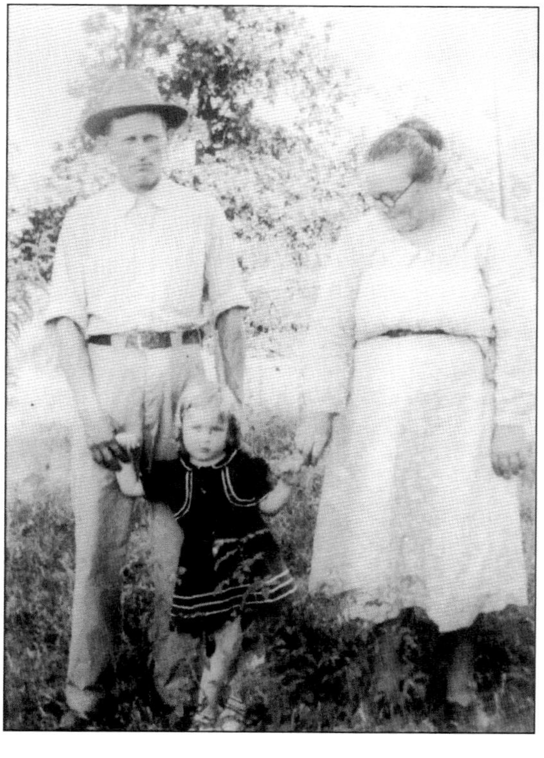

John Siah Haworth is seen here with his wife, Nancy, and their daughter, Georgia Verona, whom they nicknamed Cissy Ann. Cissy later died at age 16. They lived near Mildred.

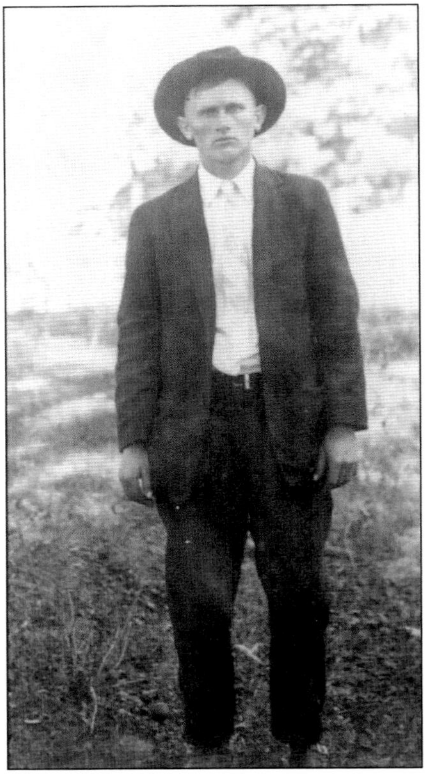

Pictured here is John and Melissa Haworth's son, John Siah, who was nicknamed "Tater." When he was a little fellow, someone once asked, "Hey John, what do ya want to eat?" He hadn't been talking long but knew enough words to jibber jabber. He looked up and relayed quickly, "Tater! Want me tater!" That's how he got the nickname.

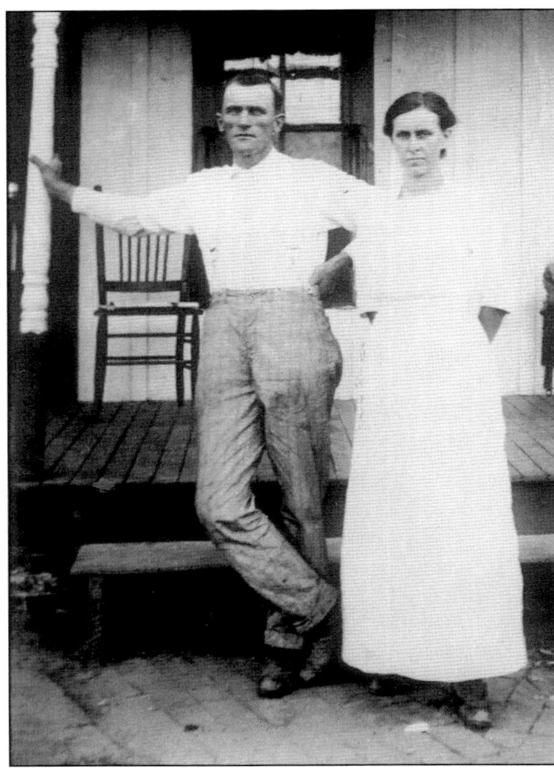

Mack and Hattie Haworth were photographed at their home in Mildred in the early 1900s. Mack was a brother to John and Melissa's son, John "Tater."

Sallie Haworth Cobb's sister, Sis Haworth Boyd, is seen here. At age 16, Sis went to town with her father, Uncle John Haworth. While he was tending to business in the general store, Sis met up with a man she knew from Oklahoma. She climbed in the wagon with him, and they headed to Oklahoma where they were married. They had two sons, Exie and Buddy.

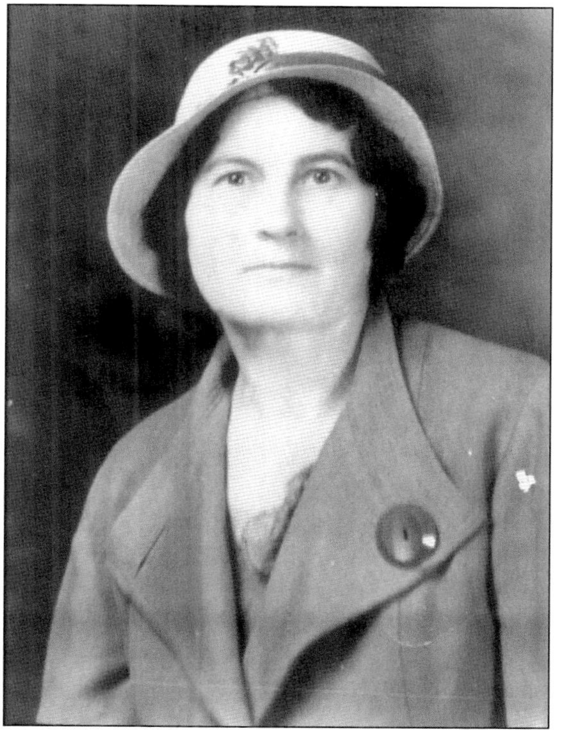

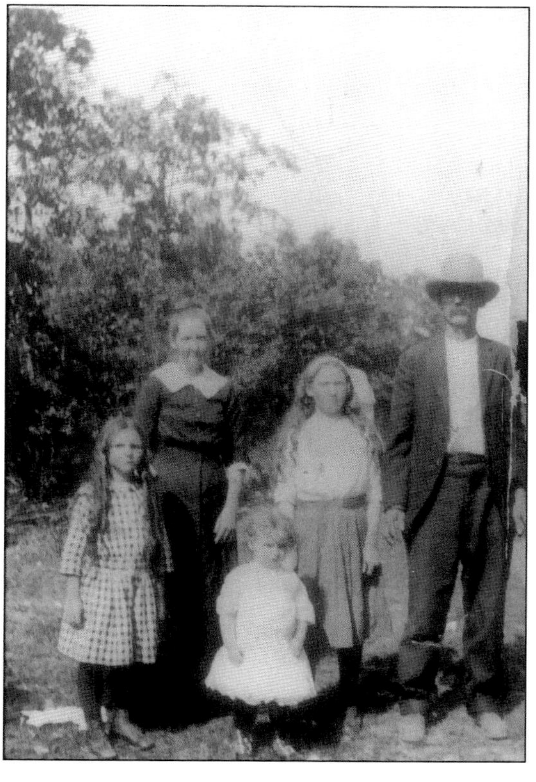

James, Mary Francis Warner Cobb, and their three daughters, Winnie, Bessie, and Edna are shown here. The Cobb family farmed in the Mildred community. James was the son of Charles and Laura Cobb, who were the first Cobbs to homestead in Taney County in 1879.

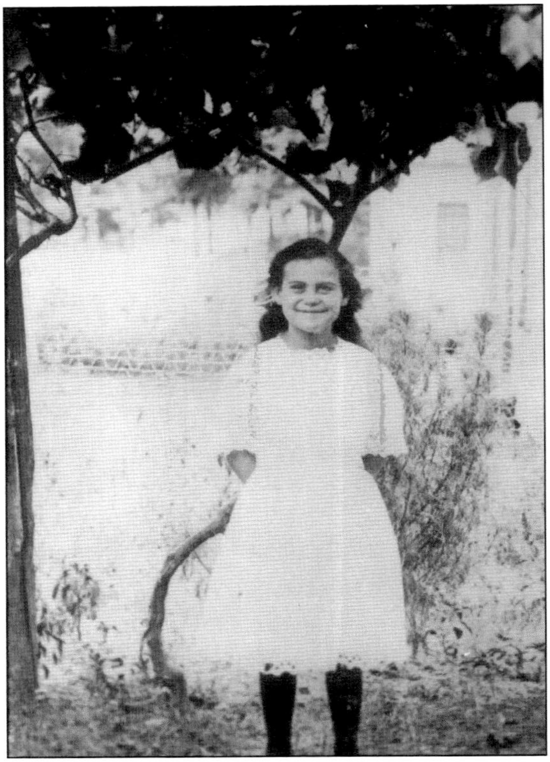

Mary Warner Cobb's half sister's daughter, Virginia (Bertie) Witley, is shown here in the early 1900s, at about the age of 10.

The children of Owen and Maggie Haworth Stallcup's daughter, Eva Yandell, are pictured here. They are: Audry, Lyman, Delmar, and Marybelle Yandell. Maggie chewed homegrown twist tobacco. She was a sister to Sallie Haworth Cobb.

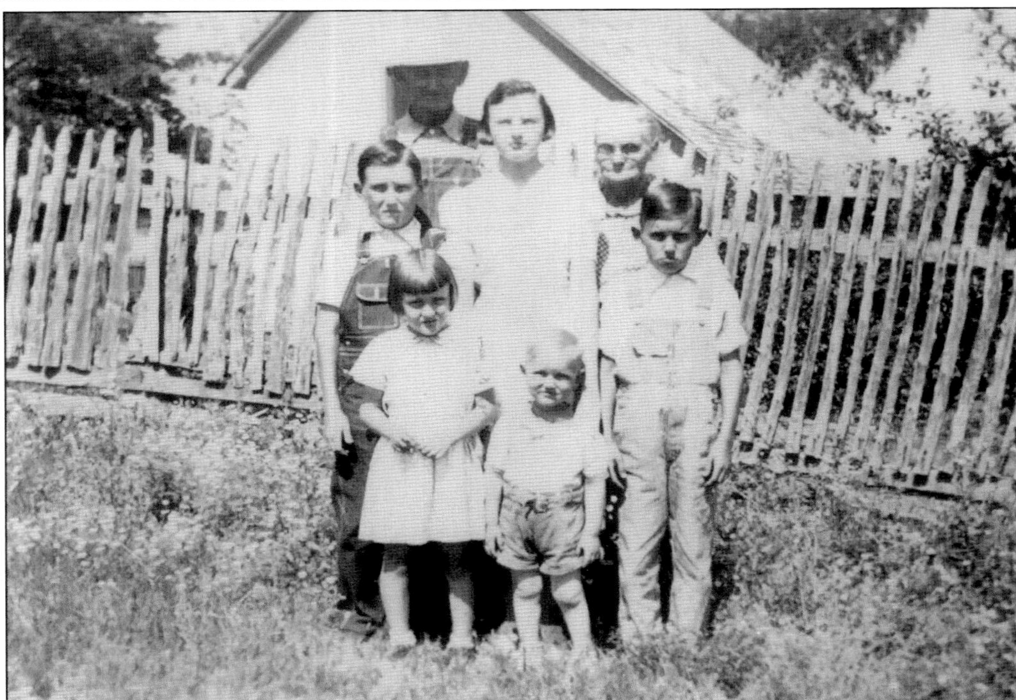

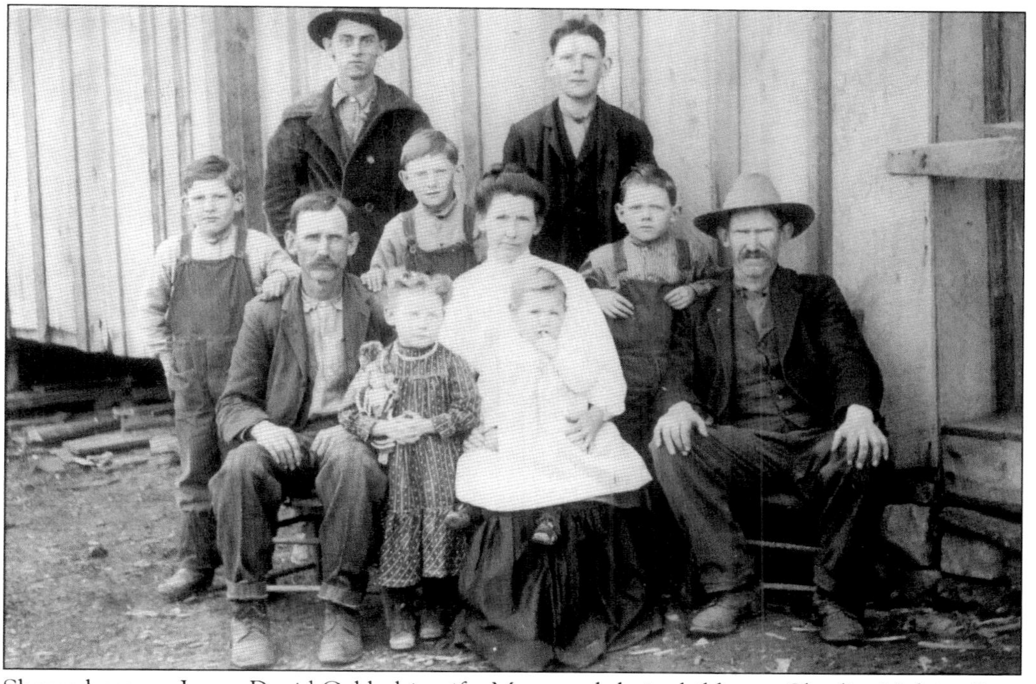

Shown here are James David Cobb, his wife, Mary, and their children—Charlie, Melvin, Roy, Alva, Bessie, and Jack; also pictured are Mary's brother, Jim Warner, and a neighbor friend, Hosea Clinkingbeard. This photograph was taken in front of the Cobb home in Mildred during the early 1900s.

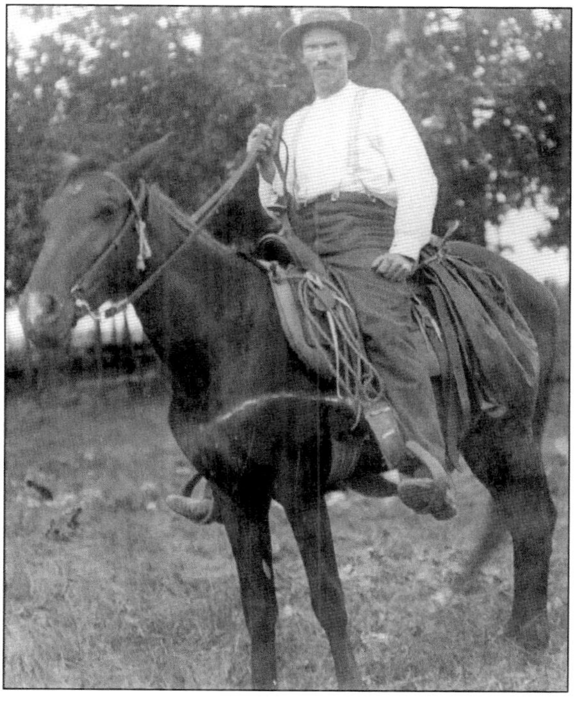

Edwin and Addie Crouch Warner's son, Jim, is pictured here. His sister, Mary, married James D. Cobb. After God called Jim to preach, Almeda Edwards Brittain taught him how to read by using the Bible. Jim took pride in his horse and riding equipment. One night, as he preached at the Mt. Olives church, one local neighbor who disliked Jim took a knife and cut the leather tie strings from Jim's saddle while everyone else listened to Jim preach inside. After service was dismissed, Jim walked out the church door toward his horse, and saw the leather tie strings had been cut. Almeda Edwards Brittain told the author in an interview that, "Uncle Jim Warner was a changed man." He figured out who did it, asked the man about it, and he confessed to the deed. Almeda said, "Jim gave that fellow a right good whipping." From that time on, no one bothered Jim's horse or his saddle.

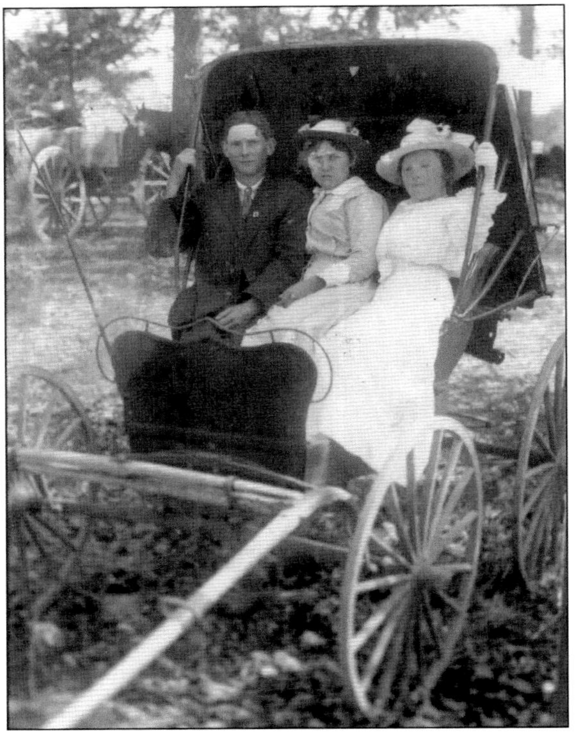

Charlie Cobb, Lucy Wade, and Nancy Blair enjoy each other's company while resting in the comfortable buggy seat, discussing the events of the Mt. Olives Sunday afternoon church gathering. Years later, after Charlie and Sallie Haworth were married, she accused him of "rocking the cradle with these two 14-year-old girls." This photo was taken about 1910.

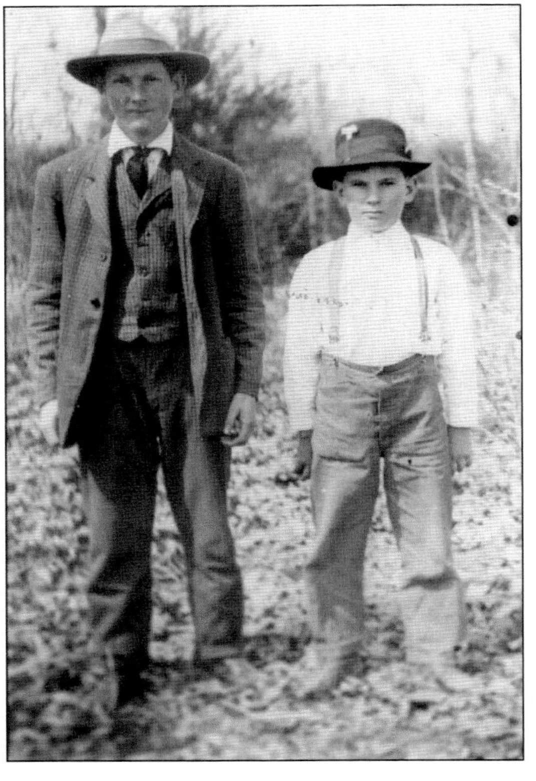

Charlie Cobb is seen in this photograph with his cousin, Ben Crouch, on a Sunday afternoon during late fall in Mildred during the early 1900s.

Mary Awberry taught school at the Hickory Grove schoolhouse. She boarded with the Tom and Mary Smith family of Mincy. The Smith's youngest daughter, Ethel, rode behind Mary on a white mule to and from school while Mary boarded with the Smith family. Mary later married Charlie Breedon. This photograph was taken in the early 1900s.

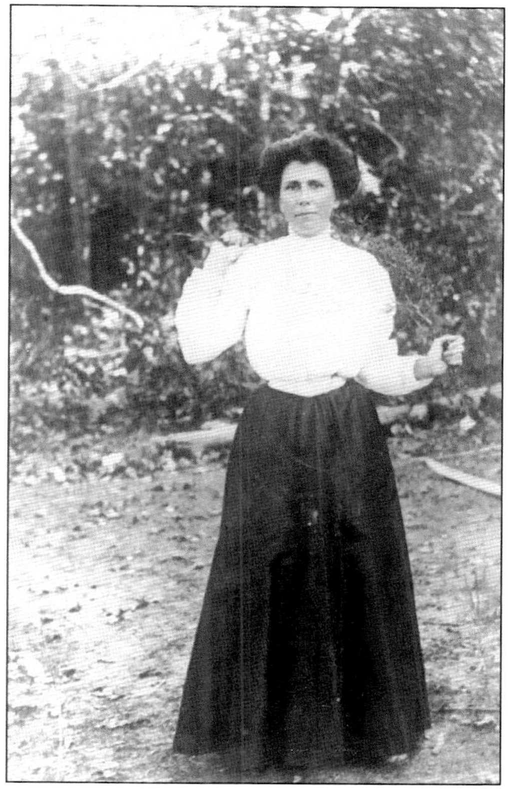

Gus Behrent, his wife Lilly, and their children, Charlie, J.D., Henry, Mable, Addie, Orpha, and Francis are seen here. Gus went to either Mulberry or Pittsburgh, Kansas, to work in the strip mines. Lilly was Jim and Mary Warner's sister. Before James and Mary Cobb's son Roy was married, he moved to Kansas, where he stayed with the Behrent family and took a job driving a team and wagon hauling goods in and out of the mines.

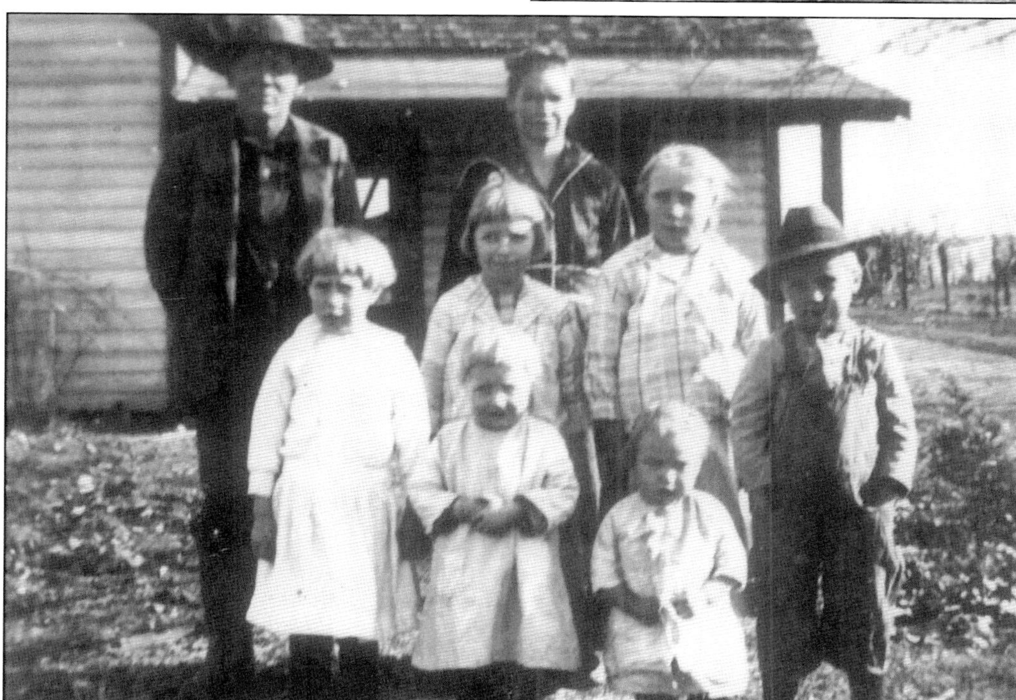

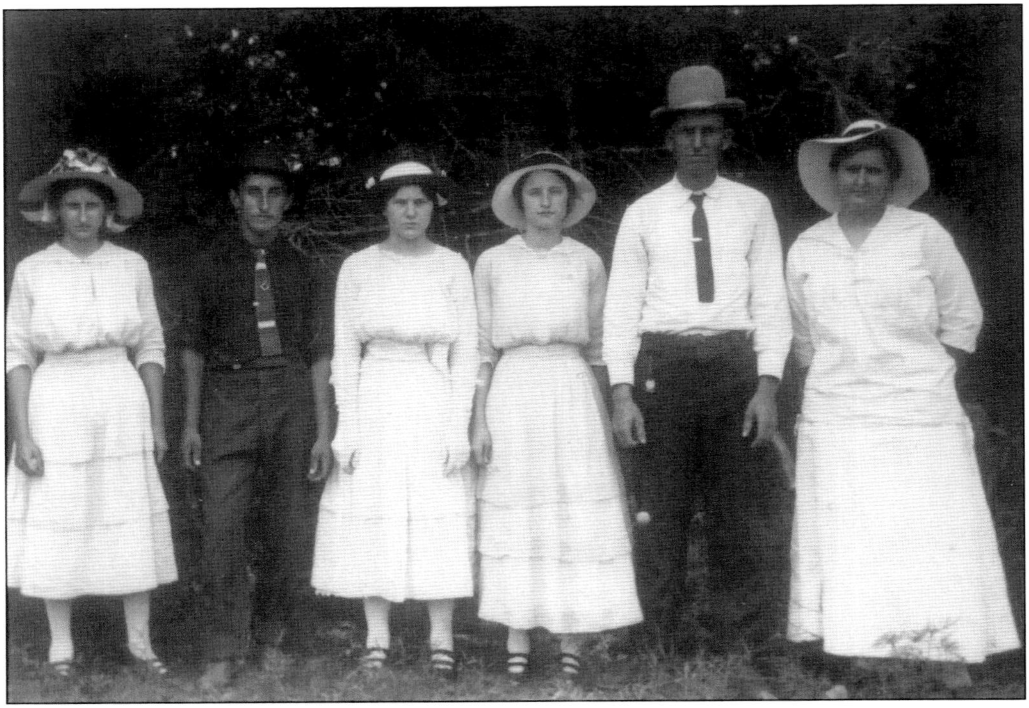

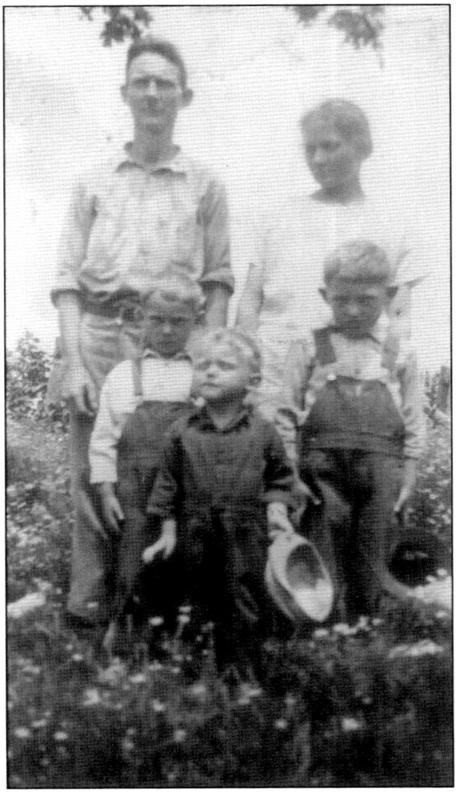

In the early 1900s, this group of young folks dressed up for a Saturday night gathering at the Mt. Olives church and schoolhouse. From left to right are: Vertie Bookout, Dewey Brittain, Lucy Wade, Zan Yandell, Jess Cobb, and Shirley Yandell. Since there were few places to go back when these young people were photographed, their means of transportation was quite different than today's modern invention, the automobile. These young people traveled to their gatherings either by a horse or mule-drawn wagon, by horseback, or they walked perhaps miles by moonlight, or by the light of a kerosene lantern, the glow often seen from one mountain top to the next.

Charlie and Sallie Haworth Cobb were photographed with their three sons, Wayne, Junior, and Johnce. Junior is the author's father. This photo was taken about 1928.

Cordie Cobb was the daughter of Charles and Laura. She later married Andrew Mahnkey, who is an uncle to Douglas Mahnkey of Forsyth, who retired after 62 years of practicing law in Forsyth, and was also a Missouri state representative.

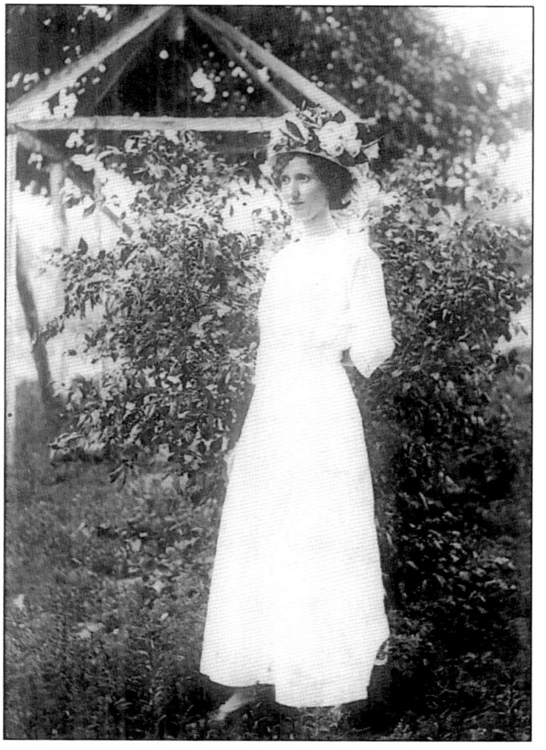

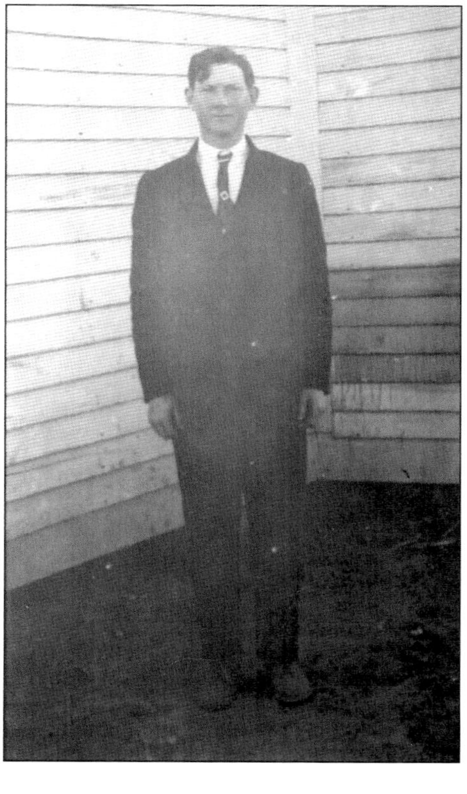

Charlie Cobb stands beside the Lone Elm school and church house in the early 1900s, when he was in his later teens. The building was moved about this time and went by the name of Mt. Olives. Charlie went to school in both locations. After he married Sallie Haworth, their three sons, Johnce, Wayne, and Junior, attended school there. In 1990, the author visited the Mt. Olives schoolhouse, now used occasionally for special church services and a frequent gathering place for local neighbors. While the author was inside the schoolhouse of bygone days, with the original desks and seats that were used by students in Taney County's earlier years, she found engraved with a pocket knife the initials "J.C." She knew immediately that it stood for Junior Cobb, her father.

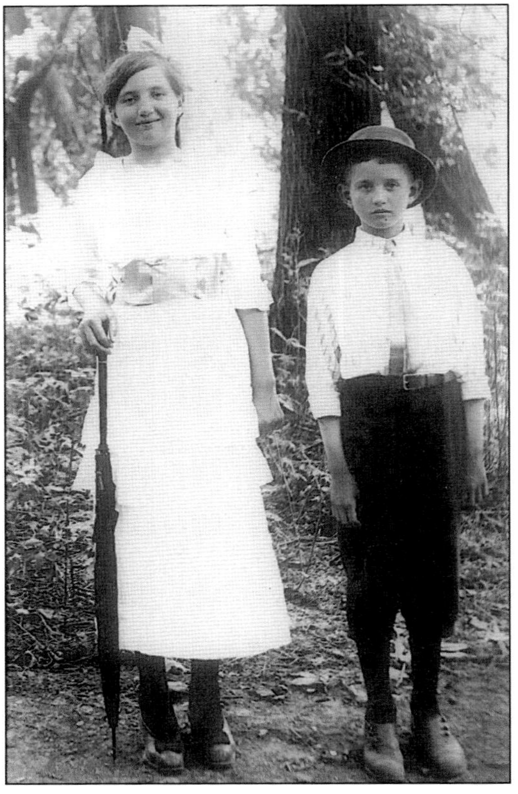

Cousins Dollie Cobb and Ben Crouch are pictured here in the early 1900s. Their homes were near Mt. Olives school and church house. One of the Crouch-Cobb descendants, Clifford Crouch, served as a Taney County judge and a lawyer in Forsyth until his death just a few years ago.

Milton P. Brittain II and his wife, Mary Ann, were the parents of Harve, John, and Milton Price Brittain III. Milton and Mary Ann owned a general mercantile store located on the Springfield-Harrison Road in Kirbyville during the early 1900s. Freighters from Arkansas en route to Springfield, Missouri, transported goods to and from Springfield and Harrison, Arkansas.

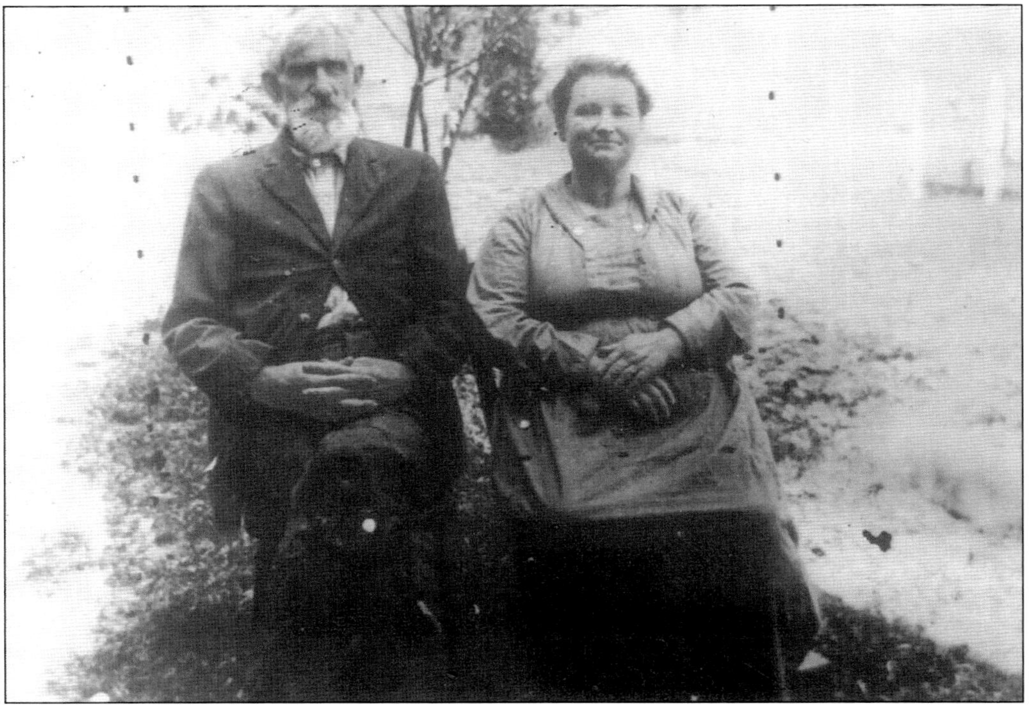

Harve and Berthie (Crouch) Brittain are shown here after they first married, about 1920. They were the first ones living on the Blackwell Ferry Road in Mildred to have a radio. They lived in a log cabin built by Tom and Annie Anderson in the later 1800s, near the Brittain Cemetery. Harve's grandfather and grandmother, M.P. Brittain I, were married in 1843, and left Henry County, Iowa, to move to Warnersville, which was later renamed "Kirbyville." Berthie's mother, Leona, was a sister to the author's great-grandfather, James David Cobb. Leona married "Uncle Jim" Crouch. The Crouch descendants were from England.

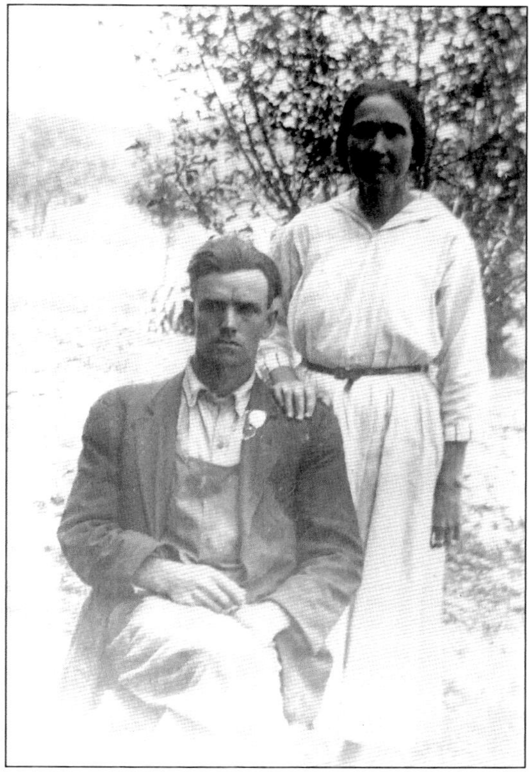

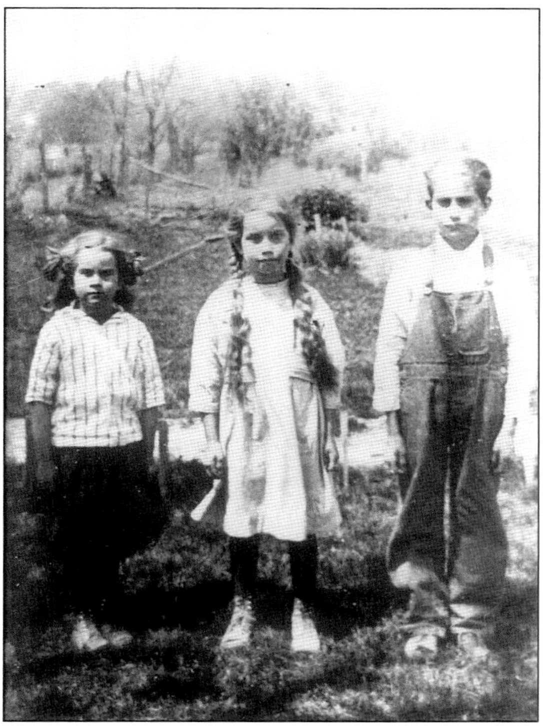

Harve and Bertha Crouch Brittain's children, Buster, Edna, and Mary, are shown here. The cabin where the Brittains raised their children remains standing today and is used to store hay. Mary married Ivan Jennings, who loved to fish. Edna married Ivan's brother Lester. Edna loved to hunt and fish, but Lester didn't. The Jennings brothers came to Taney County from Denver, Colorado.

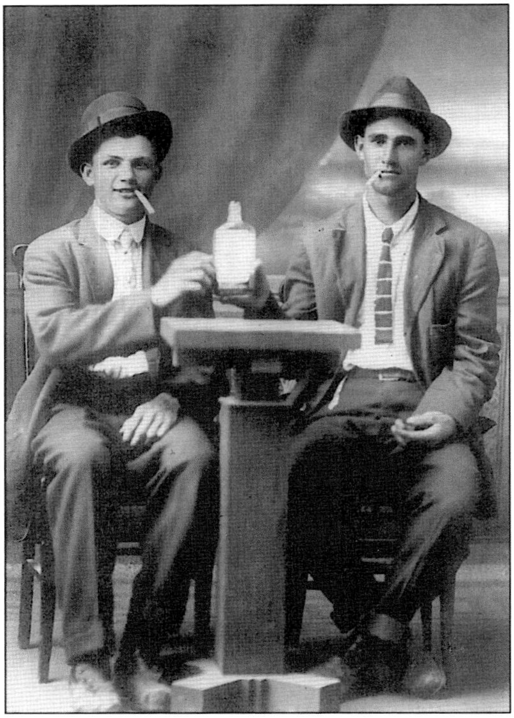

Frank and Fred Brittain, born in the later 1890s, grew up in Mildred. In the 1930s, Fred didn't have a way to refrigerate his food, and one day he bought some bologna in Branson. Upon returning to his home, he fixed a sandwich and ate it, not realizing the bologna had spoiled. He became ill. He lived close to the Otis Clinkingbeard place, and he stumbled along the road toward their house for help. He asked Queen Edwards Clinkingbeard to pray for him. She did, and while she prayed, he raised up in bed where they had laid him and said, "Aunt Queen, it's too late." They called for the doctor in Forsyth to come, but when he arrived, Fred sat up in bed again and said, "Don't anyone ever do what I have just done!" Then he died.

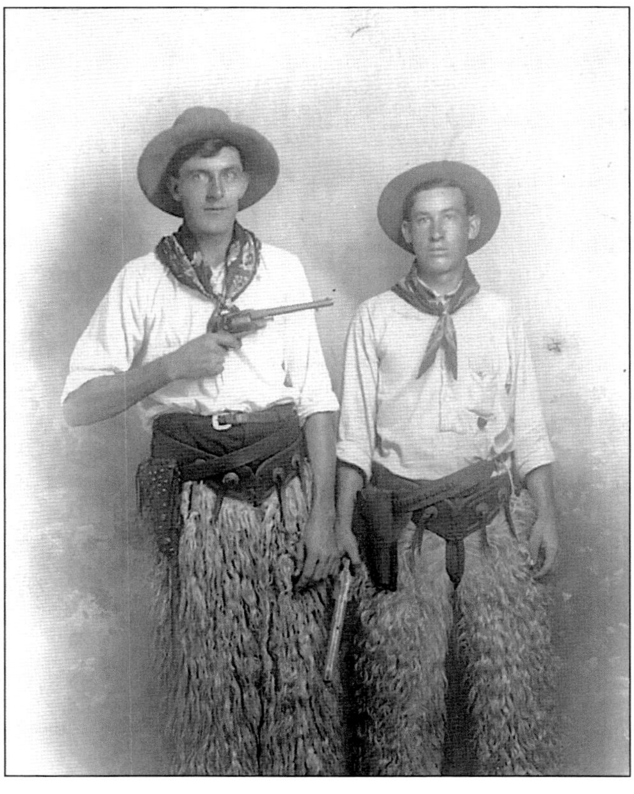

Arthur Blair and friend Harry O'Neill, both born in the later 1890s, grew up east of Branson in Mildred. Blair was known as a "fighter" among the local men, sometimes fighting two at a time. They claim he'd laugh the entire fight. His dad, Art, was the same way and had a saying about himself—"I can walk a barb-wire fence with two wildcats under each arm looking for a rattlesnake to fight!"

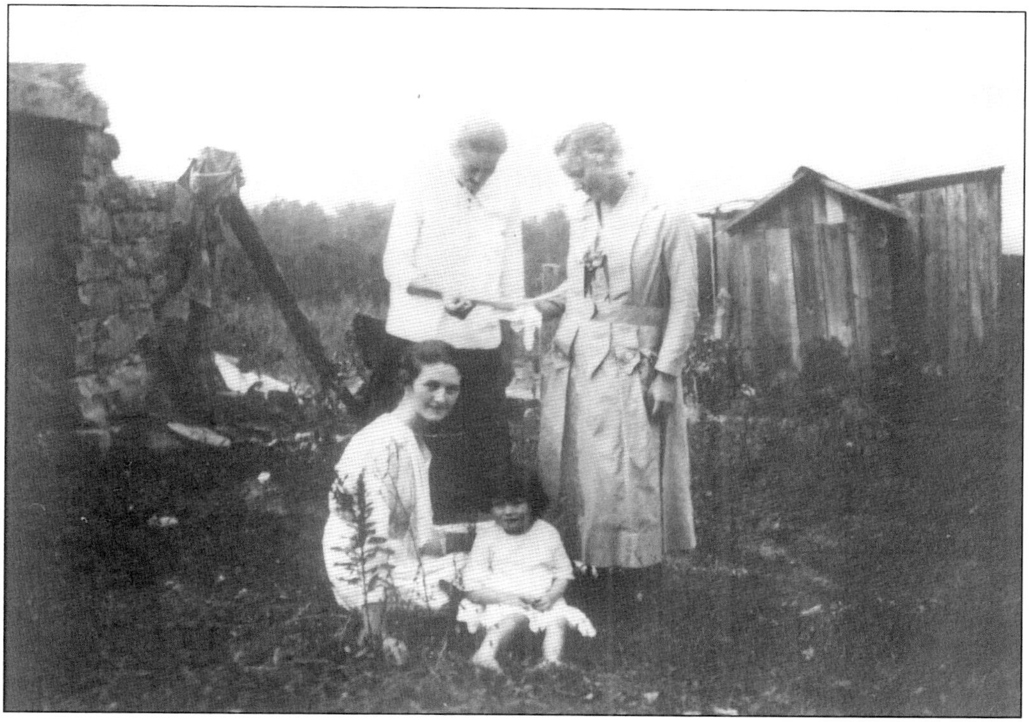

The Turrentine girls from Mildred were Myne, Joyce, Vida, and Ethel. Around the year 1915, eight members of their family contracted a serious case of the flu. The author's grandfather, Charlie Cobb, who was about 20 years old, packed his suitcase and stayed at the Turrentine home until the sick recovered. He helped tend to the sick and do the farm chores. Another neighbor woman came and stayed to do the cooking, tend to the sick, and to do whatever else she could do along with Charlie to help their neighbors in their time of need.

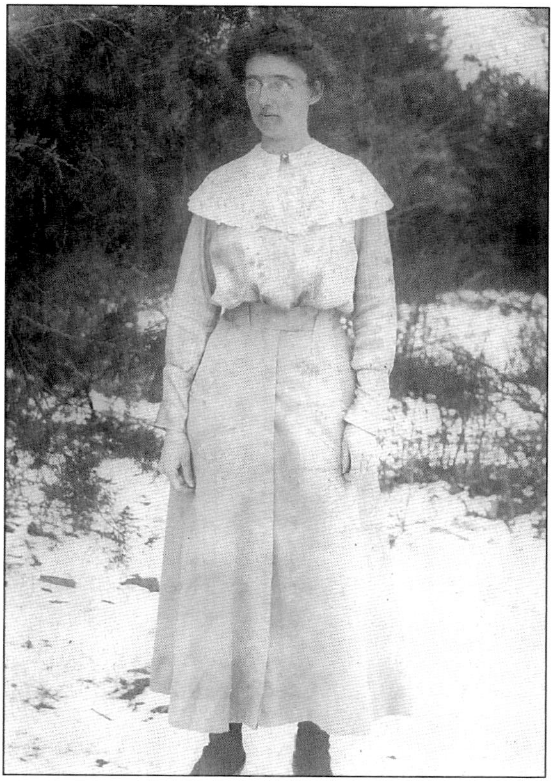

Pictured here is Mag Yandell, daughter of Wylse Yandell by his first marriage to Isabelle Brown. Wylse operated the Blackwell Ferry in the early 1900s. Mag taught school at Mt. Olives near her home.

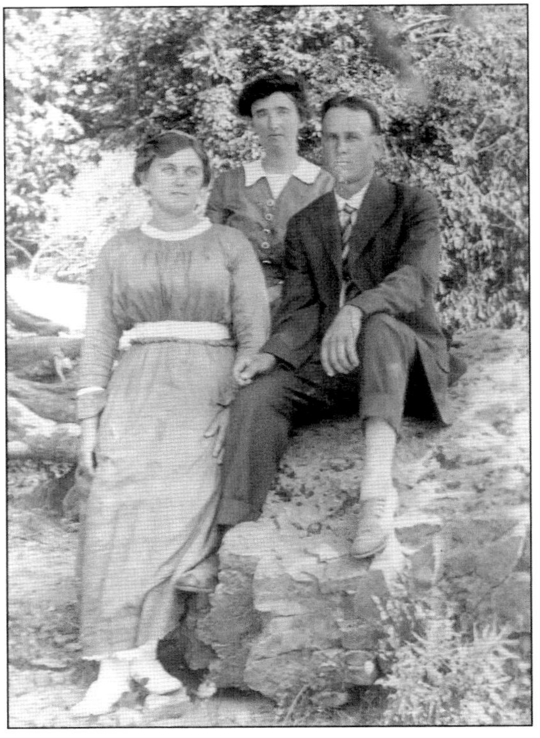

This early 1900s photograph shows three young adults from the Forsyth area. They are Susie Wade, Mag Yandell, and J.D. Coffelt.

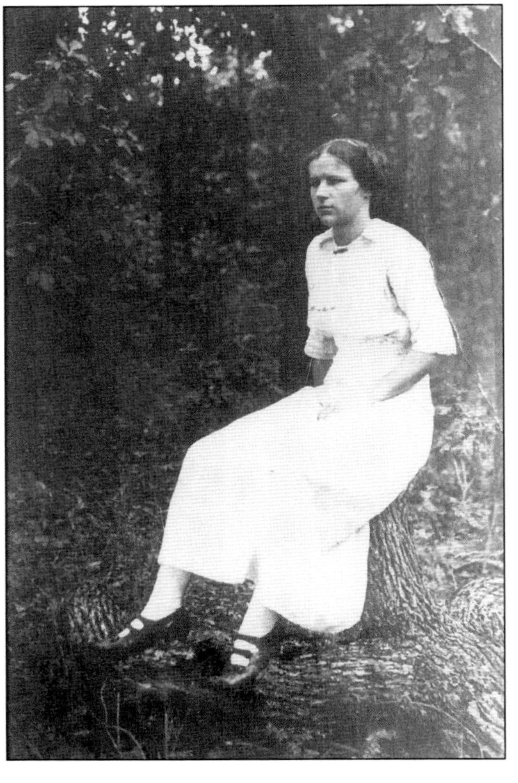

This is an early 1900s photo of Dicey Lynch, who was from Forysth.

This is an early 1900s photograph of Luella Anderson and Lucy Wade from Forsyth. The author's paternal grandfather Charlie Cobb used to "spark" Lucy, or as today's society would say, "date." Charlie's sister Bessie once carried love letters back and forth between Charlie and Lucy.

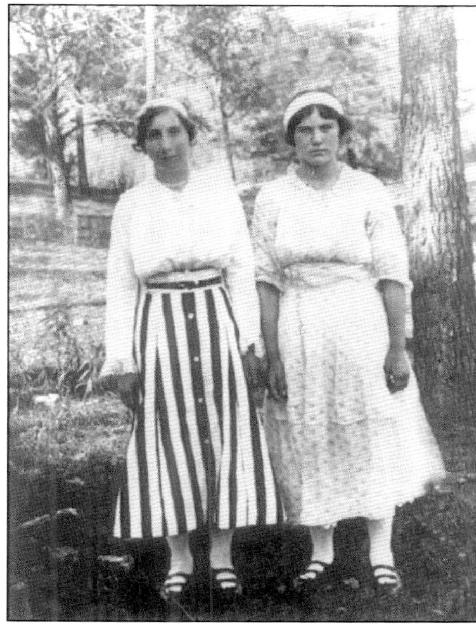

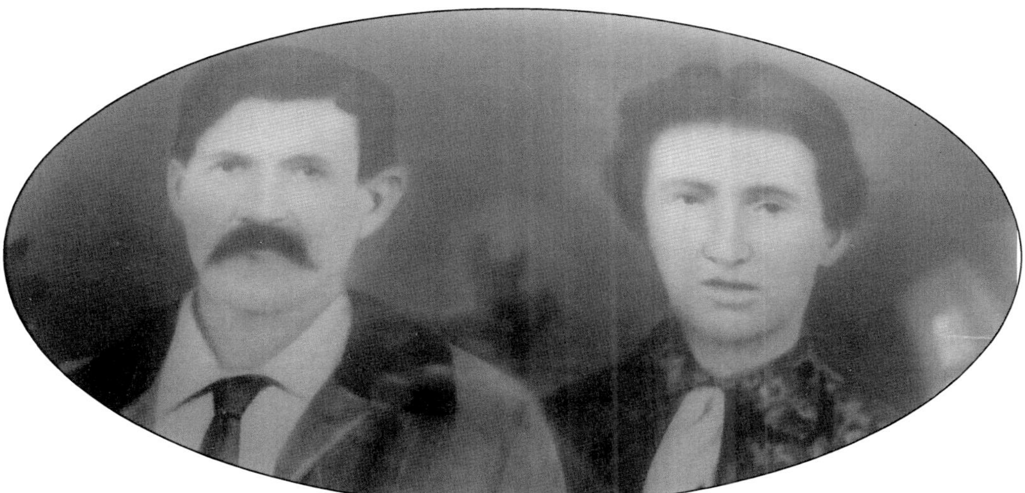

William David (Dake) Layton, grandson of Thomas and Julia Layton, and his wife, Safronea (Whorton) Layton, daughter of Randa and Sarah Whorton, are shown here. This photograph was made by combining their two images from the "Whorton Reunion" photograph, taken shortly before William's death. He'd ridden his horse from Turkey Creek to Forsyth to pay taxes and got wet while crossing Silver Creek in Powersite. When he returned home that night, Fronea knew that the fever and chills would quickly become pneumonia. Knowing he was dying, William instructed her on what to do—sell some cattle, keep the Springfield wagon for transportation, and taught her how to handle the restitution damages with the railroad. It was January 1, 1903, when William died, leaving her with two ten-week-old twins, a four-year-old girl, one six-year-old boy, and a nine-year-old boy. Soon, Safronea received $500 in restitution damages when the construction of the railroad destroyed her home and out buildings. With the money, as William advised her, she bought 160 acres from Alonzo Prather in Oak Grove, with a log cabin built before the Civil War. Safronea remained a widow the remainder of her life.

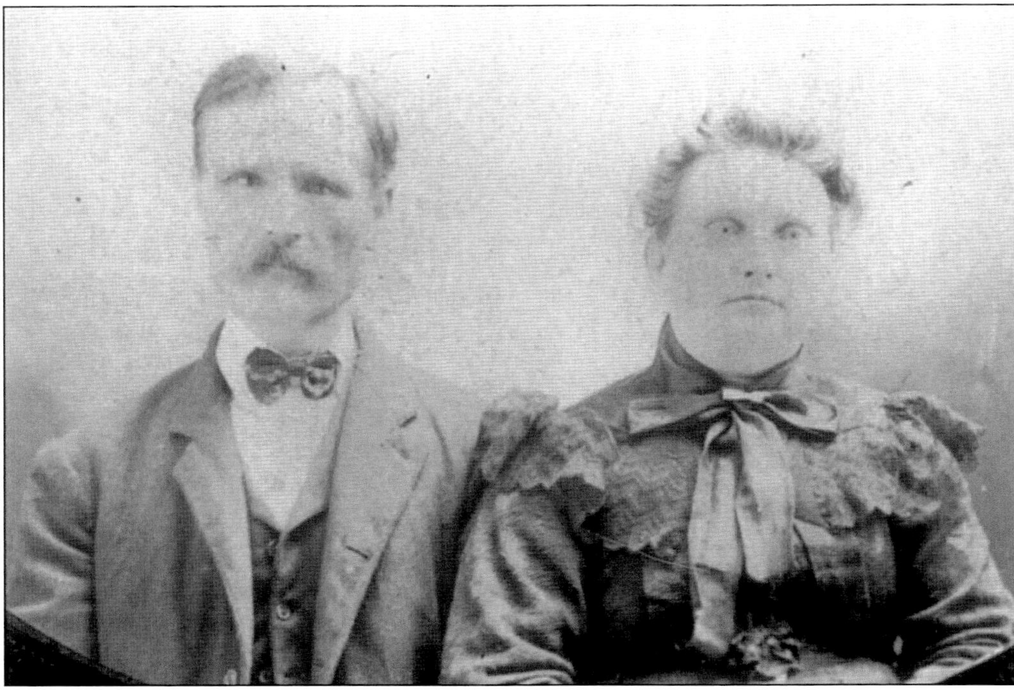

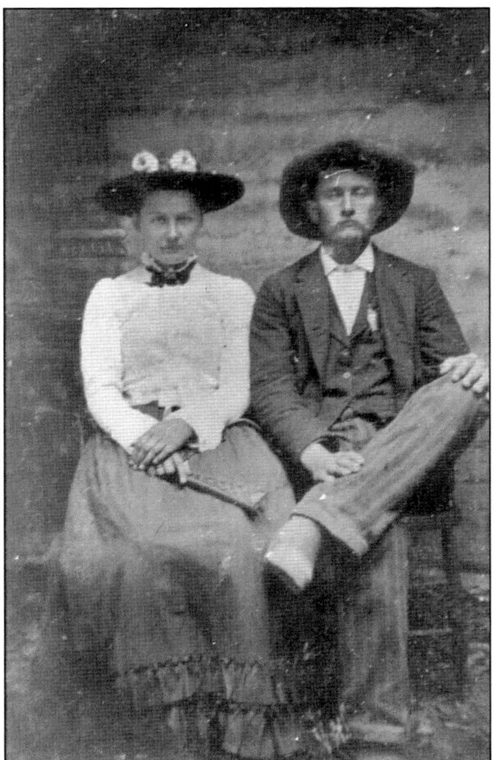

Martha (Whorton) Geeks was photographed with her husband. She was Safronea (Whorton) Layton's half-sister. Martha was Randa Whorton's daughter by his first marriage to a Miss Dotson from Kingston, Arkansas, who died shortly after the first several years of marriage.

Gemes "Uncle Jim" Whorton and his second wife, Almeda, are pictured here. He was Safronea (Whorton) Layton's brother. Jim was kidnapped by the Baldknobbers in the latter 1800s. The Whorton family and local friends, who were Anti-Baldknobbers, banded together and persuaded the group to release Uncle Jim unharmed. Almeda played the organ and piano at the Oak Grove Church house near their home. Jim and Almeda traveled wherever they went in their ox-drawn wagon. Often the back would be full of fresh farm goods to take to Branson, where they'd trade for items they needed.

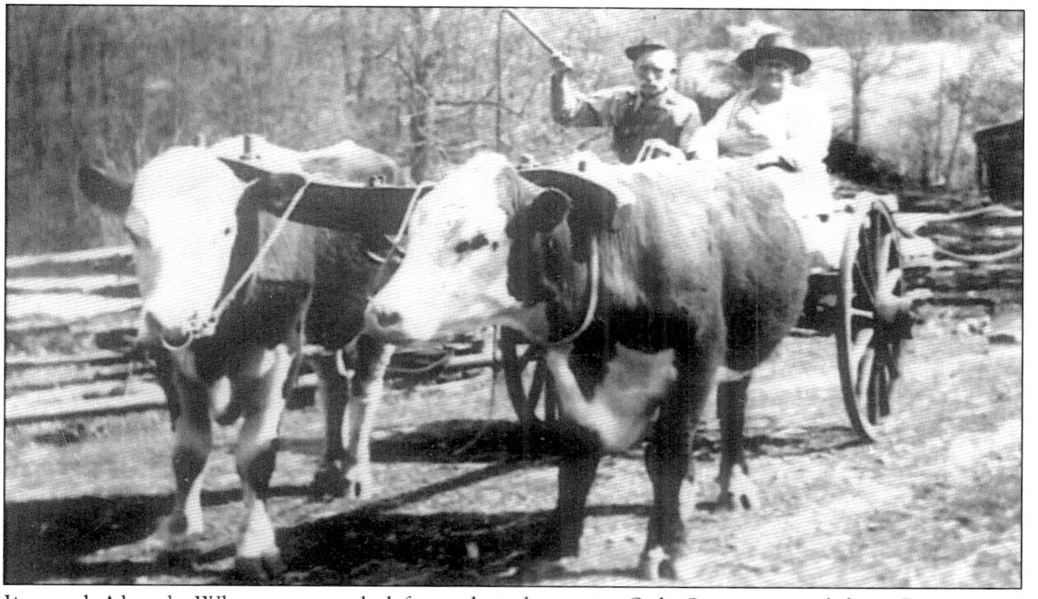

Jim and Almeda Whorton traveled from their home in Oak Grove to and from Branson in their ox-drawn wagon. An ox team consists of any breed of steer that is four years old and large enough to work and pull a wagon, teamed up with another steer of equal traits. Jim always named his ox team Duke and Line. This photograph was taken near the Whorton's barn in Oak Grove and is dated April 26, 1936.

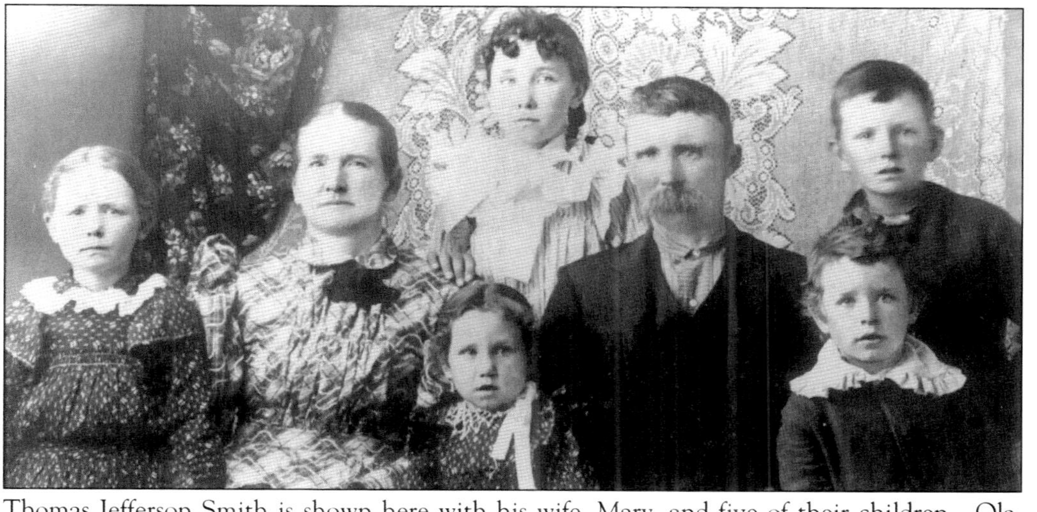

Thomas Jefferson Smith is shown here with his wife, Mary, and five of their children—Ola, Ora, June, Bob, and Truman. Their youngest daughter, Ethel, wasn't born when this photograph was taken, about 1900. Tom Smith was in charge of a freight wagon crew that hauled goods to Springfield from Taney County. The Smith family were also farmers and lived in the Kirbyville and Mincy area. Mary was a first cousin to Andrew Coggburn, the young anti-Baldknobber who was killed by Capt. Kinney, leader of the Baldknobbers. It was passed down through the generations that the day Capt. Kinney himself was buried, Mary stood by his grave, threw in a bundle of matches, and made the remark, "I want to make sure the devil has plenty of matches to keep Kinney's fire burning!"

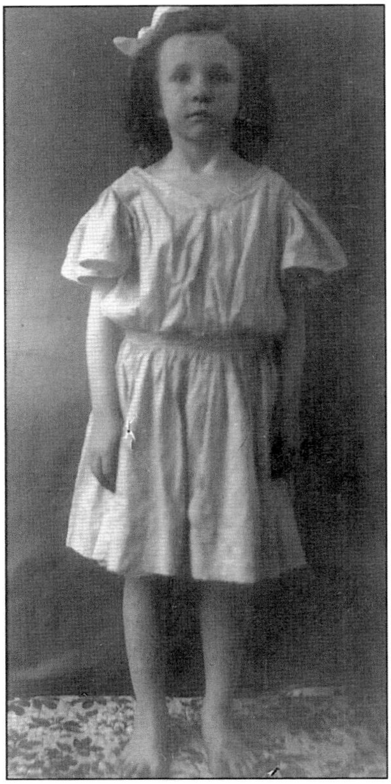

Ethel Smith is pictured here at the age of eight in July 1908. She rode in the back of the family wagon in the rocking chair her parents, Tom and Mary Smith, bought for $5 at a sale in the "Pinery" (where the town of Layton and the Layton sawmill were located). Today, the rocking chair, well over 100 years old, sits in the home of the author's mother, Hazel Layton Cobb (Ethel's daughter). As a child, the author recalls her grandmother tell of riding in the back of the wagon, traveling along the rough terrain of the Mincy area, just rocking back and forth, thinking to herself, what a big girl she was now! Ethel's family lived near Douglas Mahnkey's family when they were children growing up in Kirbyville. Ethel has spoken of the times she and Doug played together in the tree house they made in a large Catalpa tree that grew on the Smith farm.

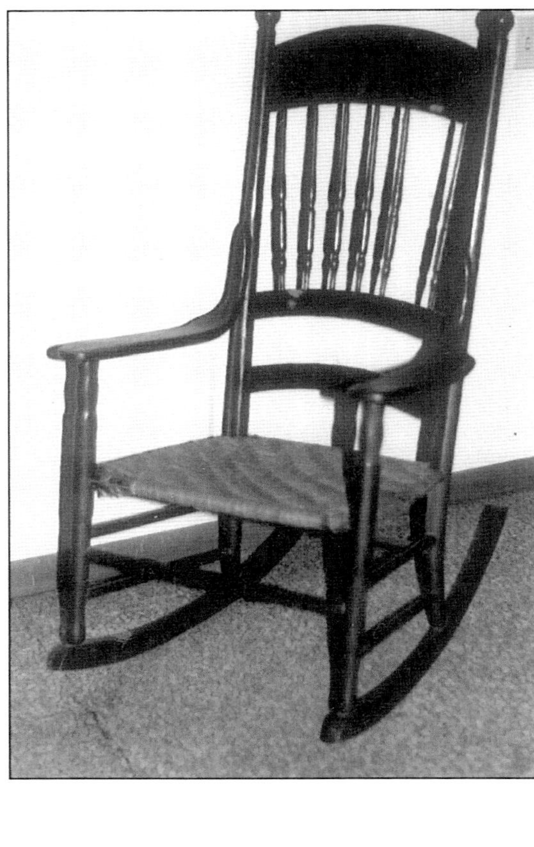

This is the rocking chair Ethel Smith rode in at age eight in back of the Smith family wagon. The chair was already old when her dad Tom bought it, possibly made during the last 20 years of the 1800s. It has been handed down to the third generation as of the year 2000.

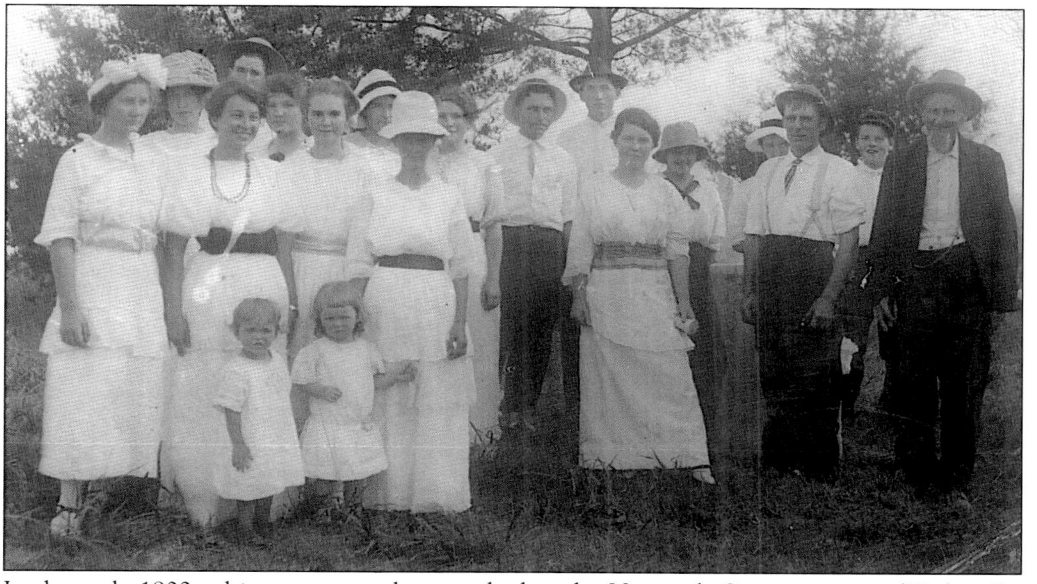

In the early 1900s, this group was photographed at the Vanzandt Cemetery east of Kirbyville. The elderly man on the extreme right with black pants and jacket is Uncle Jimmy Vanzandt. According to the author's great aunt June Smith Anderson, who had written on the back of this photograph dated 1914, said, "Uncle Jimmy is a real old-fashioned song leader and preaches it just like the Bible tells it!" June sent this postcard-photograph to her first husband, Claude Leathers, while she was back from Oregon visiting her family and friends. During her visit, Uncle Jimmy Vanzandt held a revival at the St. James church in Kirbyville. June and Ethel Smith were sisters.

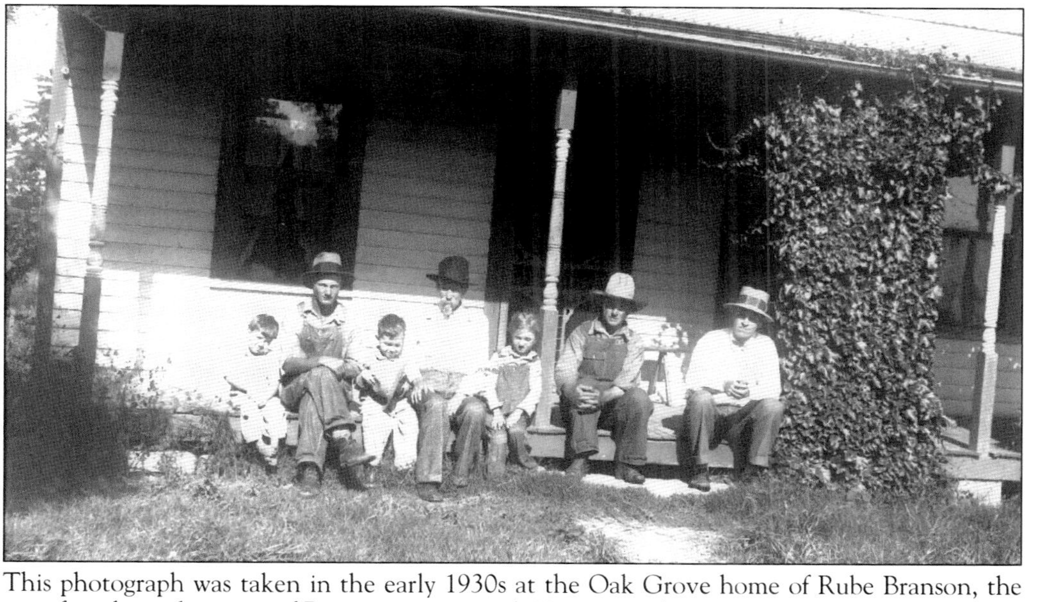

This photograph was taken in the early 1930s at the Oak Grove home of Rube Branson, the man for whom the town of Branson was named. He sits on the porch of his home along with, from left to right: Lee or Bobby Layton, Lonnie Layton, Bobby Hinkle, Rube Branson (man with black hat and goatee beard), William Layton, Randa Layton, and Clayton Hinkle. The house later burned down.

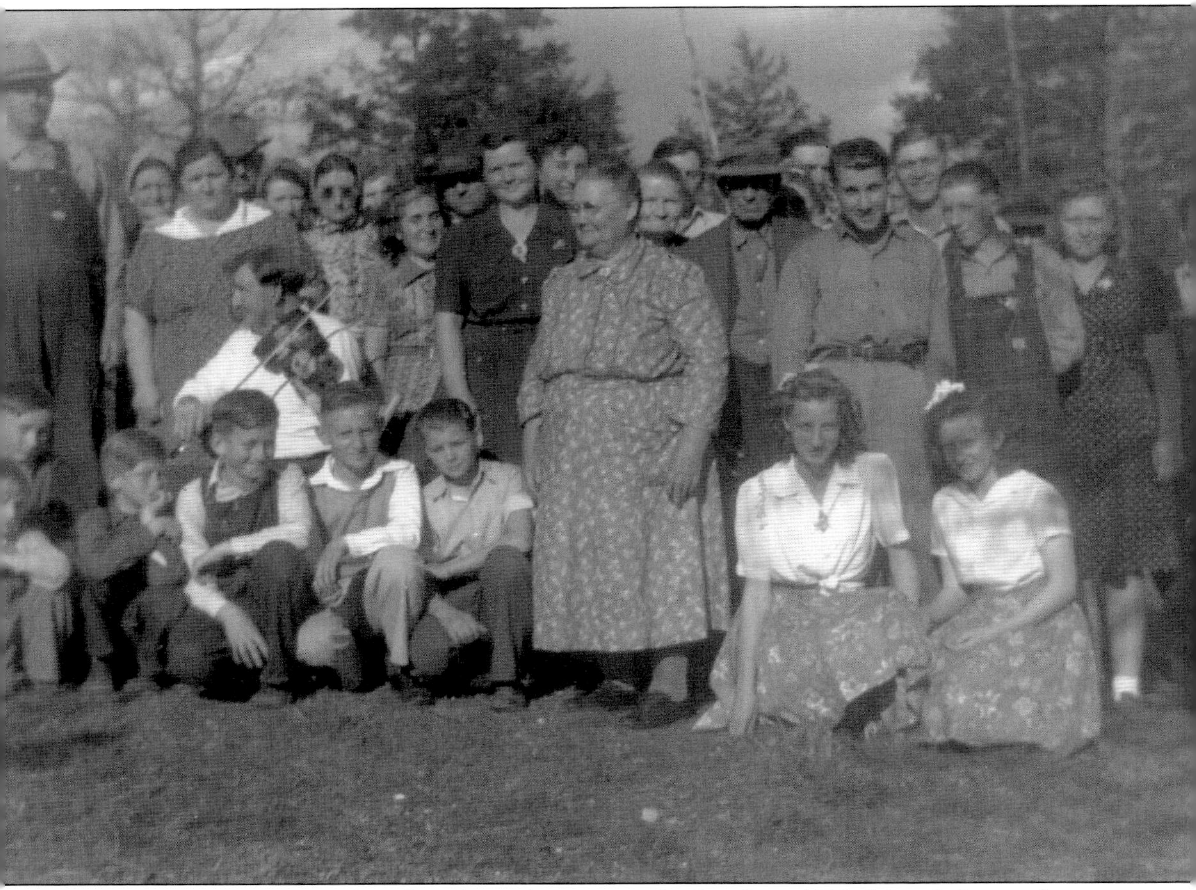

Friends and family gathered in the early 1940s at the Randa and Ethel Smith Layton home in Hollister. Wagon loads of folks, some on horseback, some on foot, brought baskets of home-cooked foods—pies, cakes, cookies, fried chicken, and chicken and dumplings, prepared on wood cook-stoves. Some of the younger men were preparing to leave Taney County to join the United States Army, so this was a get together held in their honor. Those photographed are: Price and Edna Brittain, Francis Rowland, Ollie Layton, Safronea Whorton Layton, Ben and Rosa Layton, Anna Whorton, Lennie Rittenhouse, Anise Bull, John Rittenhouse, Jessie Brittain, Lee Layton, Lester Rowland, Bill Layton, Harold Layton, Lois Rowland, Bob Layton, Almeda Whorton, and Uncle Ed Layton with his fiddle. The small boys are Don and Stanley Rittenhouse, Howard Rowland, Dallas Rowland, Don Whorton, and Gifford Boswell. The two teenage girls kneeling in front dressed similarly are Charlene and Hazel Layton.

Three

Early Schools of Taney County

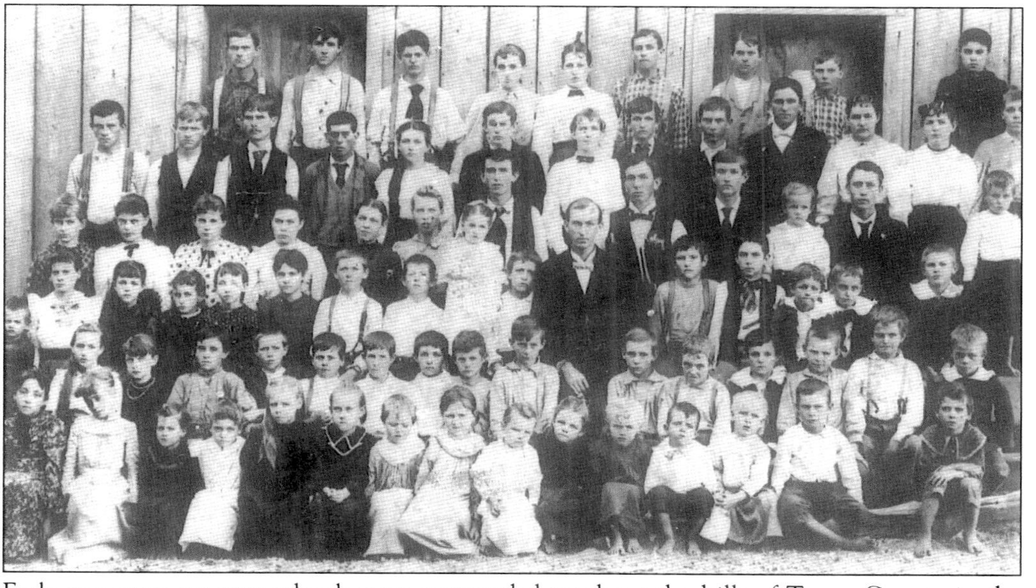

Early one-room country schools were scattered throughout the hills of Taney County in the late 1800s and the early 1900s. Not all of those in existence during that time are represented in this chapter. Their locations consisted of only miles between each other, as the methods of transportation in those days was limited to either walking by foot, by horseback, or by wagon. So they had to be relatively close and were the center of each community—not only serving as a source of education but often also as the local church houses. Below is the Mincy School group of 1897. The Pruitt family brothers and sisters are as follows: David, Sidney, Cordelia, Robert Howard, Lula Clay, Benjamin Harrison, Ernest William, and Commie Andrew Pruitt. Others shown include: Mamie Brown, Andy Moore, Robert Brown, the Biles children, and the Puterbaugh children. Many are ancestors to numerous descendants still living in Taney County. At the top, second row from the right, the second couple to the left are Andy Moore and Cordelia Pruitt, who married in 1902. This photograph was contributed by Bobby Pruitt of Grants Pass, Oregon, a descendent of the Pruitt and Thomas Foster Layton families.

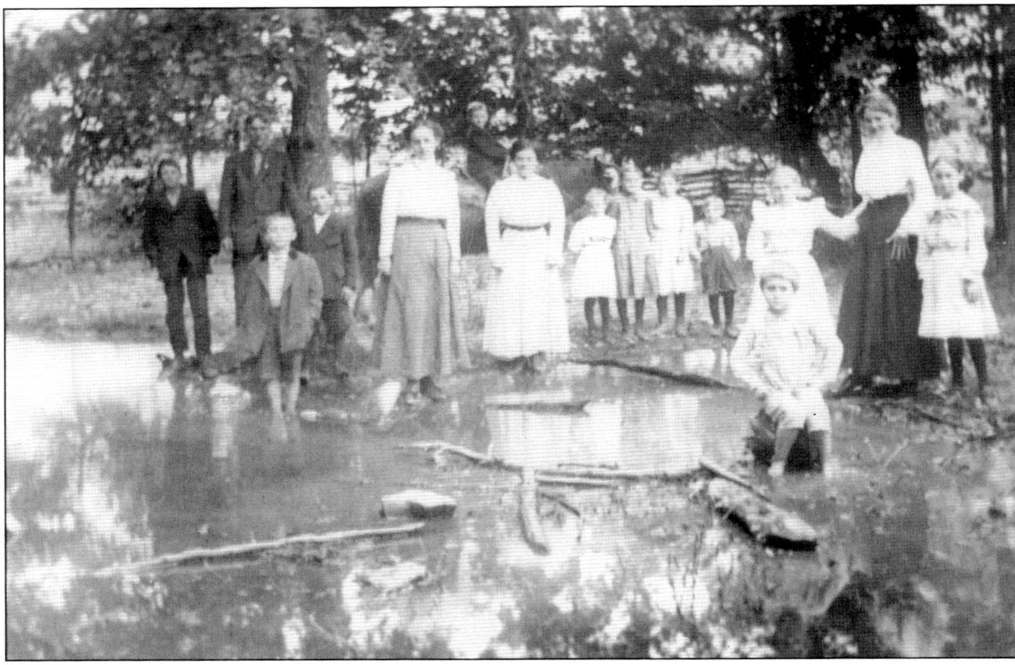

The Pleasant Hill school, also known as Sardis, is located on Highway 76 east of Branson, between Kirbyville and Mildred. Pictured here from left to right are: Harry Moore, John Haworth, Emmett McCann, Van Moore, Lula Rose, Gum Thurman, Maude Jennings, Beatrice Thurman, Eva Stallcup, Georgia Moore, Valus Winters, Sallie Haworth (author's paternal grandmother), Benton Moore, teacher Pearlie M. Hicks, and Bernice Thurman.

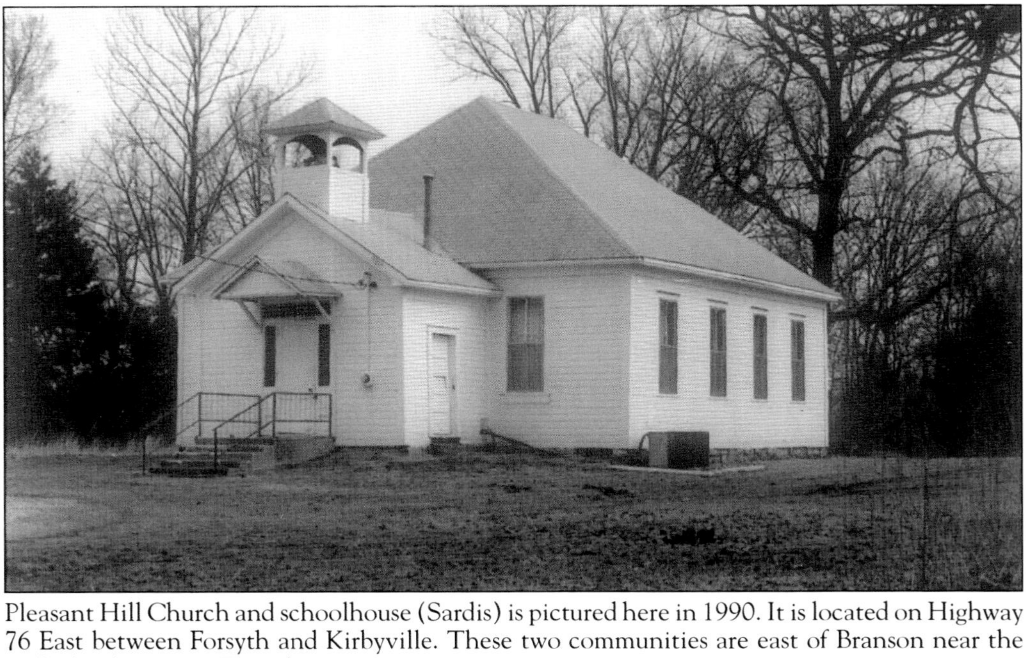

Pleasant Hill Church and schoolhouse (Sardis) is pictured here in 1990. It is located on Highway 76 East between Forsyth and Kirbyville. These two communities are east of Branson near the Bull Shoals Dam in Forsyth.

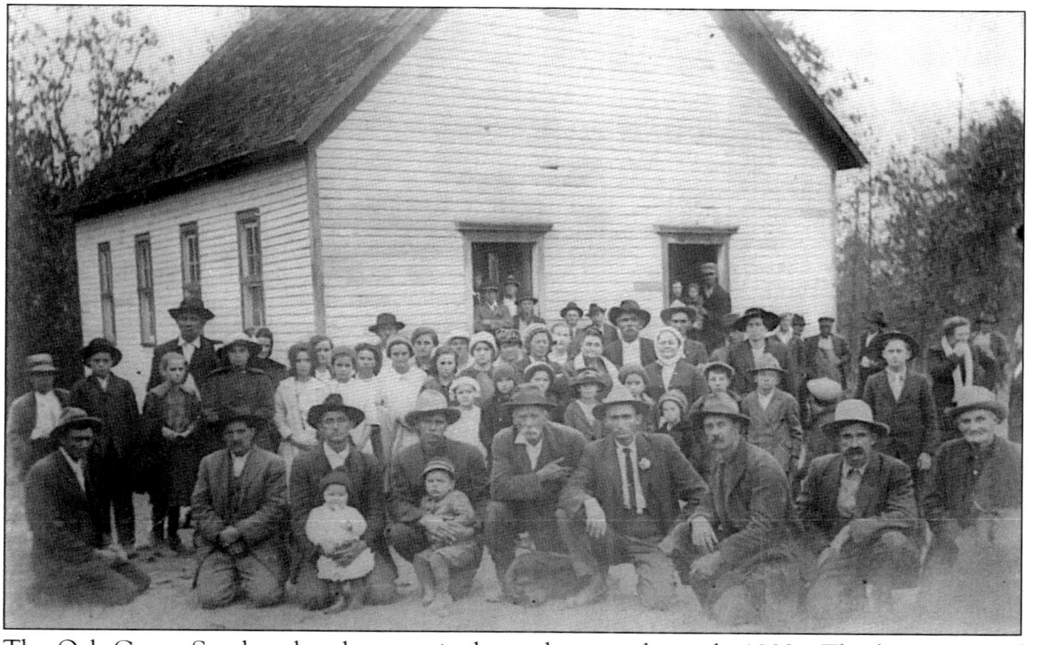

The Oak Grove Sunday church group is shown here in the early 1900s. The last names of some present include: Hodge, Rose, Kaneaster, Cornealison, Brown, Layton, Whorton, Snapp, Howard, Branson, and Haggard.

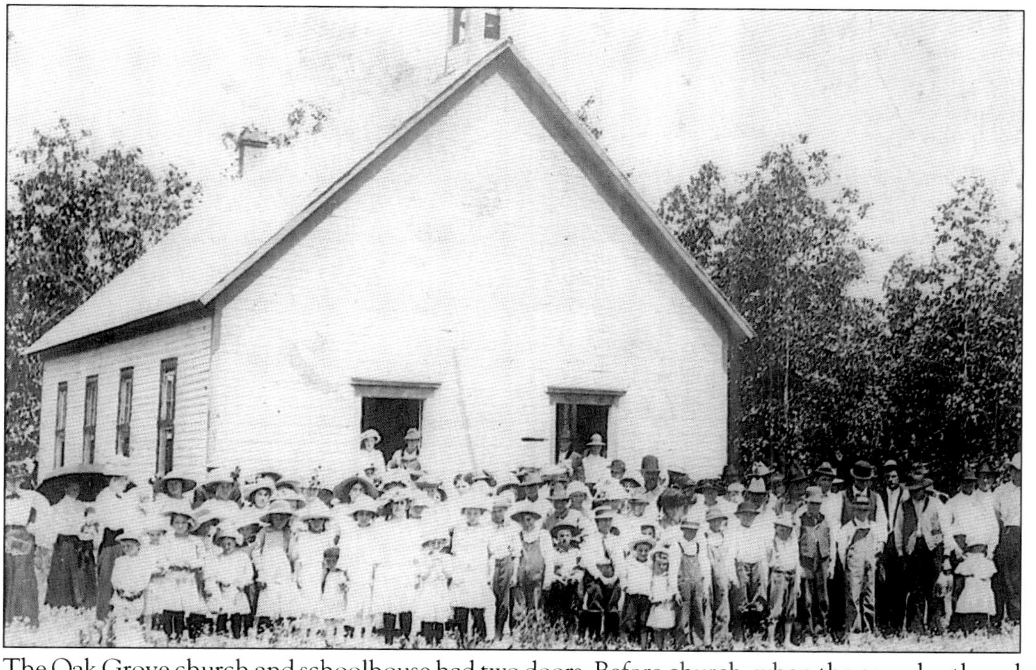

The Oak Grove church and schoolhouse had two doors. Before church, when the crowd gathered for services, the men entered one door, and the women entered the other. The men sat on one side, and the women sat on the opposite side in the pews. Young boys lined up in the back, or outside, where they listened and watched through the windows.

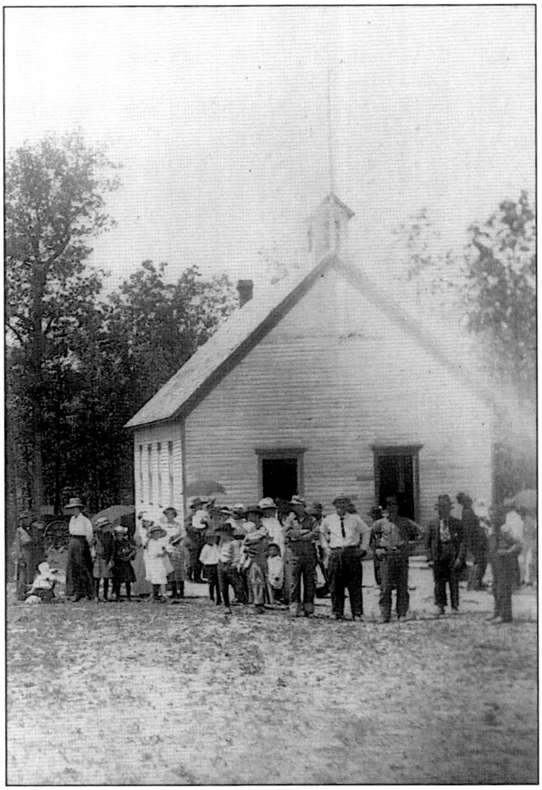

At the back of the church on the left side, a horse stands beneath a shade tree hitched to a buggy awaiting the trip home. The country church served the community as a source of spiritual guidance and a place for the education of the community's children. In those days, the basic subjects taught were writing, reading, spelling, arithmetic, and history, with all grades and ages in the same room. It was also a community-gathering place for social events such as pie suppers on a Saturday night. This gave the young people near the age of "courtship" the opportunity to get acquainted outside of church and school activities.

This mid-1920s photograph depicts the inside of the Oak Grove school as it appeared during school session. Oak Grove is east of Branson, off what is known as "T" Highway, or the Long Beach Road.

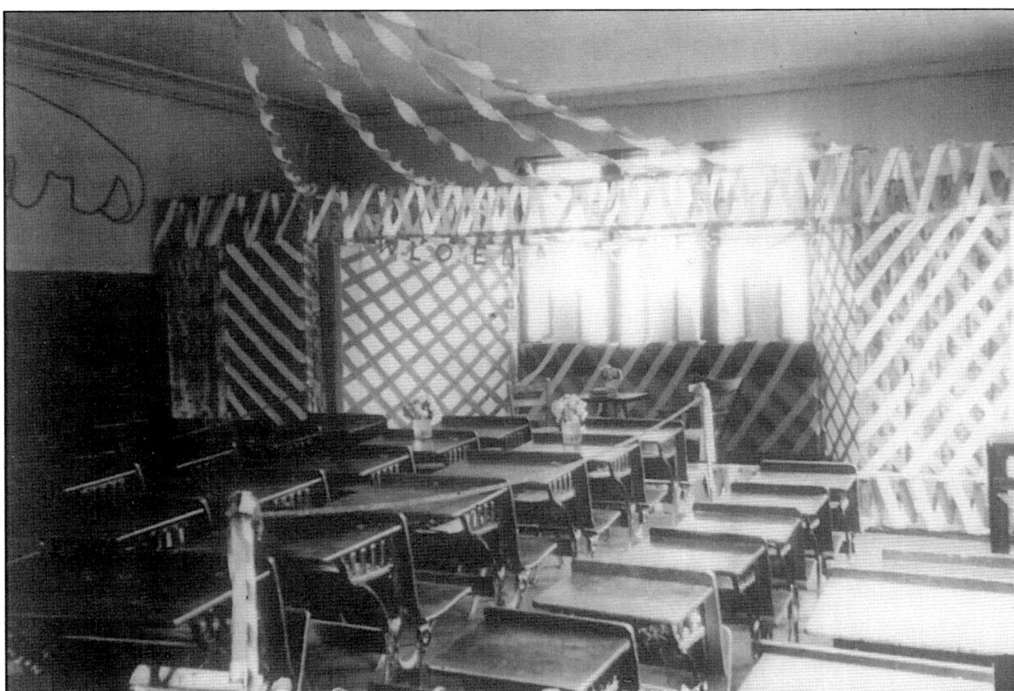

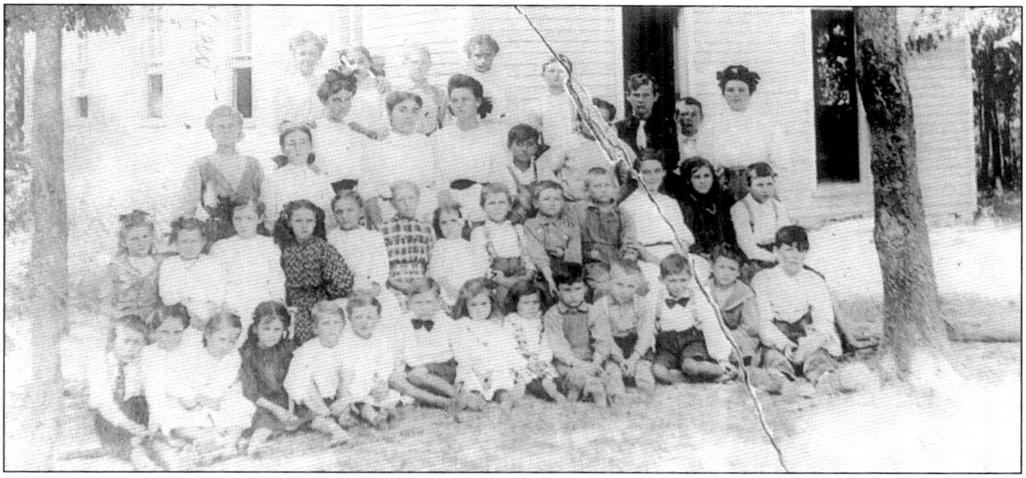

Pictured here is an Oak Grove School group of 1908. They are, from left to right: (front row) Matt Snapp, Gracie Russell, Emma Russell, Alma Rooks, Lonnie and Ollie Layton, Martin Davis, Agnes, Mable, and Clarence Rose, Sam Kaneaster, Buddie Davis, Gertie Rooks, and Georgia Purtel; (second row) Emma Rooks, Opal Firmin, Esther Berry, Mae Cornealison, Edna Layton, Mamie Hensley, Bell McGill, Robert Snapp, Lee Firmin, Martin and Maude Baldwin, Addie Snapp, and Randa Layton; (third row) Ellie Hensley, Bessie Kaneaster, Josie Gloyd, Betty Kaneaster, Rosa Gloyd, Ben Russell, Rose Kertner, Leo Firmin, Frank Baldwin, and teacher Mamie Johnson; (fourth row) Mary Wright Muller, Rosa Kaneaster, John Baldwin, Bessie Russell, and Albert Whorton.

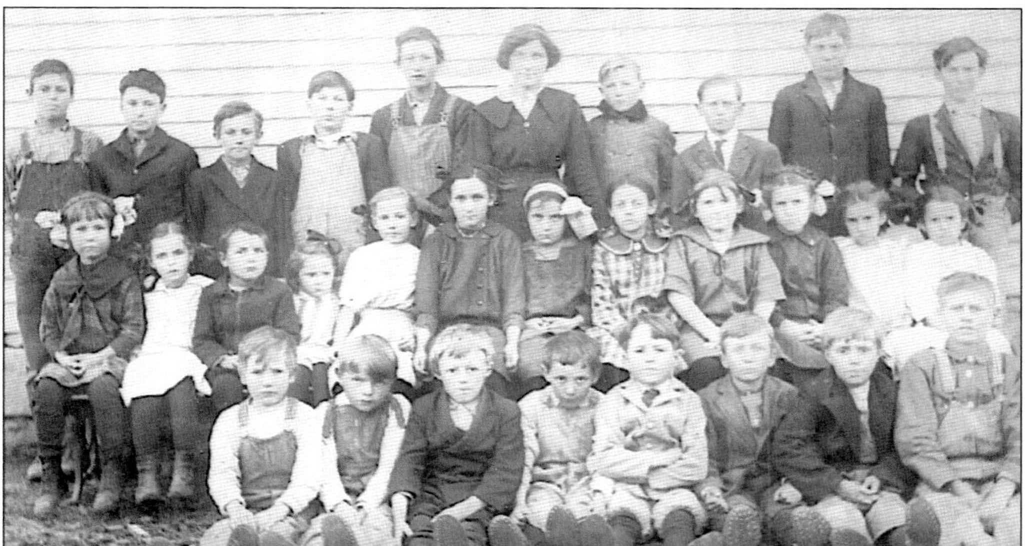

The Oak Grove School students are pictured here in 1918. They are: (back row) Ray McFarland, Lonnie Layton, Clinton Whorton, Sam Kaneaster, Ernest Crouch, Clyde Crouch, Loral McFarland, Clarence Rose, and Athas Stacy; (middle row) Freida Coggburn, Mamie Rose, Ted Hall, Blanche Hall, Beryl McFarland, Mable Rose, Esther Lee Hall, Della Betts, Tommy Branson, Maggie, Lottie, and Agnes Rose; (first row) Leonard McFarland, Dewayne Eismen, Teddy Warn, Owen McFarland, Ray Coggburn, Harmon Rose, Fletch Kaneaster, and Ed Clarkson.

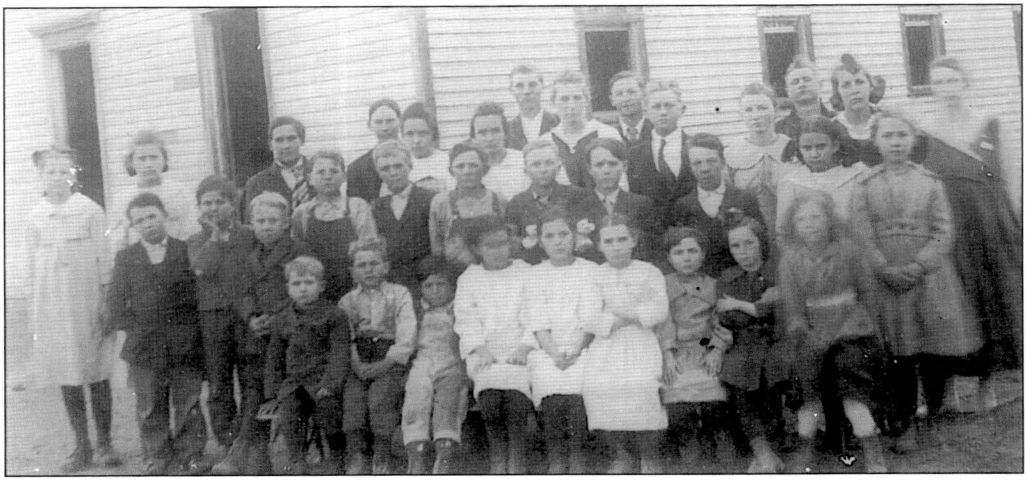

This is the Oak Grove School in 1920. They are, from right to left: (back row) Jesse Sutherland (the teacher), Bertie Pleake, Ed Carson, Ollie Layton, Clinton Whorton, Martin Baldwin, Gertie Pleake, Sam Kaneaster, Mable Rose, Esther Lee Hall, Ernest Crouch, James McGill, Maggie Rose, and Beryl McFarland; (middle row) Ted Hall, unidentified, Leonard McFarland, Fletch Kaneaster, Owen McFarland, Harmon Rose, Ray Coggburn, Frank Hall, Lottie Rose, and Frieda Coggburn; (front row) first two unidentified, Mamie Rose, Clara Belle Rose, and the others are unknown.

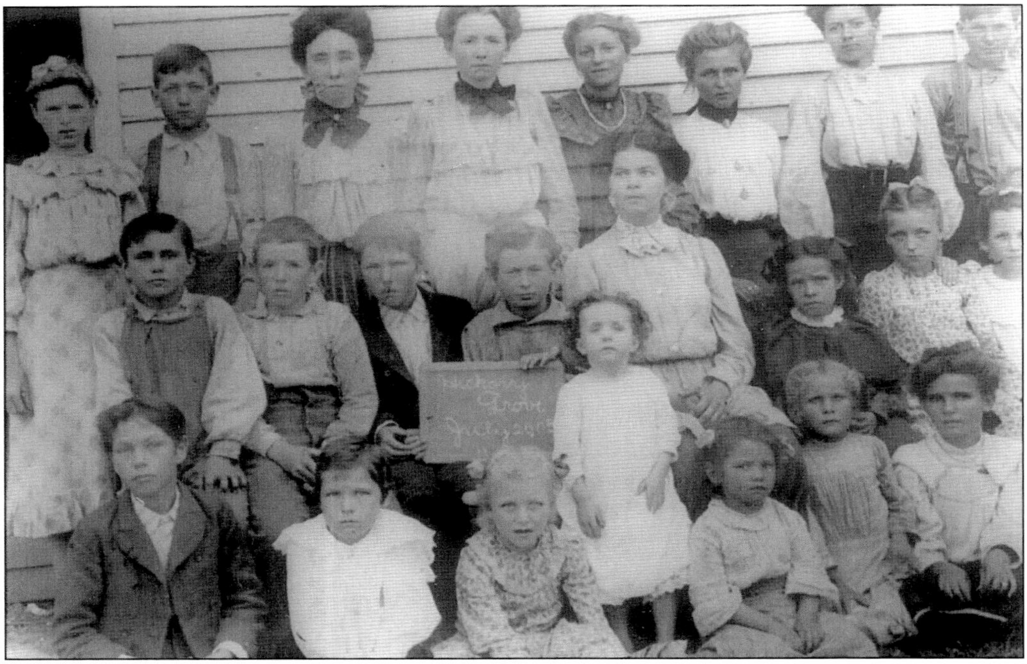

This is the Hickory Grove School on July 25, 1905. The school is located in Taney County off Highway J, near Kirbyville. Pictured here, from left to right, are: (front row) Mary Renylous, Jim Humphry, Ola and Ora Smith, Mamie Trout, Annie Parnell, Minta Trout, and Bob Smith; (second row) Vince Nelson, Truman Smith, Allen Pleake, Frank Language, Ethel Smith, Lillie Brazeal (the teacher), Golda Pleake, Neta Humphry, and June Smith; (third row) Vernie and Chess Pleake, and Minnie Humphry; the other three girls' last name is Gargarus.

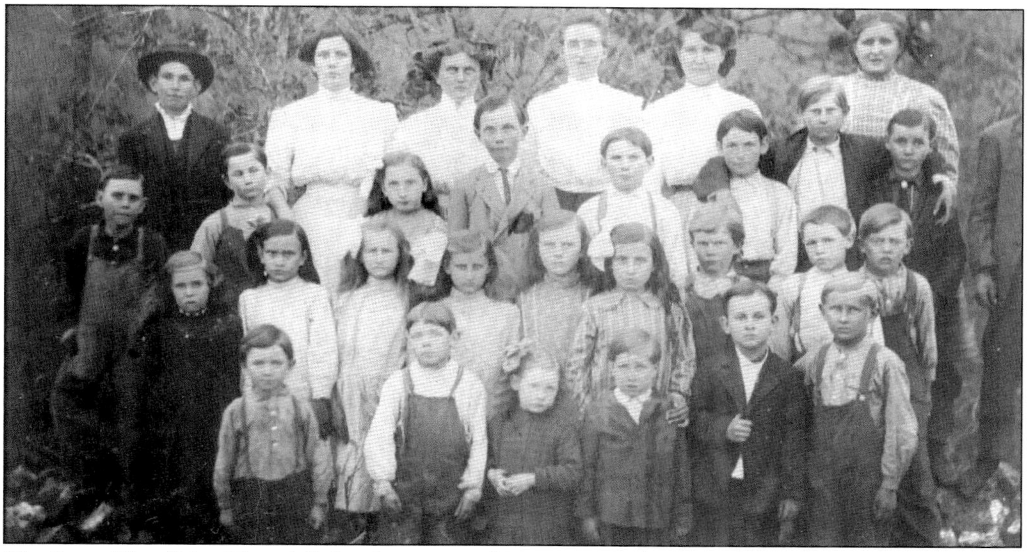

The Lone Elm (Mt. Olives) School is pictured here in March 1912. This photograph was taken by Markus Clayton, with the old tintype camera. Pictured are, from left to right: (front row) Ray Edwards, Alva and Bessie Cobb, Eugene Kinney, Lester Clayton, and Lee Yandell; (second row) Velma Kinney (Edwards), Chloe Casey (Thurman), Thelma Yandell (Johnson), Lucy Wade (Green), Ethel Casey (Pickett), Claude Edwards, Bill Lynn, and Herman Edwards; (third row) George Cobb, Ralph Crouch, Luella Anderson (Brittain), Zedic Anderson (Brittain), Ben Crouch, Ernie Lynn, Albert Branson (who later married Bessie Cobb), and William (Bill) Cobb; (back row) John Crouch, Sidney Casey (Fulkerson), Susie Wade (Coffelt), Mag Yandell (O'Neal), the teacher Ellie Flint, Shirley Yandell (Stallcup), and Colonel Clayton.

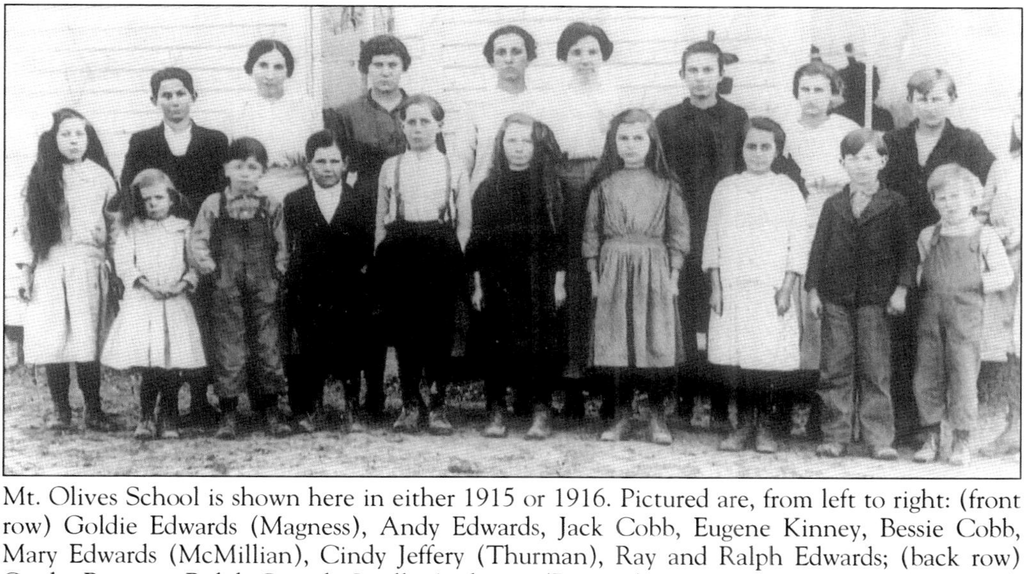

Mt. Olives School is shown here in either 1915 or 1916. Pictured are, from left to right: (front row) Goldie Edwards (Magness), Andy Edwards, Jack Cobb, Eugene Kinney, Bessie Cobb, Mary Edwards (McMillian), Cindy Jeffery (Thurman), Ray and Ralph Edwards; (back row) Cordie Branson, Ralph Crouch, Luella Anderson (Brittain), Lucy Wade (Green), Ethel Casey (Pickett), the teacher Tilda Stafford (Brown), Chloe Casey (Thurman), Zan Yandell (Edwards), Lee Yandell, and Velma Kinney (Edwards). The author's great-aunts Bessie Cobb Branson and Winnie Cobb Yandell of Kirbyville contributed the photograph and identifications.

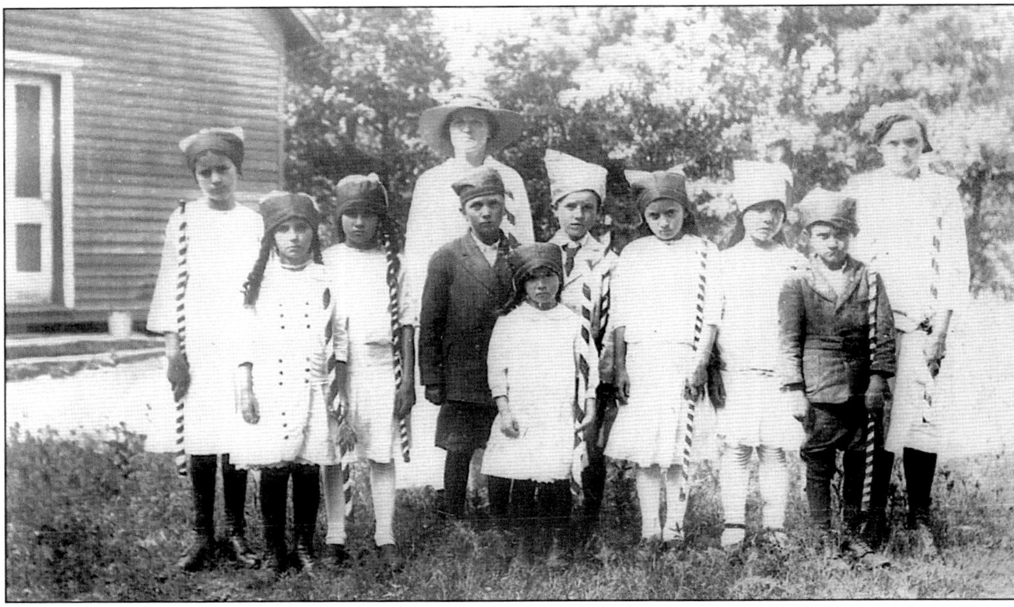

Mt. Grove School, east of Branson, is shown here in the early 1900s. The teacher, Bertie Tompson Coggburn, taught these children a recital for Memorial Day. Those present include: Maggie Agnes, Lottie and Harmon Rose, Ray Coggburn, Clara Belle Rose, Freida Selsor, Mamie, Mable, and Maurice Rose.

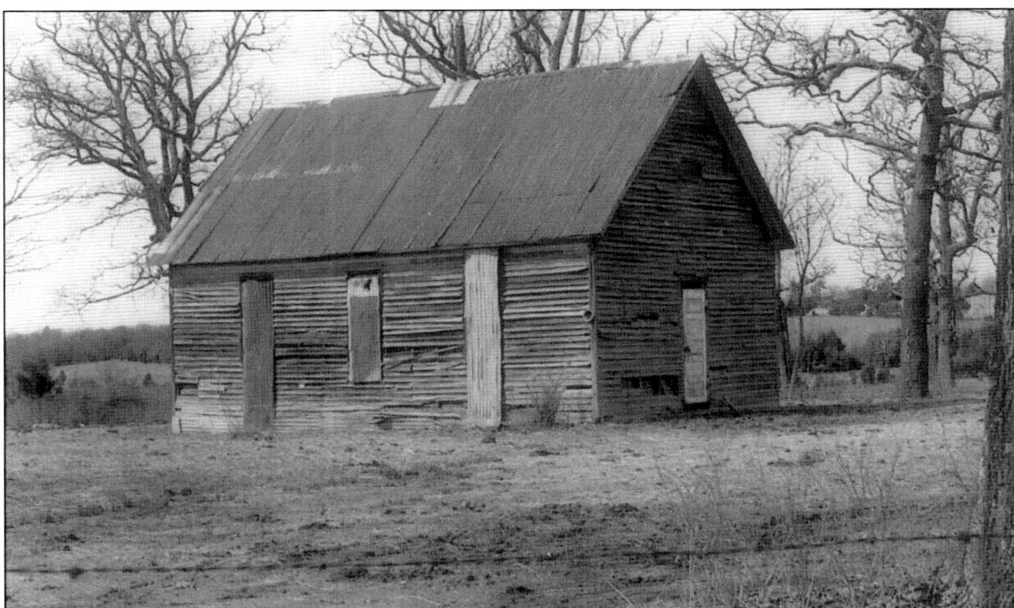

This is Hickory Grove School in 1990. The vacant one-room school, once the educational facility for all grades taught by one teacher, is a lonely reminder of Taney County history. The simple days of the one-room country school are forever lost. Once the sound of children's laughter and footsteps filled the abandoned school and church house. Now silence prevails, along with memories of the remaining ones who knew it in their lifetime.

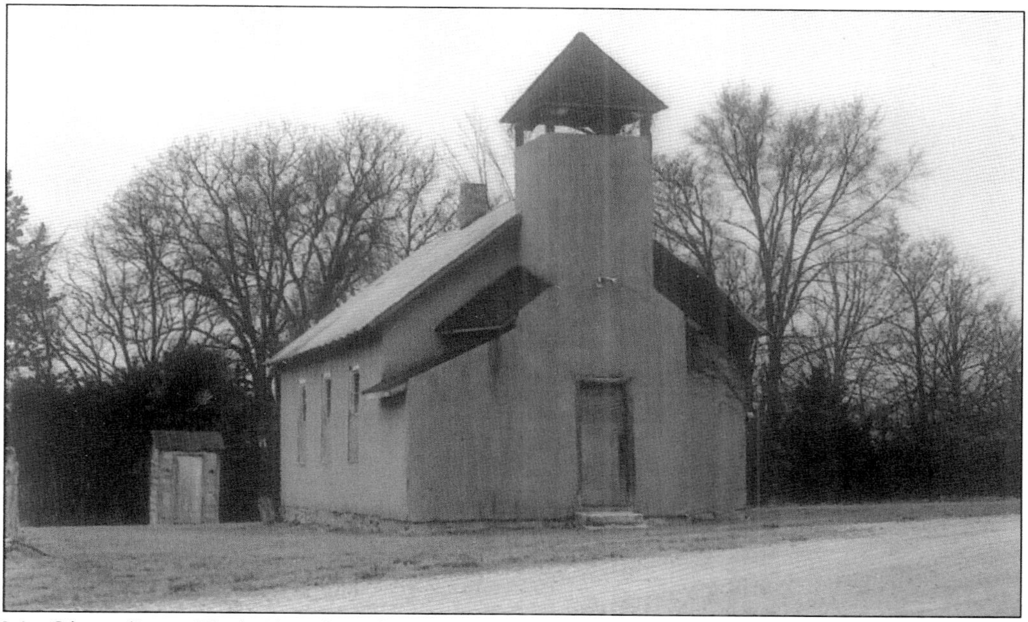

Mt. Olives (Lone Elm) Church and schoolhouse is shown here in 1990, on the Blackwell Ferry Road in the Mildred community, east of Kirbyville. The rock steps to the door came from the original Lone Elm school and church, which was moved from the hollow to its present site at the turn of the 20th century.

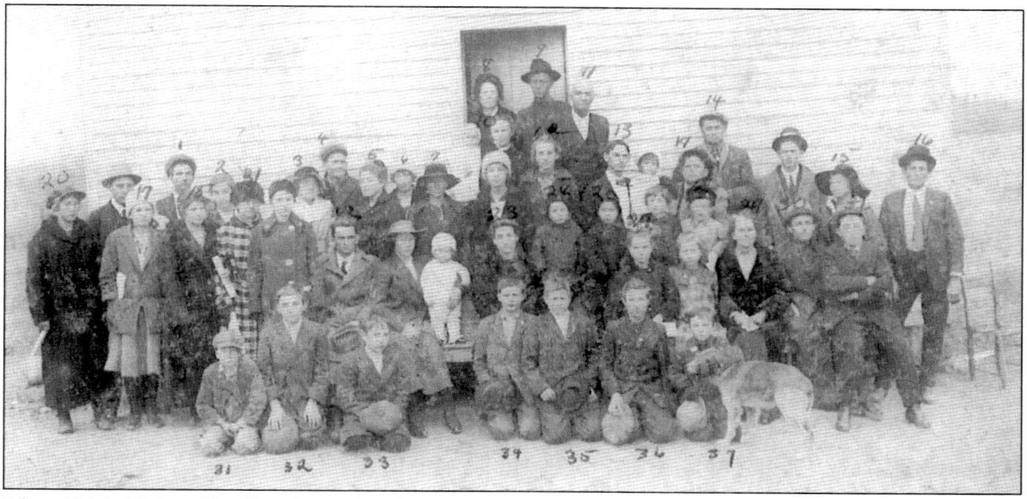

The 1914 Kirbyville Sunday school group is pictured above. They are, from left to right: (front row) Charley Speers, Jim and Lee Chaney, Lawrence Haggard, Ed Carson, and Douglas Mahnkey and his brother Reggie with his dog Rex; (second row) Miss Dehl, Miss Layton, Bruce and Violet Coggburn, Mr. and Mrs. Bert Chaney, Bill and Roberta Mahnkey, Mary Elizabeth (Prather) Mahnkey, C.P. Mahnkey, and Lee Brown; (third row) first man is unidentified, Floyd White, Ethel Chaney, Iva White, Bill Brazeal, Nora and Nezzie Coggburn, Myrtle Campbell, Bernice McClary, C.L. Stottle with child in arms, Hiram Larabee, Maude White and Harding King, teacher Miss Wilson, in the doorway with Ben Speers in front, Winnie Stottle, Uncle George Brazeal, and Paul Brazeal. (Photo courtesy of Douglas Mahnkey.)

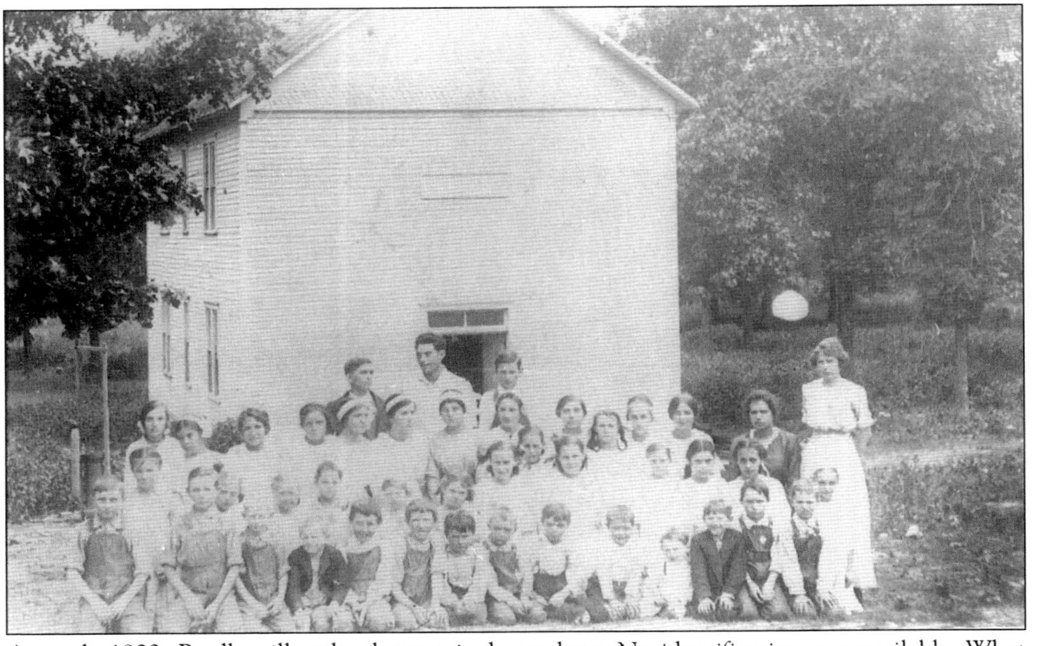

An early 1900s Bradleyville school group is shown here. No identification was available. What social life the early Taney County citizens knew usually centered around the one-room church and schoolhouse. Pie suppers were held on Saturday nights, with girls and women baking pies that were later auctioned off and sold to the highest bidder. The buyer got to eat the pie with the girl who baked it. This was how many of the country boys and girls became acquainted. Often the ritual of "courtship" followed, as did many local marriages. (Photo courtesy of Douglas Mahnkey.)

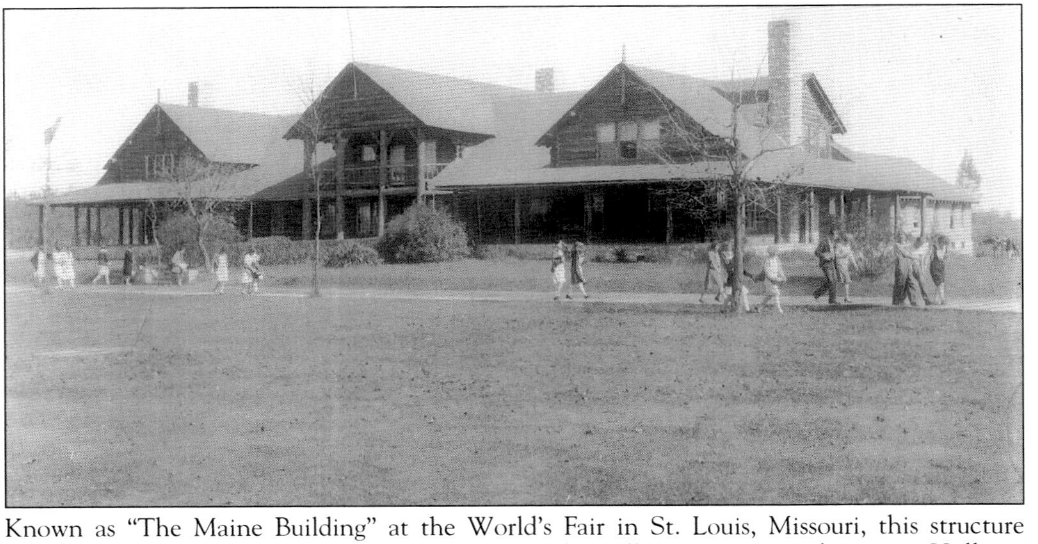

Known as "The Maine Building" at the World's Fair in St. Louis, Missouri, this structure became the first building on the School of the Ozarks College at Point Lookout near Hollister and Branson. It served as a girls' dormitory and dining hall in 1917 and 1918, when Douglas Mahnkey attended the college along with Roy Southard, Ernest Redfern, Jess Stultz, Clarence Parkey, and Lee Moore—all from Taney County. Later, the building was destroyed by fire. (Photo courtesy of Douglas Mahnkey.)

Four

WHEAT FIELDS AND BATTLEGROUNDS

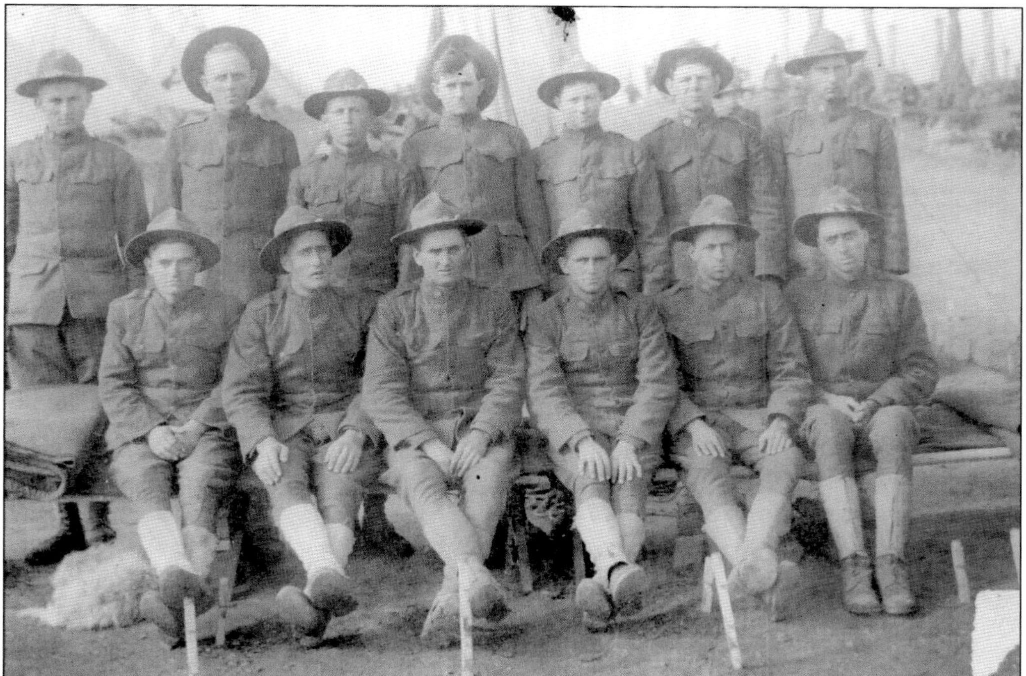

Pictured here are a group of World War I soldiers stationed in Camp Bowie, Texas. The author's grandfather, Randa Layton, is the third man from the right in the back row. Others from Taney County, along with Randa, include: Ed Stallcup, Harry Moore, and Dophus Layton. The other soldiers are: Ernie McMillian, Homer Moberly, Pailey Swigler, John Randolph, Johnny Mullin, Maynard Lamberth, Art White, and Orval Wallace.

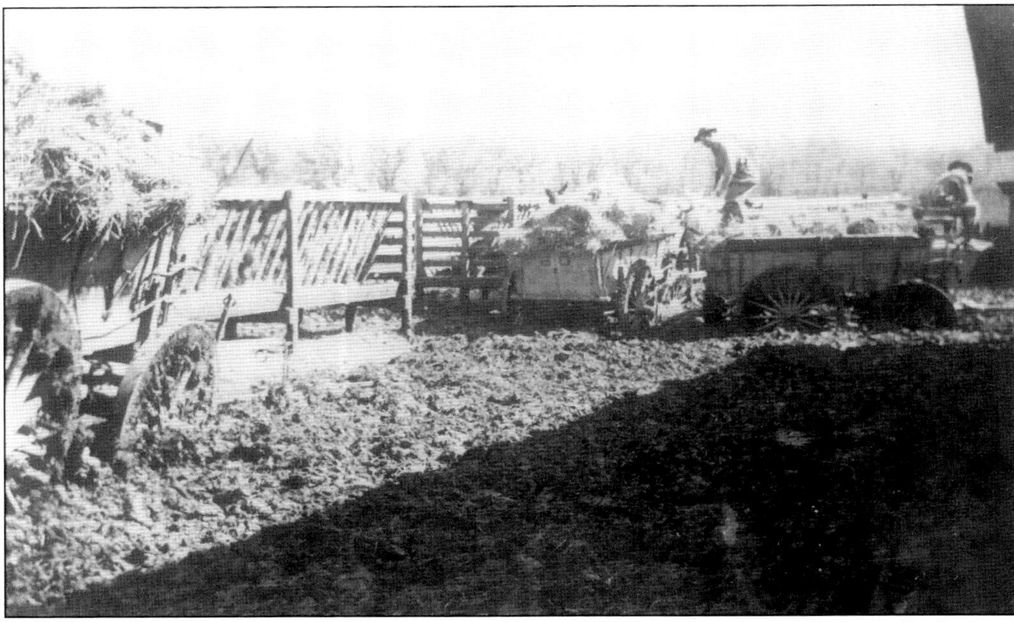

In World War I, Randa Layton, the man on the left, pitches hay from the wagon into the feed bin. He was in charge of the care and feeding of over 3,000 head of mules. As he often recollected those days, he said the mud would be so deep at times that it nearly reached his knees. Often times along with the soldier crew working under his command, the mud would pull their boots off.

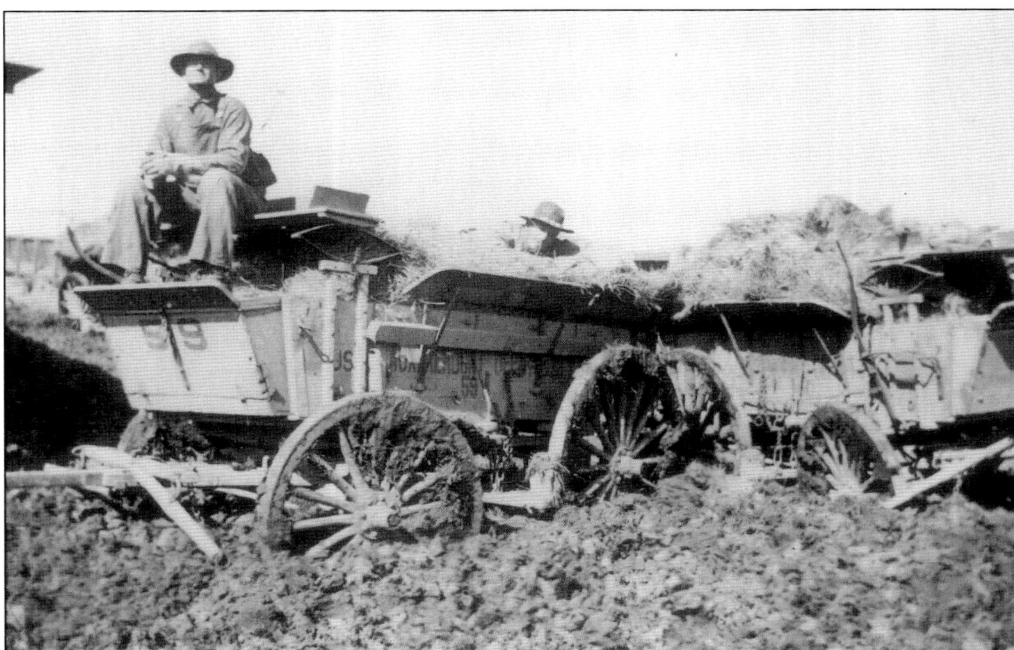

Randa Layton sits in the wagon seat as one of his Army buddies stretches across the loose hay in a more relaxing moment. The mud was so deep at this time from frequent and heavy rains that they were unable to move the wagons, because the wheels would be buried hub deep in the mud.

Albert Whorton was a World War I soldier from Taney County. The Whorton family and the Layton family were a few of Taney County's earliest pioneer families. The Whortons came to Hollister after the Civil War.

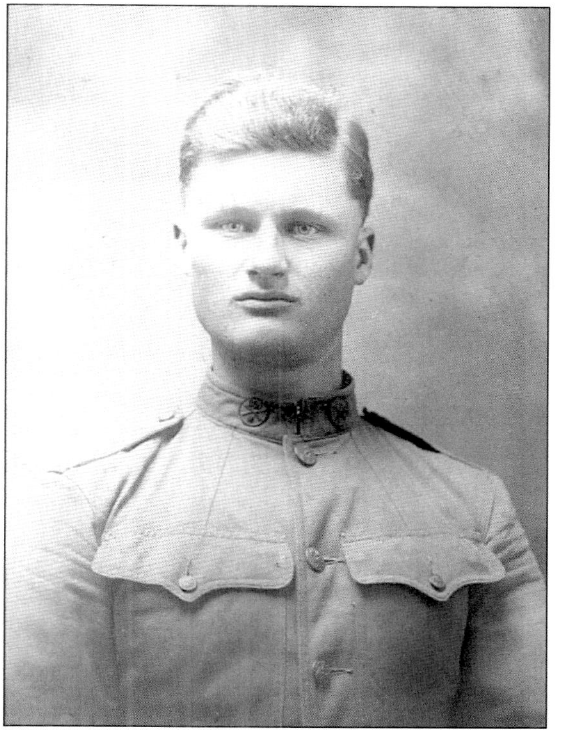

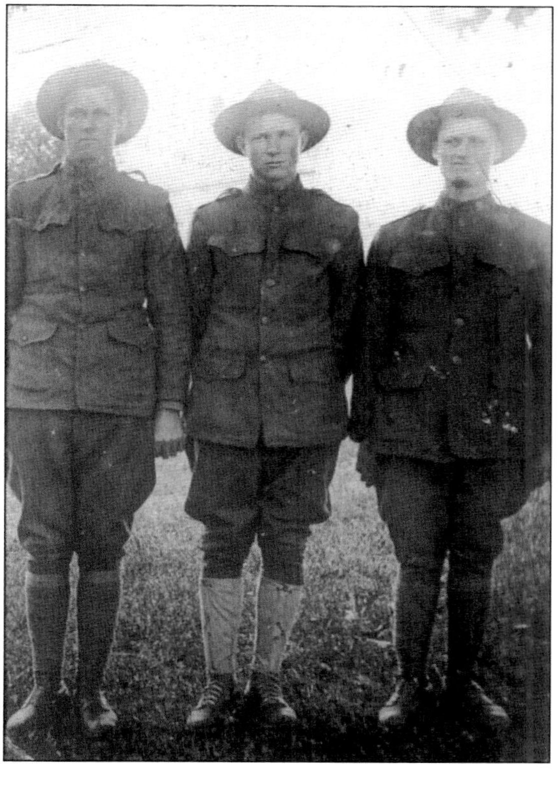

Randa Layton stands between his cousin Albert Whorton on the right, and the soldier's name on the left is not identified. Randa and Albert grew up within a mile of each other in the Oak Grove community near Branson, Missouri, in Taney County. Not only were they in the service together, but they also traveled to the wheat fields of Kansas, and as far north as South Dakota.

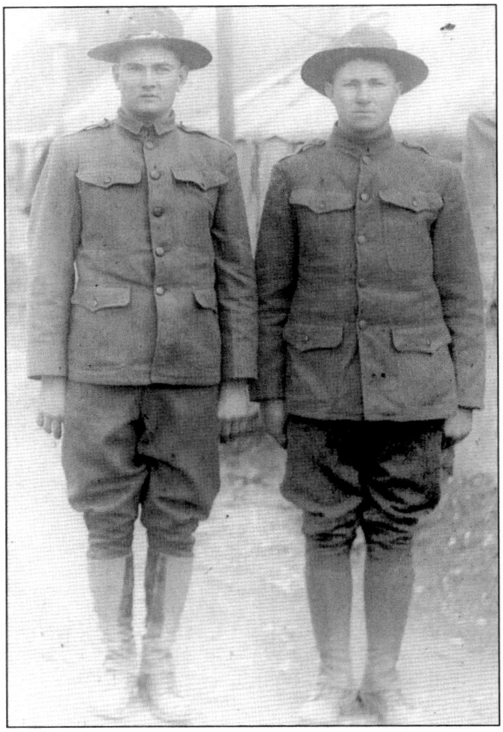

Randa Layton and another Taney County soldier, Sam Awberry, are pictured here.

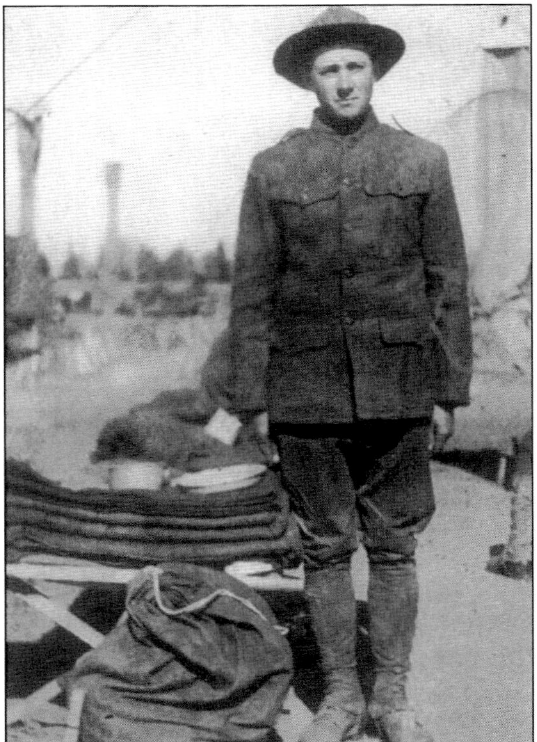

Randa Layton stands beside his Army cot and belongings while stationed in Camp Bowie, Texas.

The author's paternal grandfather, Charlie Cobb, was the grandson of Charles and Laura Cobb, who homesteaded in Taney County during the latter half of the 1800s. Charlie claims that one time while he and an Army buddy were en route by train back to Taney County, his buddy took ill one night. Not knowing what do, Charlie said that the first time the train made a stop was near a fruit orchard. He jumped from the train and grabbed a handful of peach tree leaves and told his buddy to chew on them. He did, and by morning, his buddy had recovered.

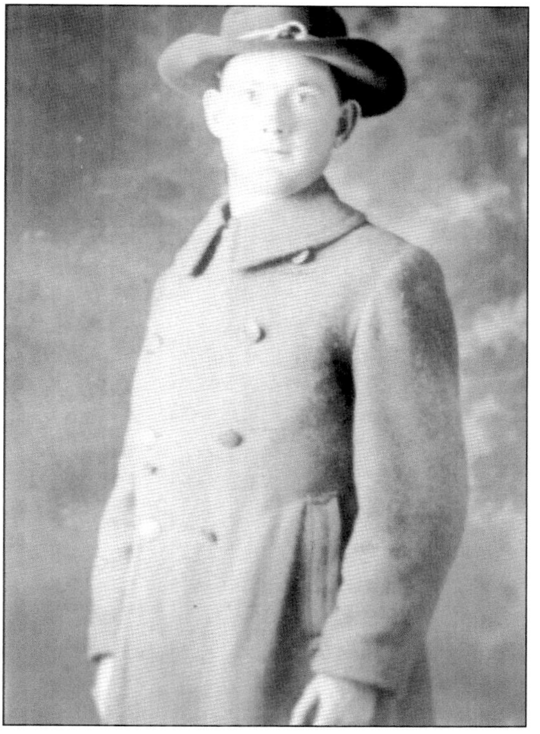

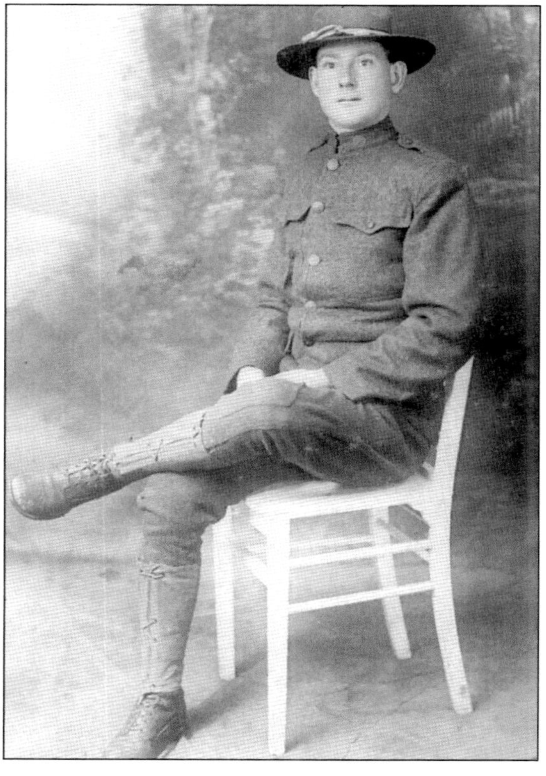

Charlie Cobb poses for another Army photograph.

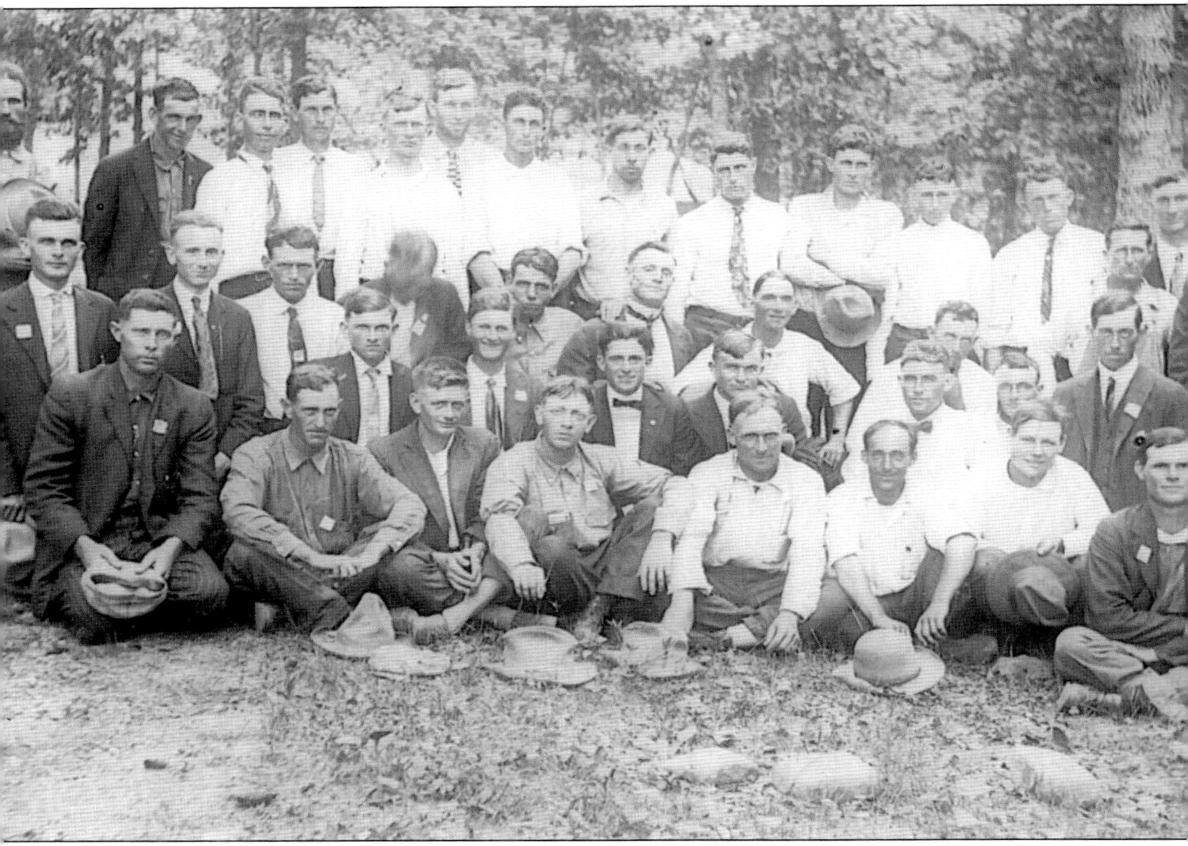

This group of men from the Kirbyville and Oak Grove communities were given a special dinner at the Oak Grove General Baptist Church. It was held in their honor as they prepared to leave their homes and families to be inducted into the Army during World War I.

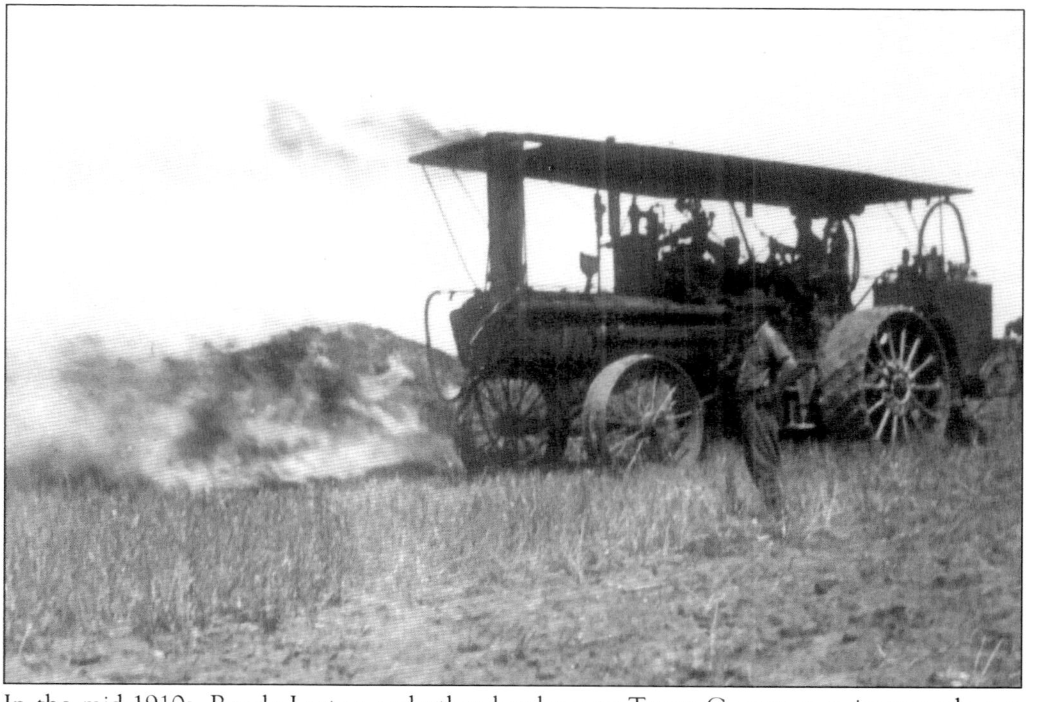

In the mid-1910s, Randa Layton and other local young Taney County men journeyed once a year to the wheat harvest fields of Kansas, and as far north as the South Dakota cornfields. There, they earned money to send back home to their families to help support them. In this photograph a spark ignites, setting the wheat stack on fire.

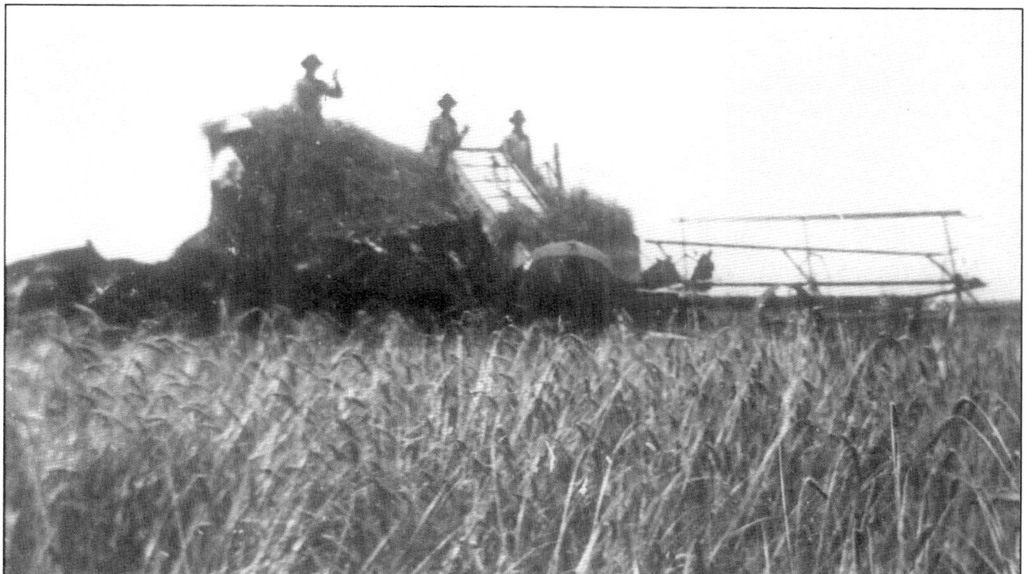

Pictured here is a wheat harvest crew in Kansas. Once, Randa and his cousin, Albert Whorton, were stranded several days on a snowbound train in South Dakota, en route back home to Taney County.

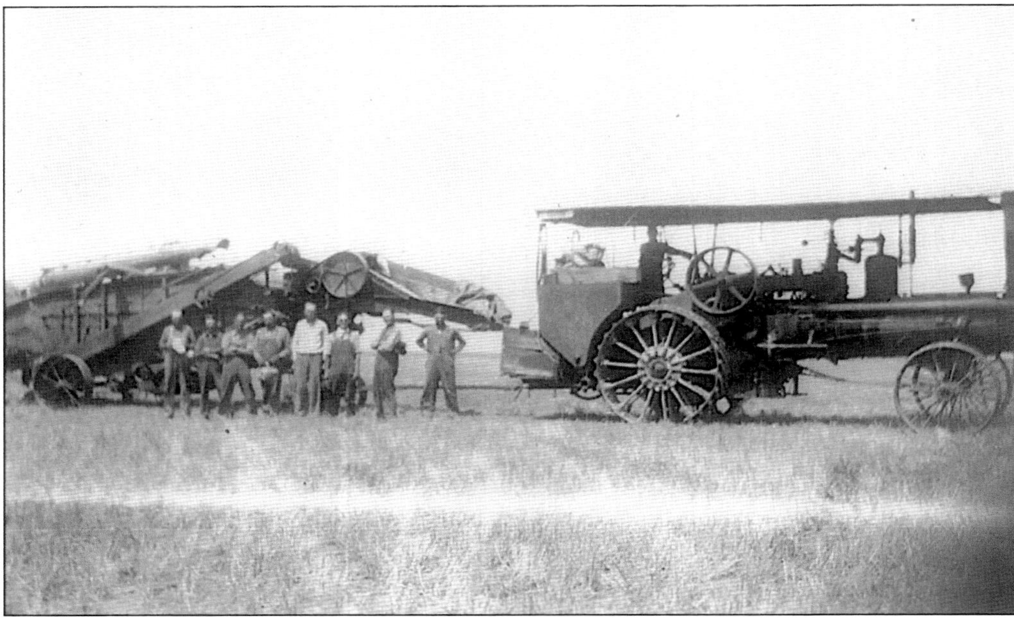

Randa Layton and his brothers, Lonnie and Ben, stand with the threshing machine crew in Kansas. Randa said the wheel to the engine was tall enough for a man to stand in it.

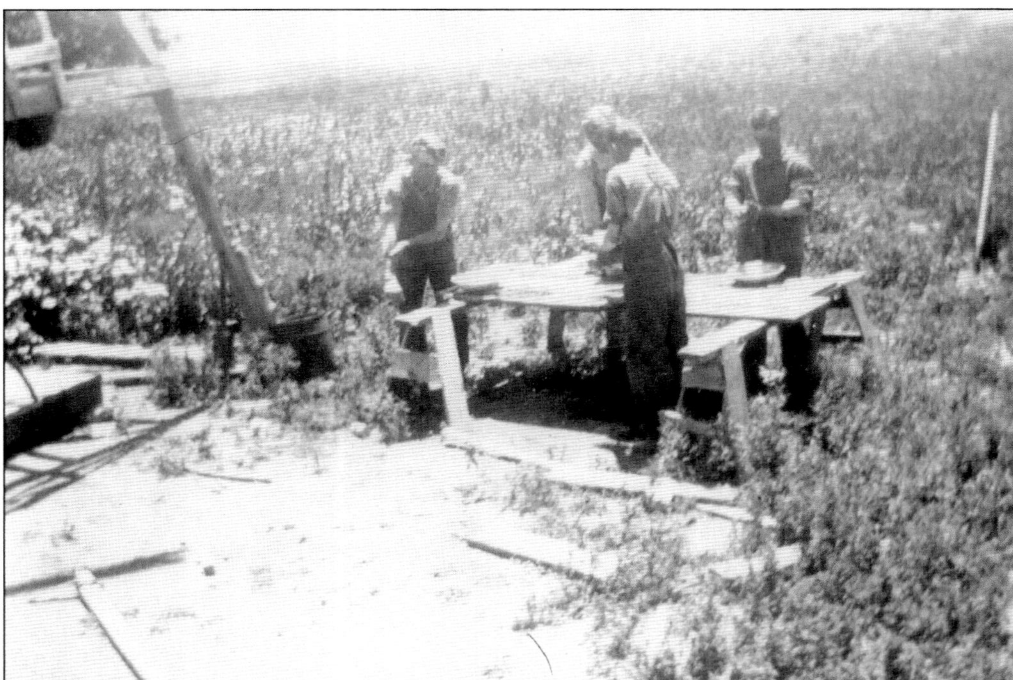

Randa Layton's two cousins, Albert Whorton and Ira Rittenhouse, traveled with Randa, Ben, and Lonnie Layton. Albert and Ira with two other unidentified individuals stand beneath the windmill and "wash up" for the midday meal.

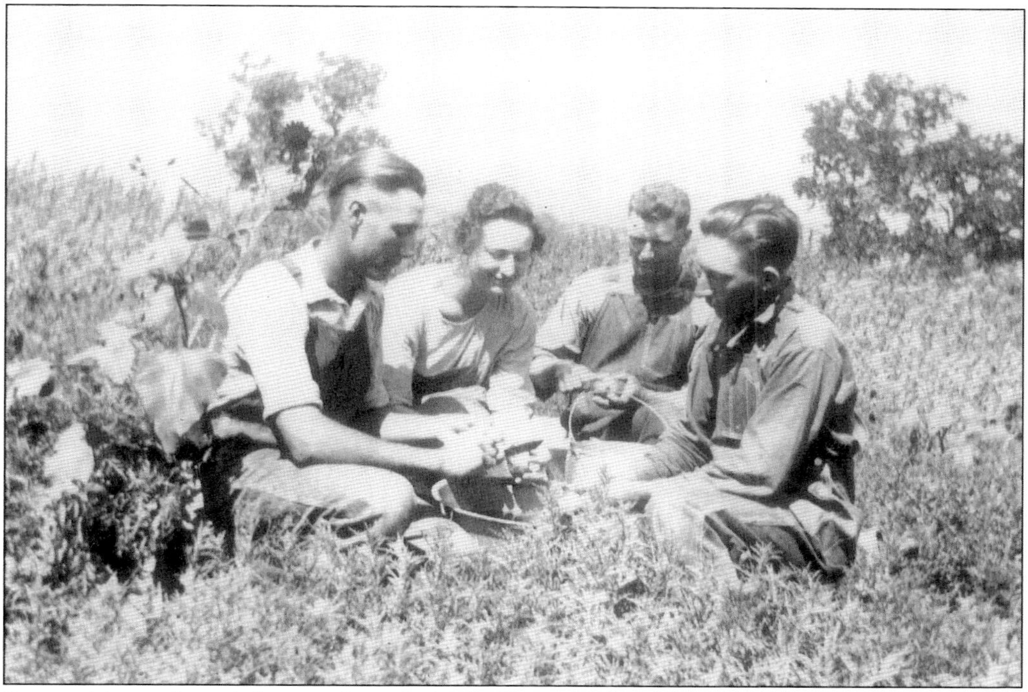

Pictured here, from left to right, are: Tully Sims, Vida Oglenis, Albert Whorton, and Ira Rittenhouse. Vida was in charge of the cook shack. Here she is with the fellows helping her "peel tater's" for their noon meal.

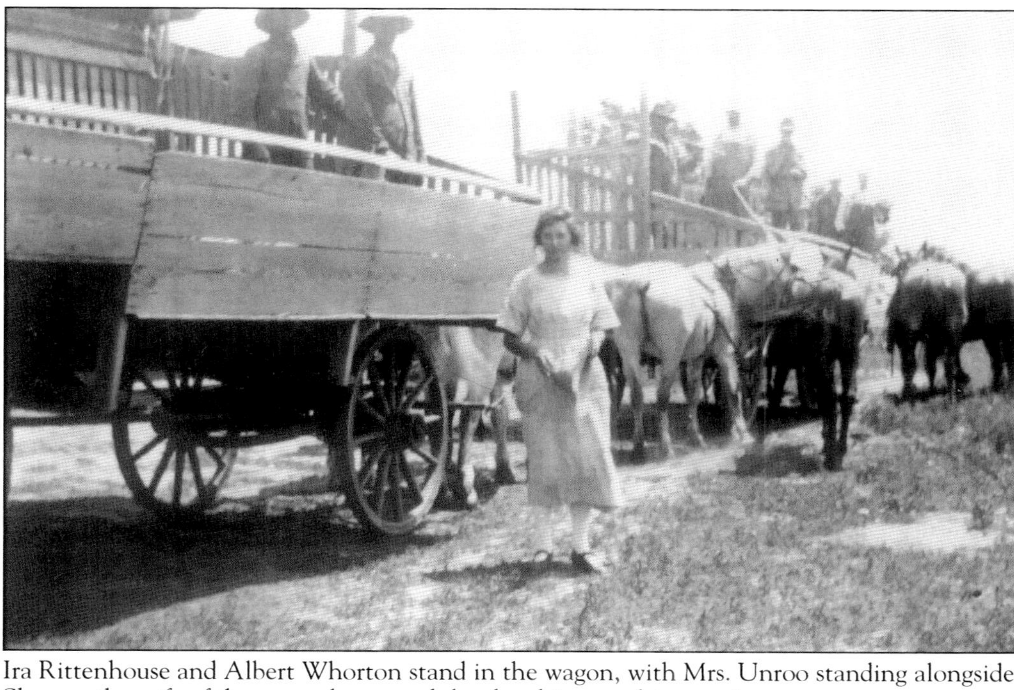

Ira Rittenhouse and Albert Whorton stand in the wagon, with Mrs. Unroo standing alongside. She was the wife of the man who owned the threshing machine equipment.

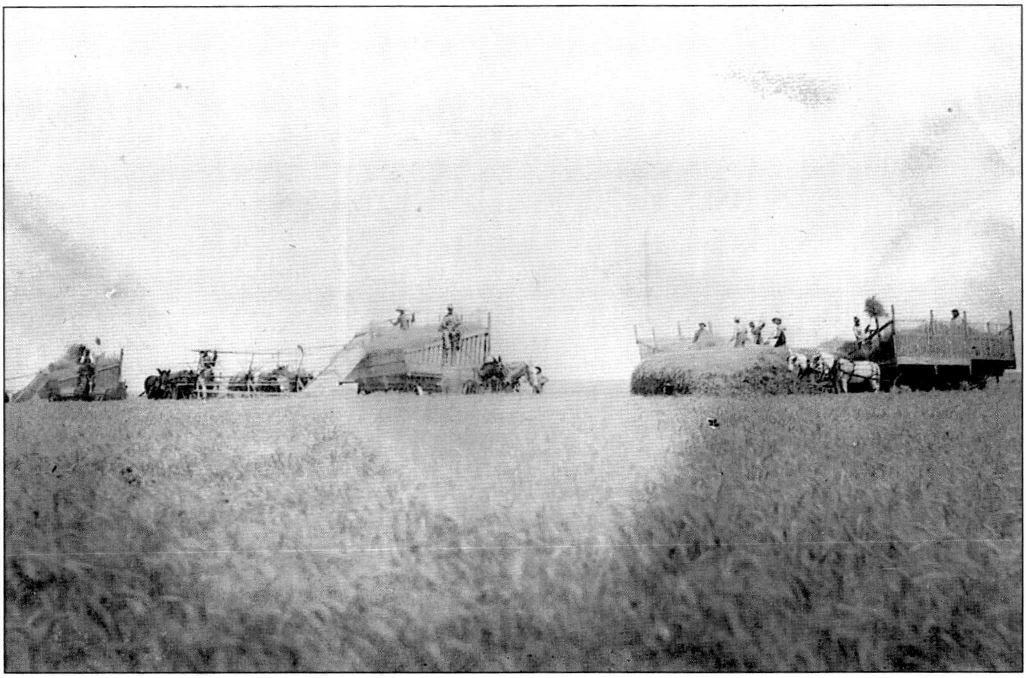

Randa, Ben, and Lonnie Layton; Ira Rittenhouse and Albert Whorton; and cousins of the Layton brothers are photographed with the wheat harvest crew in Kansas.

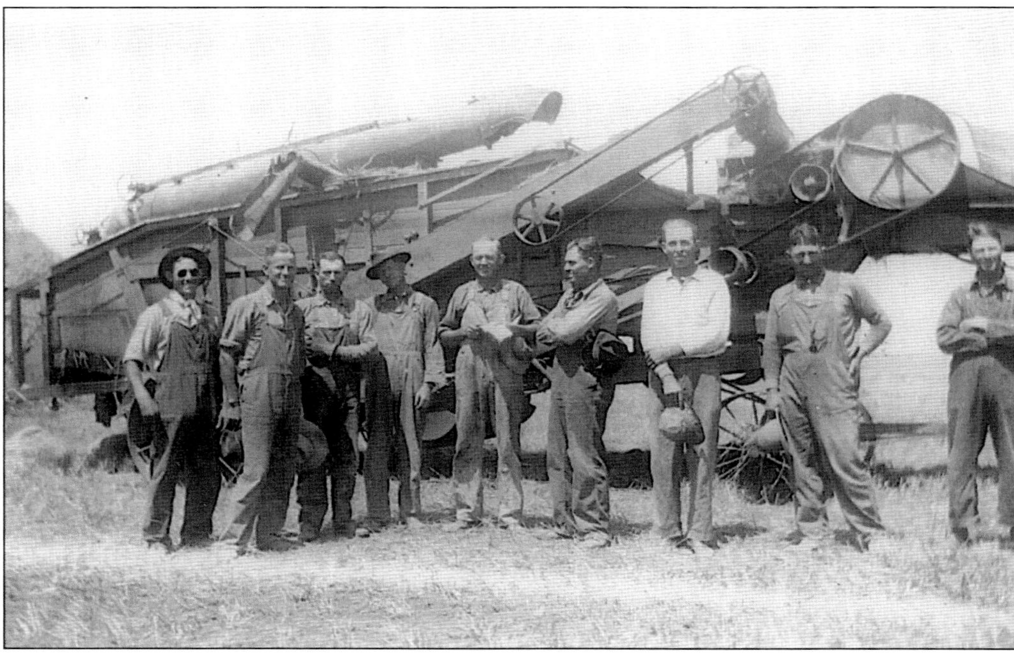

Randa and Ben Layton are the first two men standing on the far right by the wheat harvest threshing machine in Kansas.

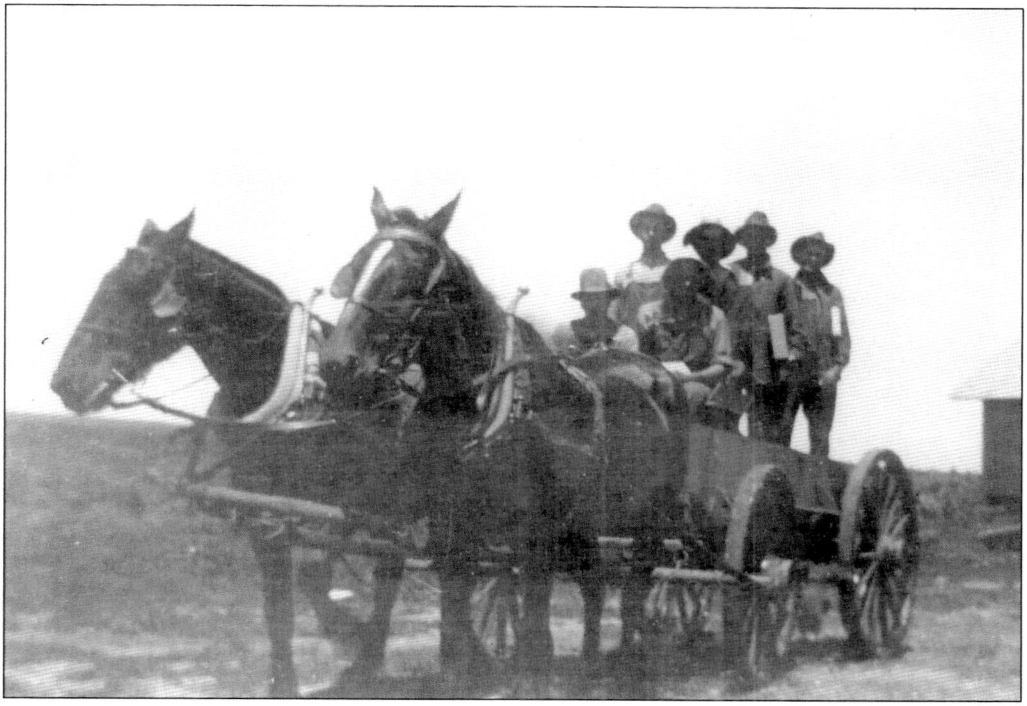

The wheat harvest crew loaded up in the wagon and headed back to the cook shack and their sleeping quarters at the end of a work day in the harvest field.

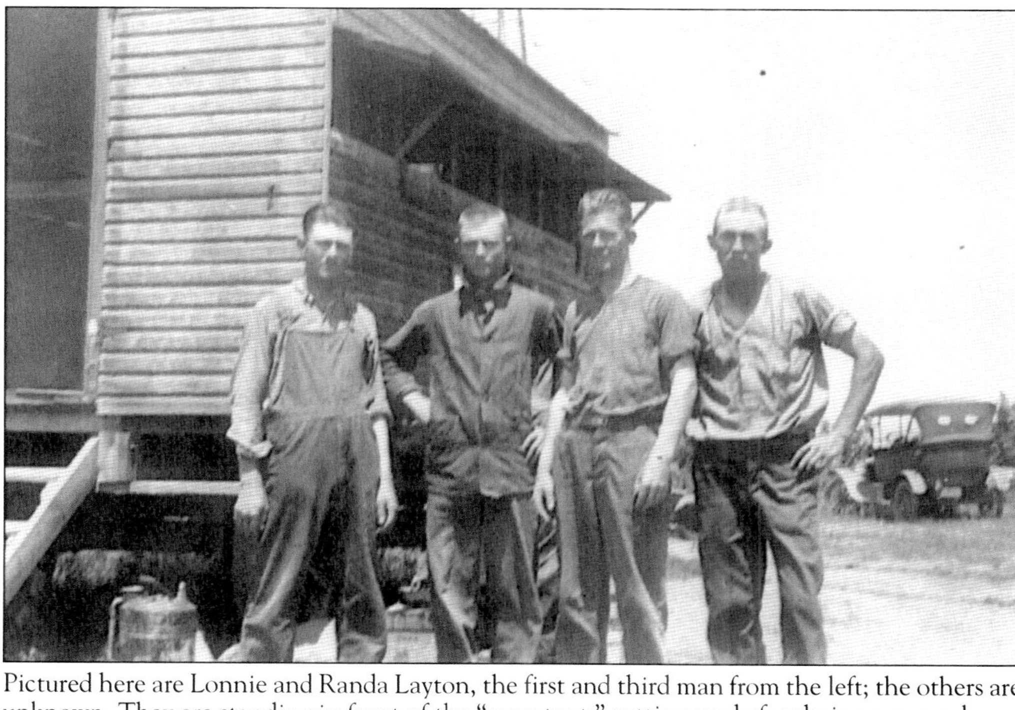

Pictured here are Lonnie and Randa Layton, the first and third man from the left; the others are unknown. They are standing in front of the "mess tent," getting ready for their noon meal.

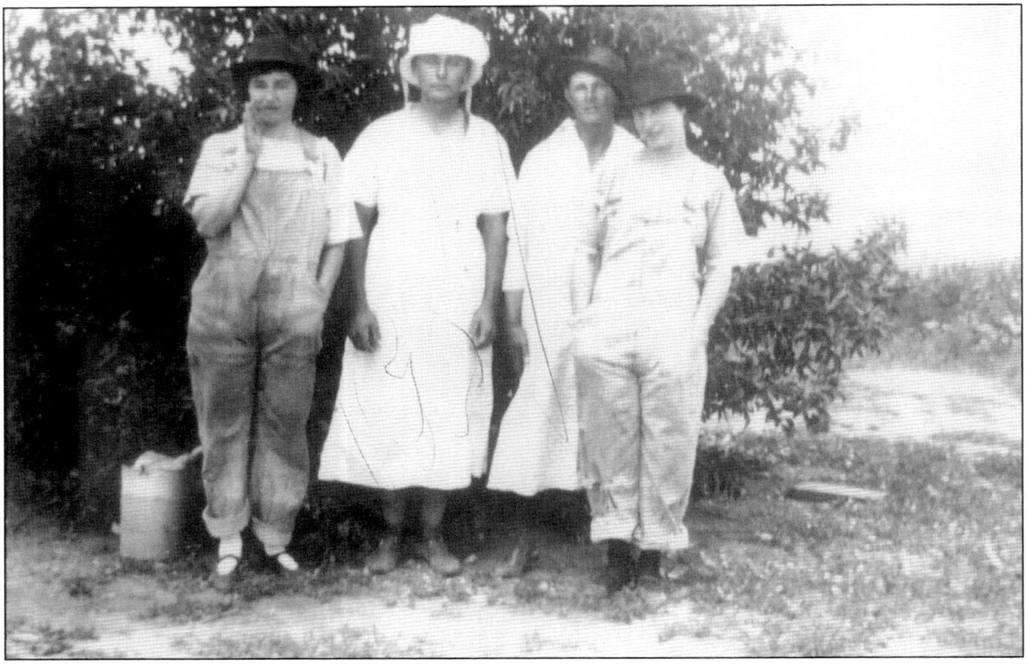

Pictured here, from left to right, are: Mrs. Unroo, Tully Sims, Randa Layton, and Vida Oglenis. This photograph depicts them together in a more humorous moment, aside from the hard manual labor involved in harvesting the wheat, as they trade places in each other's work clothes for this particular photo.

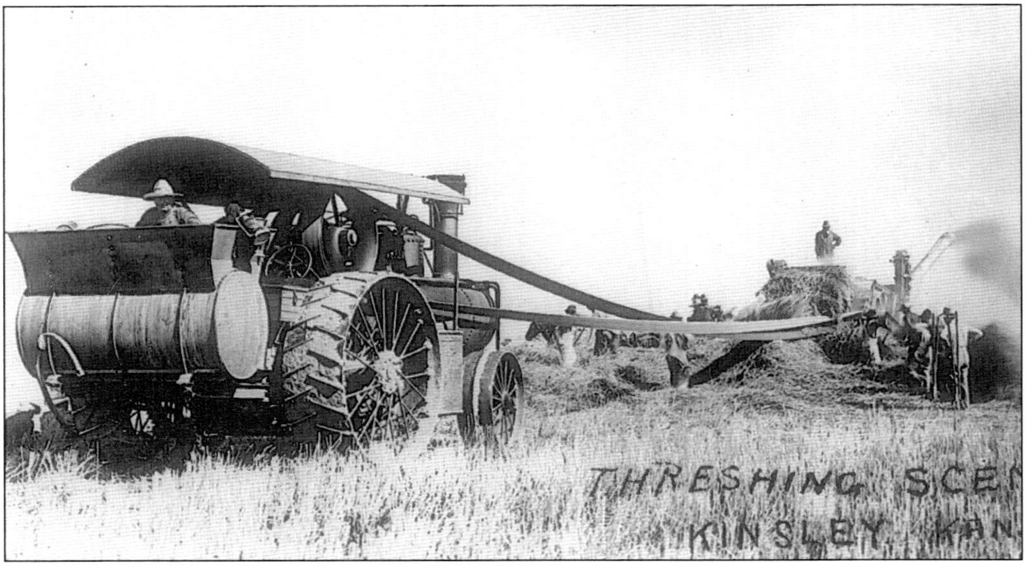

This photograph belonged to Ira Rittenhouse. It was taken when many of the local Taney County young men traveled by train together from their homes to work during the wheat harvest season. There, they earned enough money to help support their families for the months that lay beyond harvest time. This shows a wheat harvest crew in Kinsley, Kansas, in 1920. Ira traveled with his cousins, the Layton brothers, and another cousin, Albert Whorton.

Five

Douglas Mahnkey's Contribution

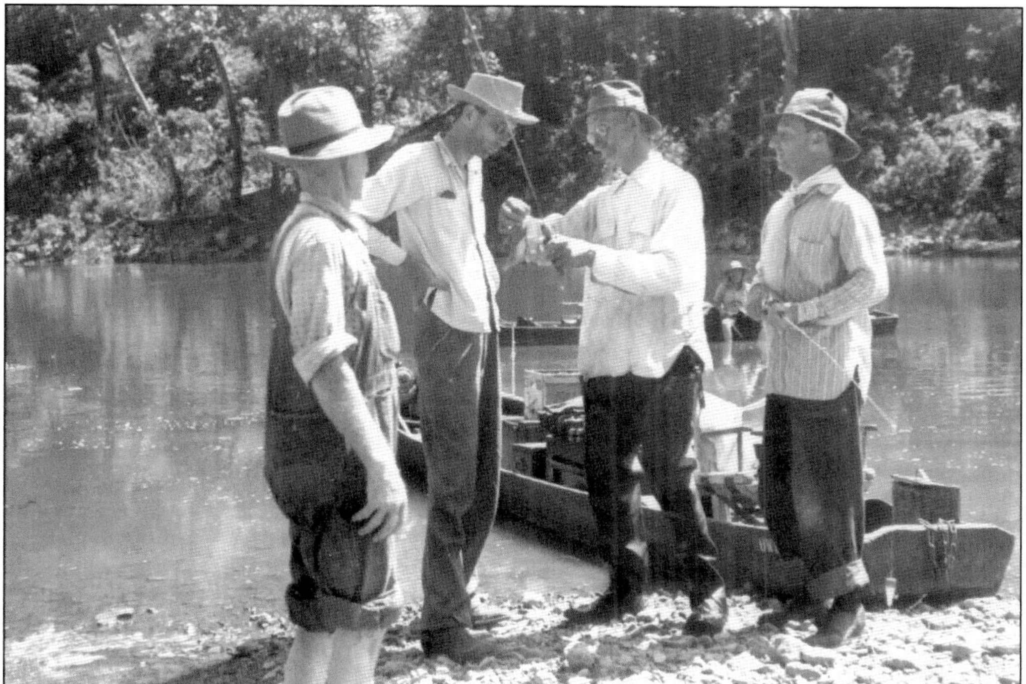

"Now this here's how you put a minnow on your hook," Charley Barnes explains to a St. Louis *Globe Democrat* reporter. Barnes originated the famous river fishing boat known as the "jon boat." Bill Kinyon of Forsyth stands on the far left, and Douglas Mahnkey, Taney County pioneer family descendent and lawyer, stands on the far right. The White River was famous for float trips in the 1930s through the '50s, before the lakes came into existence with the construction of Table Rock Dam.

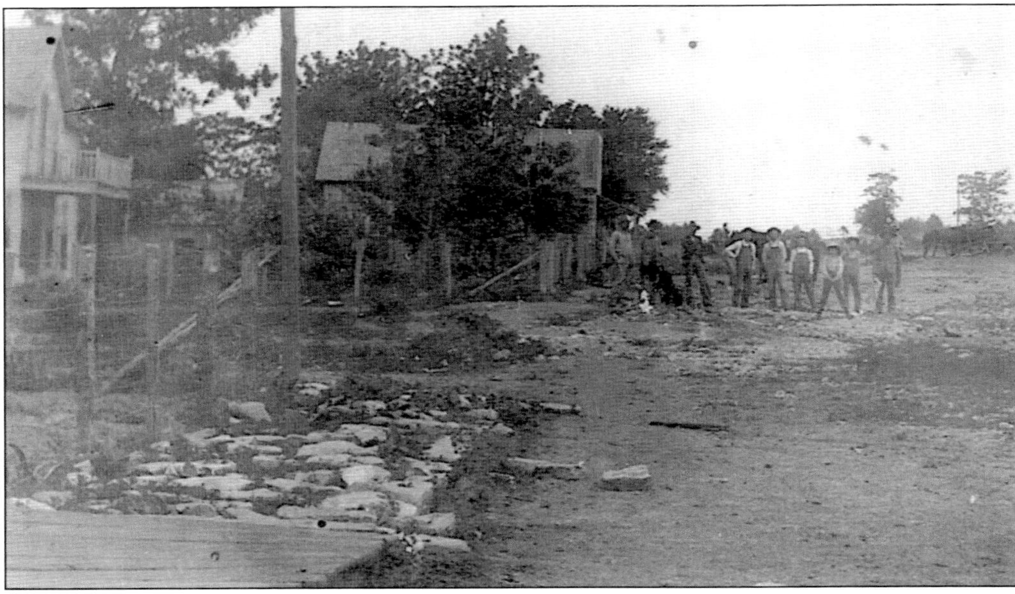

This is an early street scene of Kirbyville about 1907. The building on the right was originally the Parnell Store, but later C.P. Mahnkey and Joel Johnson took it over. The second building was a blacksmith shop first operated by J.E. Trout and later run by Bill Brazeal. The third building was the mill. The first building on the left was the home of Captain James Vanzant, a Civil War veteran. The next belonged to Sol Linzy. The main street was 100 feet wide and known as the old Springfield-Harrison Road, which ran north and south. It was a three-day journey between Harrison and Springfield

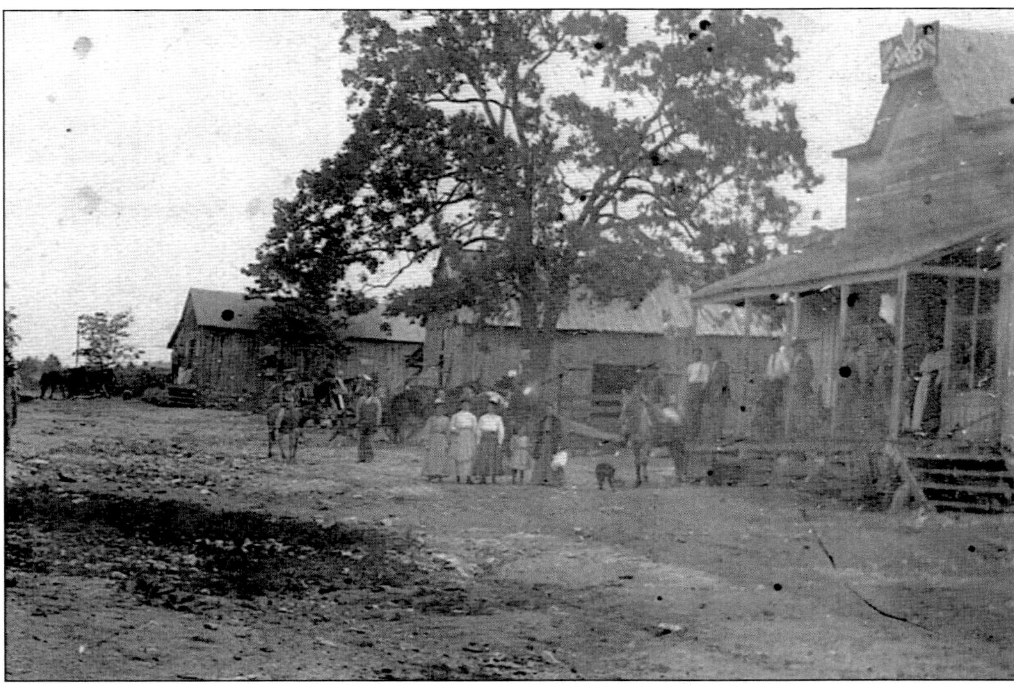

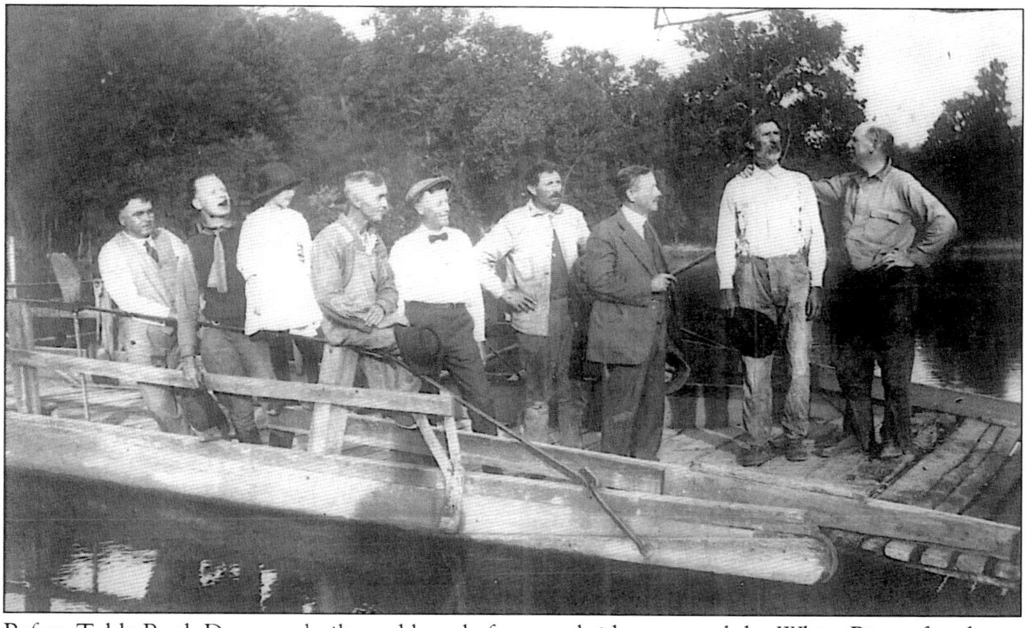

Before Table Rock Dam was built, and long before any bridges crossed the White River, ferryboats were located at various locations all along the waterway. This one is Moore's Ferry, pictured about 1920. Wylse Yandell, the ferryboat operator, stands second from the right. John Ray is fourth from the right. Many of the farmers who lived nearby the ferries often sold corn and hay to the wagon freighters who crossed the river on the boat. Even jugs of whiskey exchanged hands.

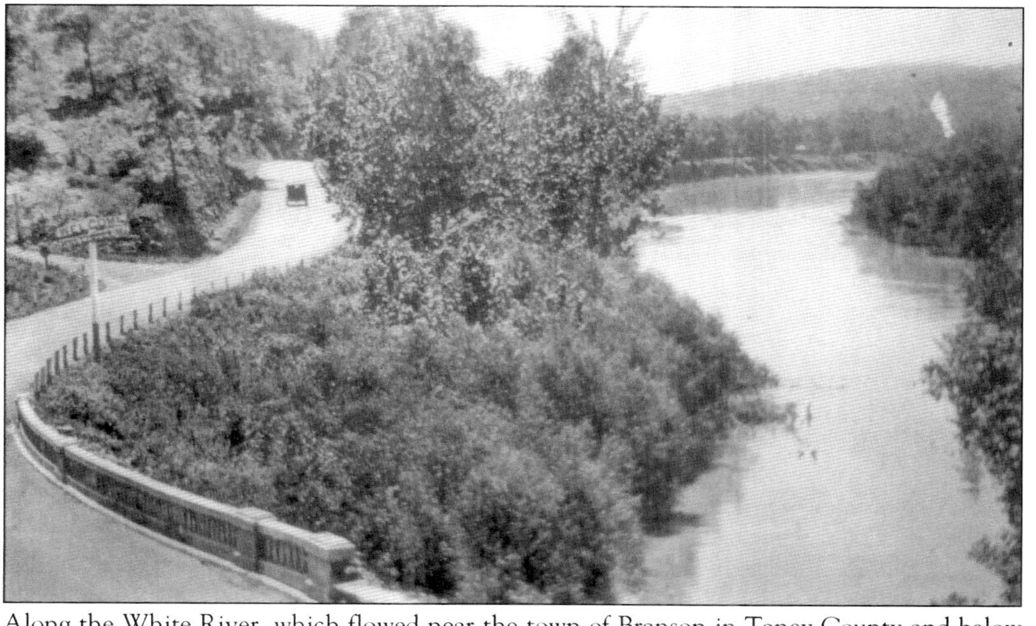

Along the White River, which flowed near the town of Branson in Taney County and below Presbyterian Hill, an automobile journeys southward across the Coon Creek Bridge in the early 1930s. This was before Table Rock Dam was built and Lake Taney Como came into existence. To this day, automobiles still cross the Coon Creek Bridge.

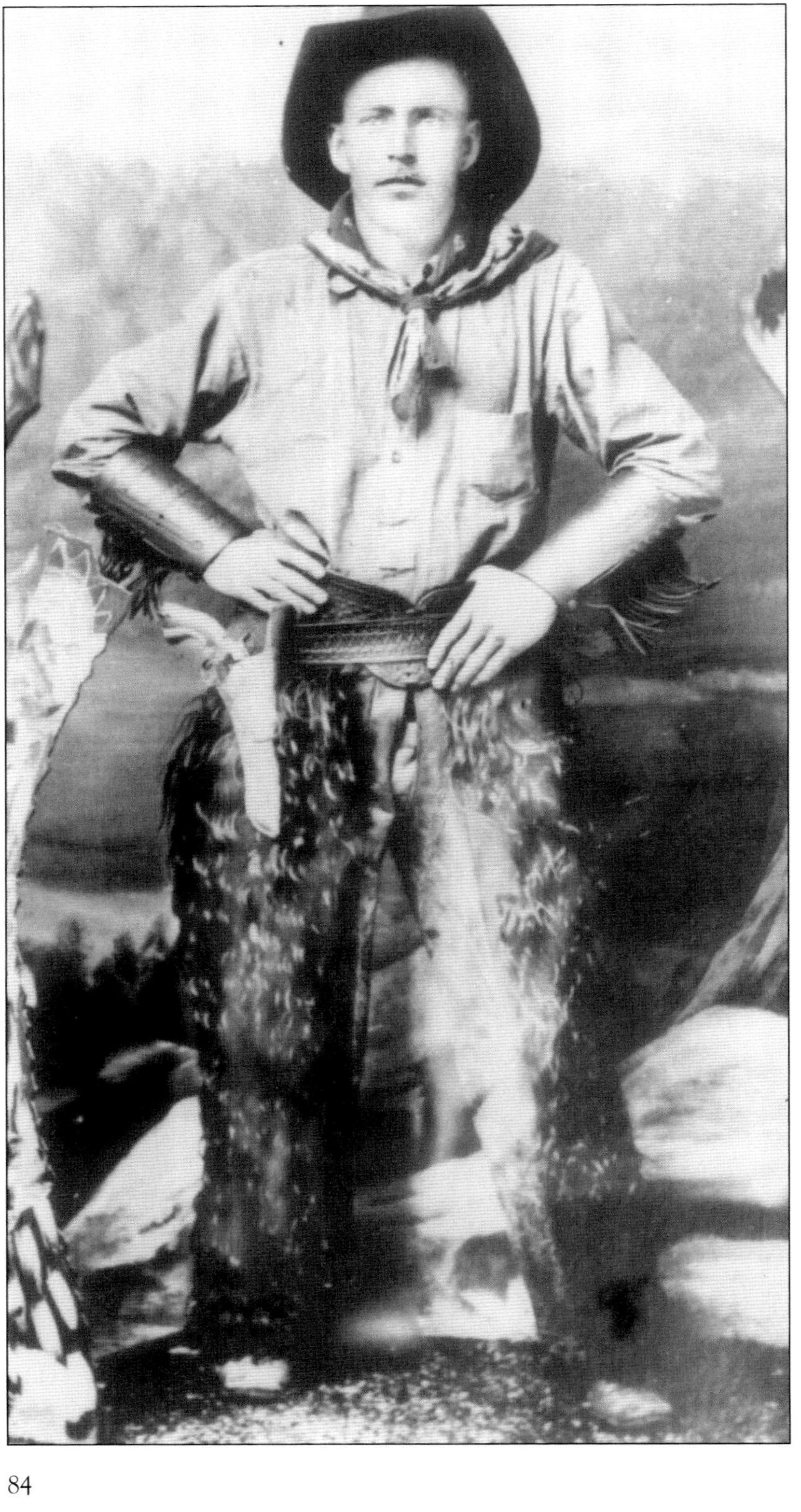

Robert "Bob" Ramsey served over 20 years for the murder of Taney County Sheriff Newt D. Boles, following the robbery of the Protem Bank in the early 1900s. He received a life term but was paroled. Ramsey went to California, where he died of cancer. Randa Layton knew Bob when they were boys playing along the banks of Turkey Creek near Hollister. Even then, Randa claims that Bob enjoyed playing with make-believe revolvers and pretended to be a gun fighter. Randa said he always knew that Bob's actions as a youngster with guns would get him into trouble when he became a man.

Colonel Alonzo S. Prather is pictured here. The back of this photograph reads: "From the Old Soldiers Home, Los Angeles, California, received June 22, 1910. 'Poor old dad, oh why couldn't this have had for a background a fine old country home with his family and little grandchildren around him?'"

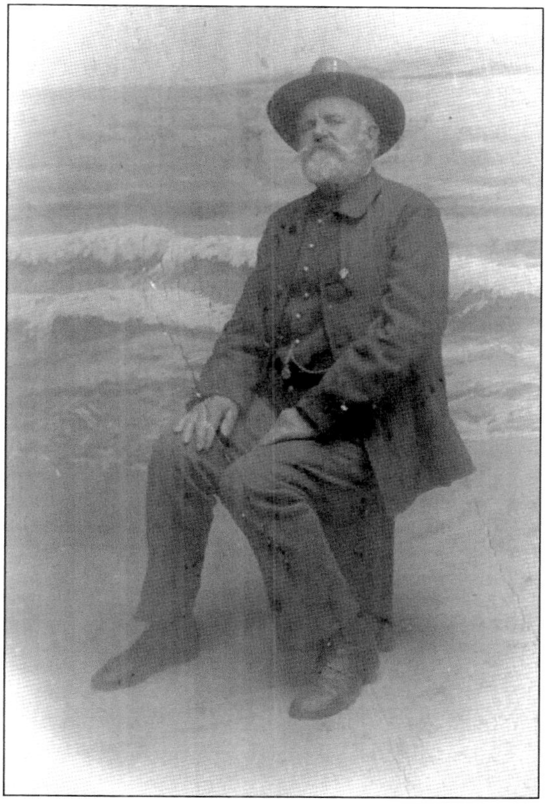

Colonel Prather was an officer during the Civil War. He later became a commissioner of education in Northeast Arkansas during the reconstruction days and a leading figure of the Baldknobber organization in Taney County following the days of the Civil War and the late 1800s. State Representative Colonel A.S. (Alonzo) Prather, grandfather of Douglas Mahnkey, managed to obtain state money in 1889 in order to build Taney County a new courthouse.

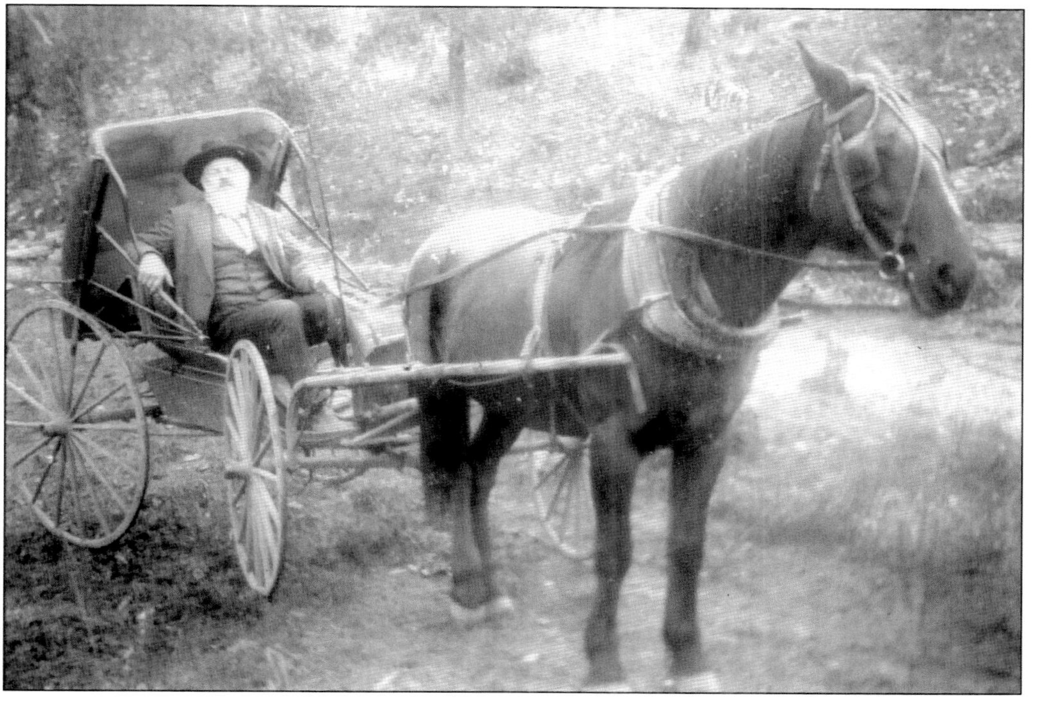

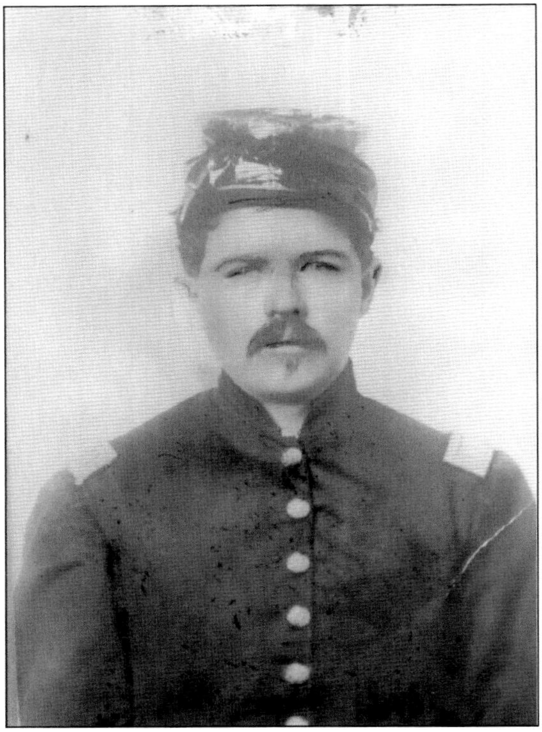

This photograph was taken during the time of the Civil War. Alonzo S. Prather was Second Lieutenant in Co B. 6th Indiana Infantry. This photograph was made from a tintype.

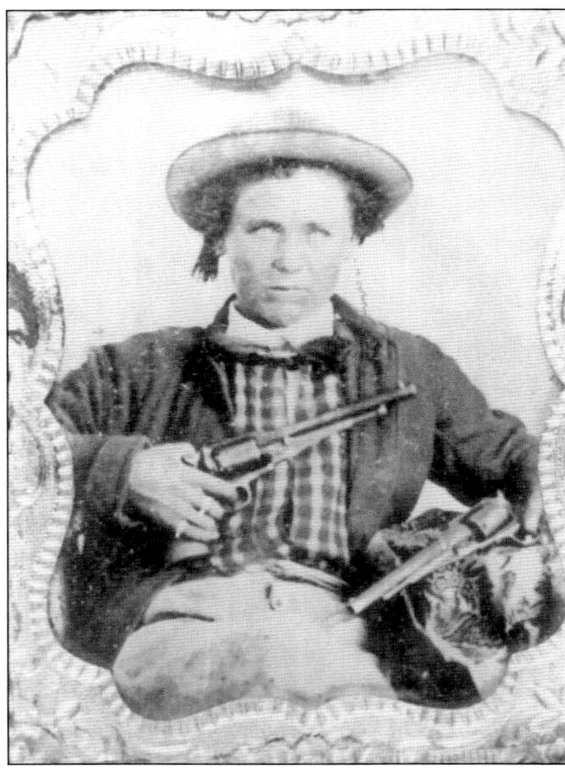

Ben Cummings, a Union soldier from Bee Creek, Taney County, is pictured here. Ben was a friend of the Mahnkey family.

Taney County Civil War soldiers are pictured here. They are, from left to right: Rufe Brazeal, Maurice Fulkerson, and Andrew Mahnkey. Andrew was the uncle of Douglas Mahnkey, who married the author's great-great aunt Cordie Cobb.

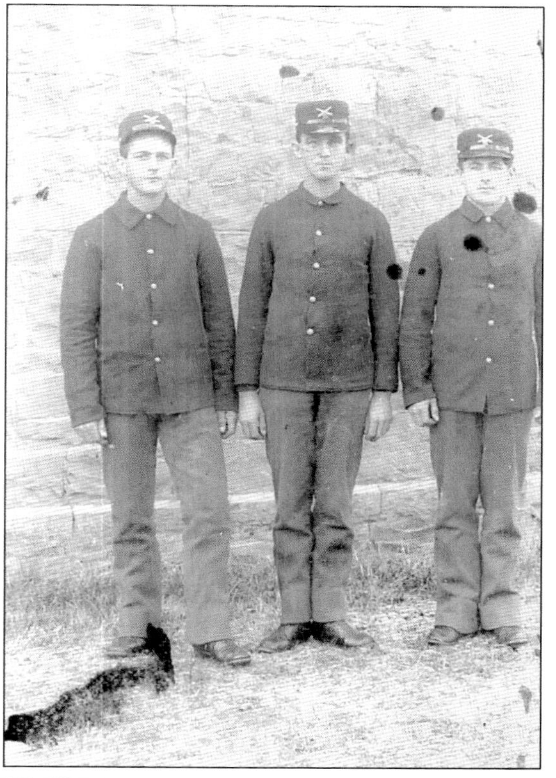

Pictured here, from left to right, are: Jimmy Jones, Robert L. Gideon, C.A. (Chub) Bennett, Bill Williams (worked on the Powersite Dam in Forsyth), and E. Wilton Adams. They are shown with their turkeys and guns following a hunt near Forsyth about 1928.

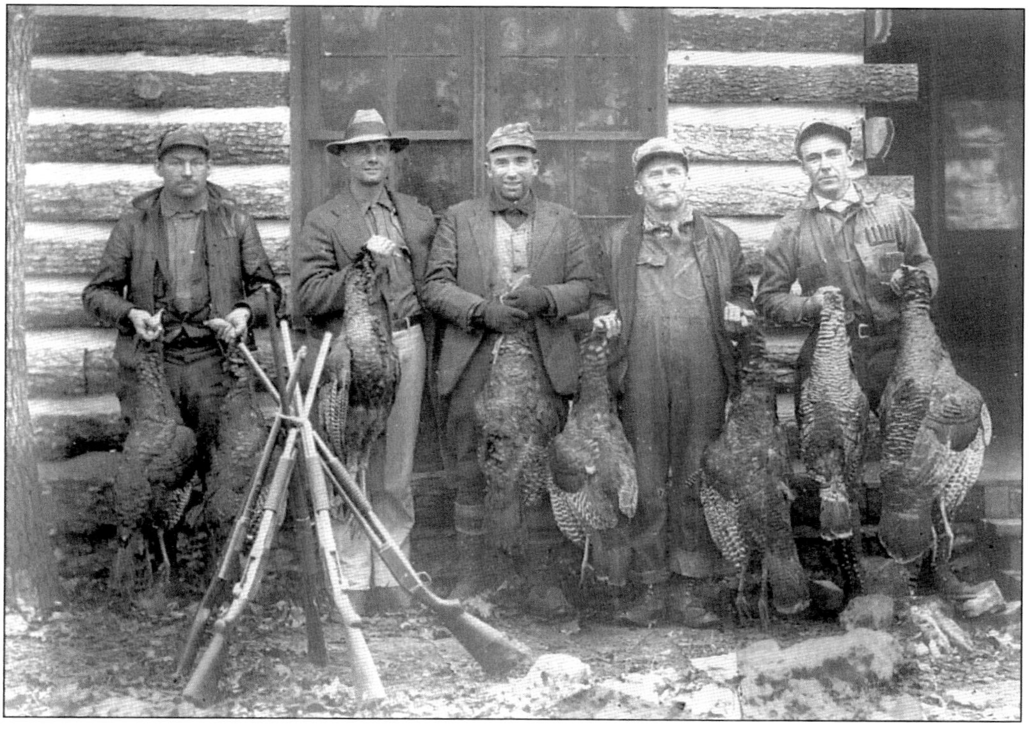

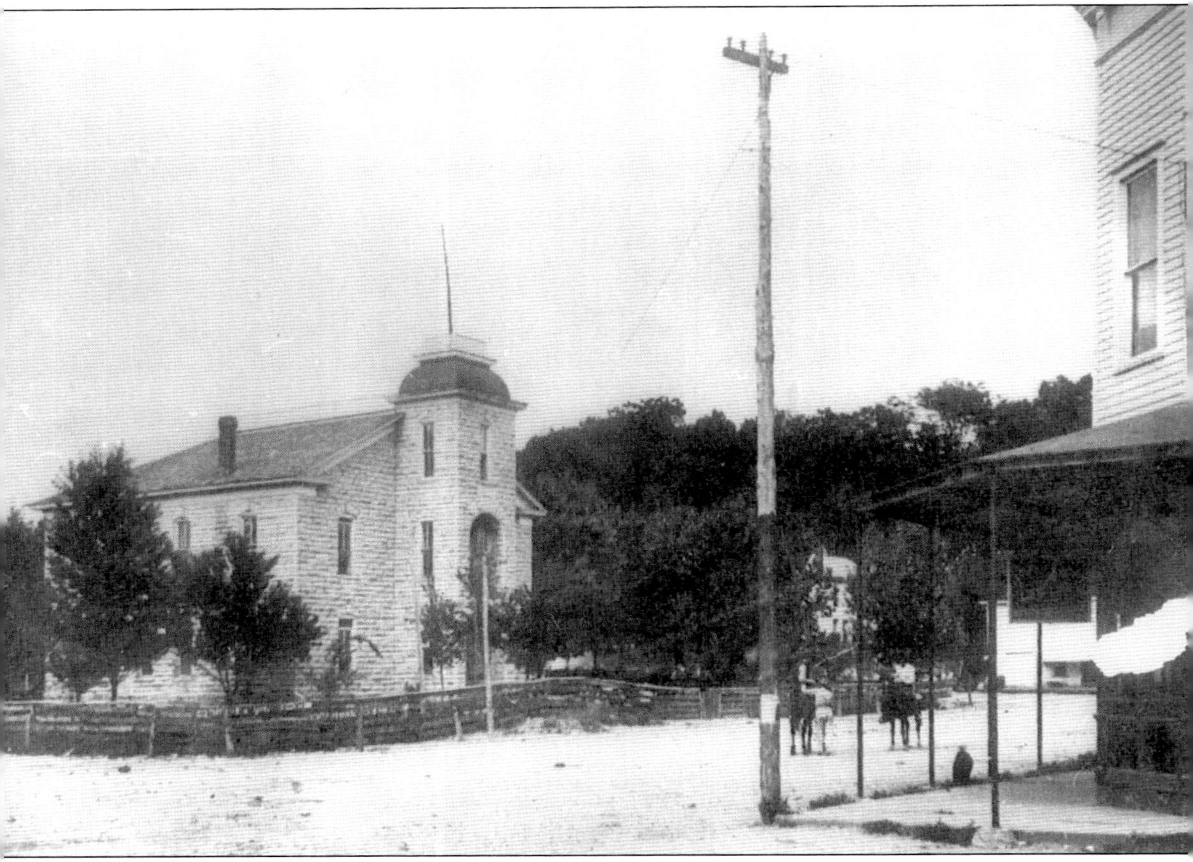

This is an early street scene of Forsyth taken about 1908, before electricity was available. In 1911, the construction of the Powersite Dam began, and in 1919, electricity brought lights to Forsyth for the first time. In later years, Forsyth was moved to its present site from what is now known as "Shadow Rock Park," which is still referred to as the "Old Forsyth" locale. The stone building photographed was the new courthouse, erected with funds appropriated by the state legislature.

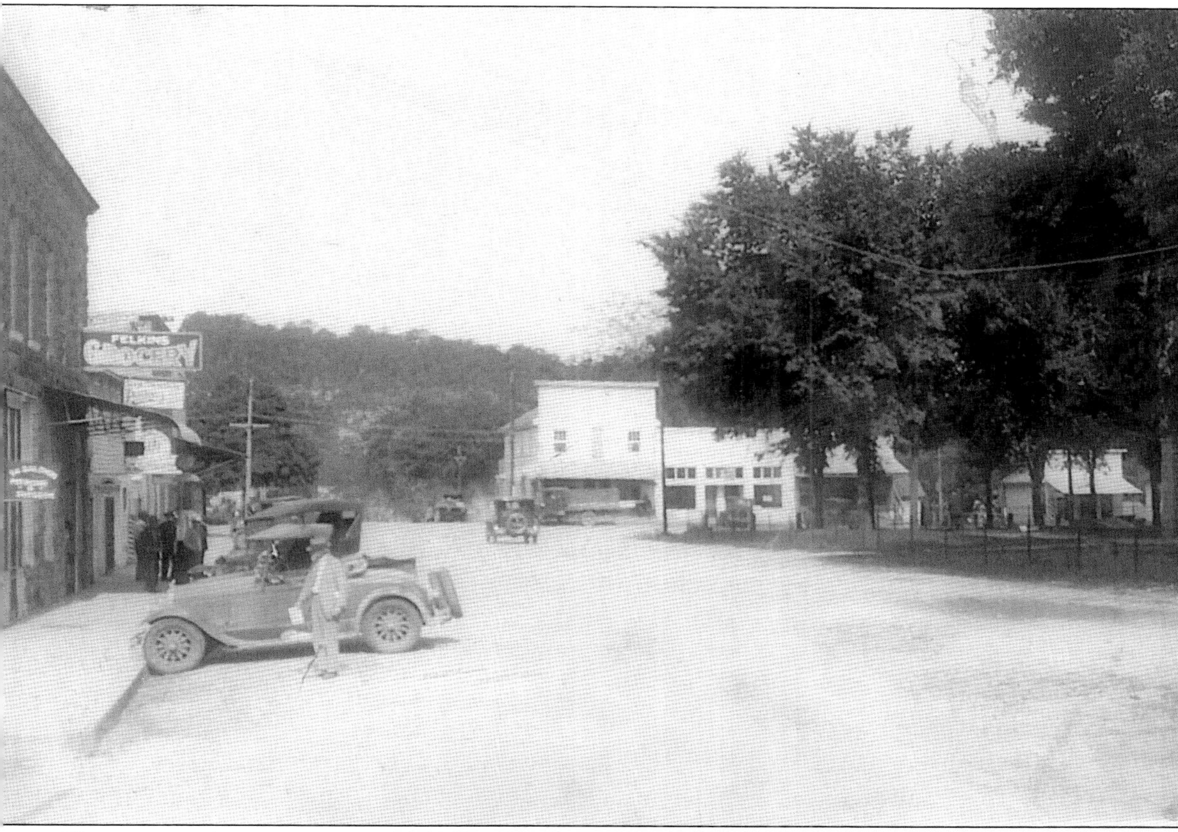

This is an early street scene of Old Forsyth about 1930. The man standing in front of his car is Dr. Frank Baldwin. He was a coroner from 1914-1916. He was also a county healh officer in 1927.

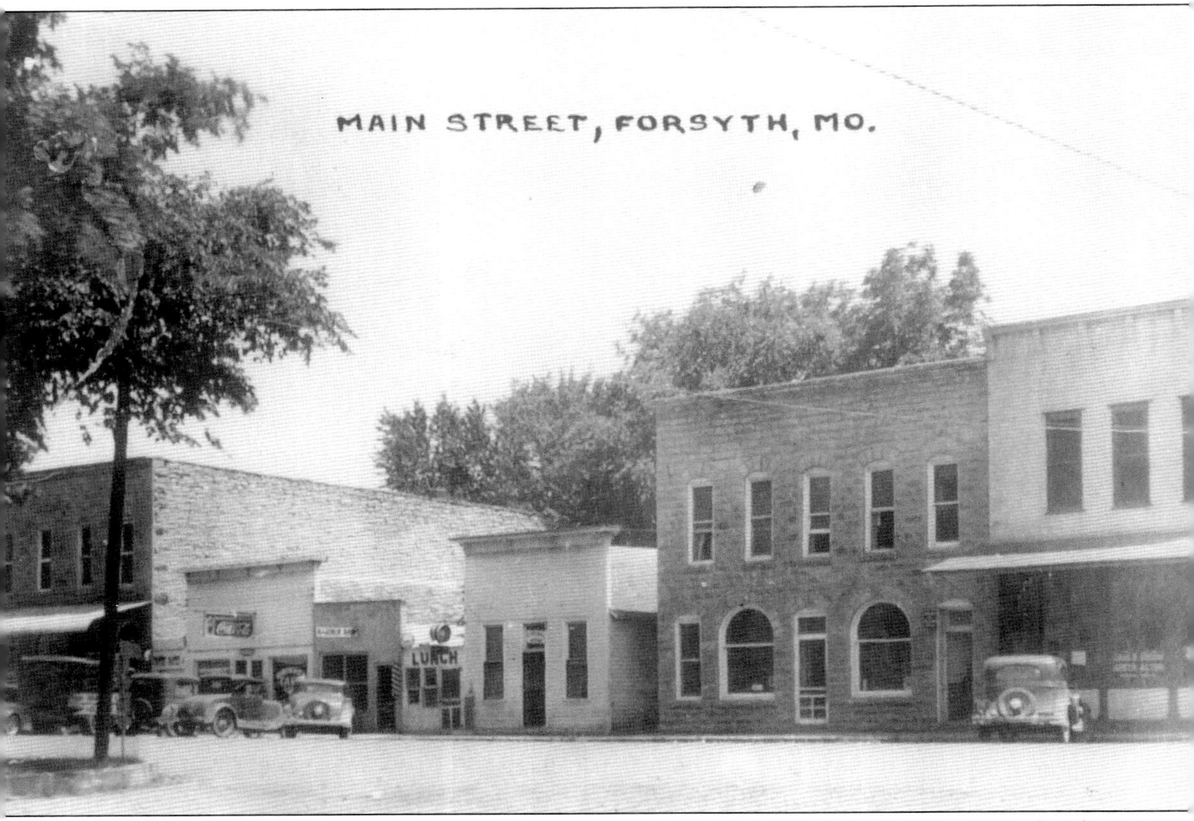

Old Forsyth is shown here before it was moved from its original location on Swan Creek, where Shadow Rock Park is currently located. This was Main Street. The gentleman standing beside the car is Dr. Frank Baldwin M.D., the coroner for Taney County from 1914 through 1916. Note the hill in the background where Old Forsyth was moved due to the construction of the dam.

Six

Float Fishing and Gravel Bars

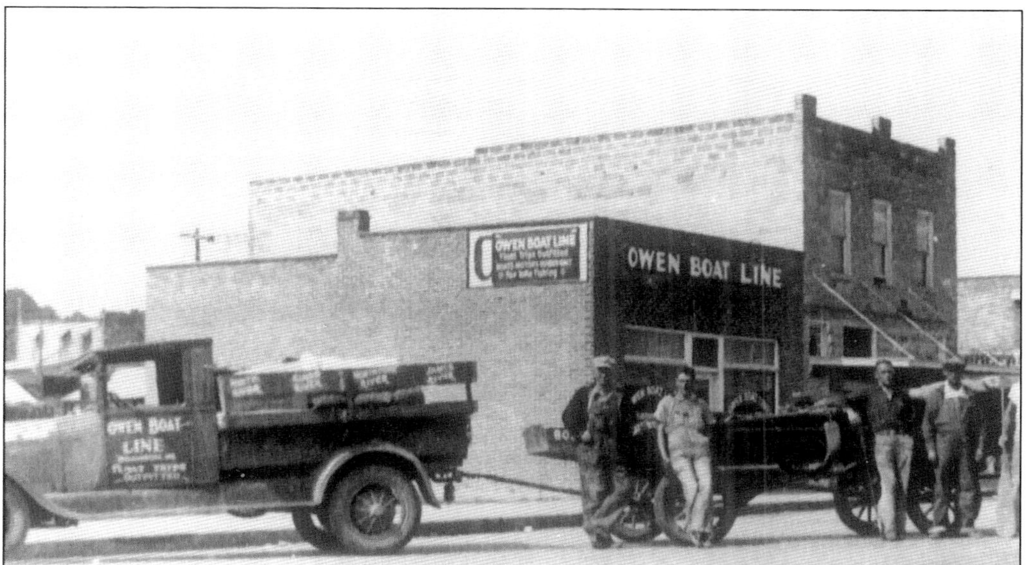

This photograph of the Jim Owens Boat Line's truck and trailer was taken in 1953, in downtown Branson. This trailer hauled 20-foot jon boats to and from the rivers on float trips. Randa Layton is the first man on the left. Randa began his guide career in May of 1918, for Charlie and John Barnes, who operated the Galena Boat Line. Randa left that morning with two commissary and 14 fishing boats. He earned $2 a day and received a tip and a pair of shoes. He sold the shoes to Charlie Barnes for $2.

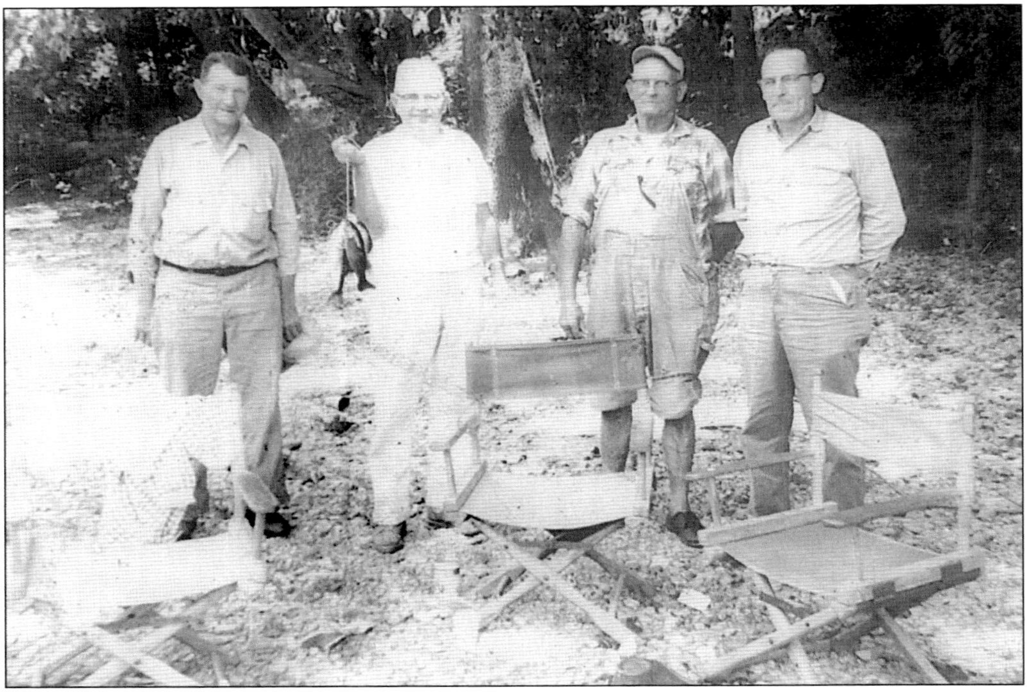

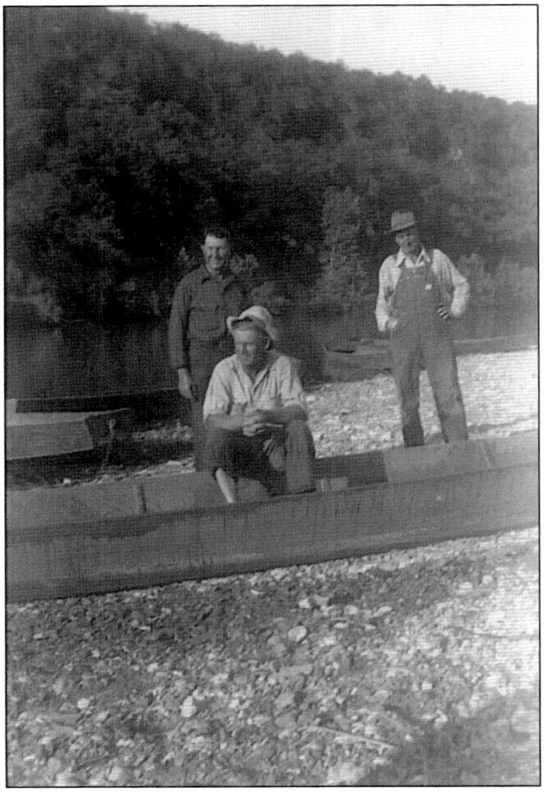

Depicted here is a Jim Owens float trip in the late 1950s. River guide Randa Layton is first man on the left. The second man is unidentified, the third man is river guide Clint Maxwell, and the fourth man is also unidentified. This location was somewhere on the White River. Randa began guiding for Owens in the early 1950s, earning $10 a day. He guided for Jim Owens Boat Line for many years.

Three river guides pause along one of the many obsolete gravel bars of the legendary White River, also now a part of history since the construction of Table Rock Dam. Pictured from left to right are: Randa Layton, Ollie Biles, and Henry Gibson.

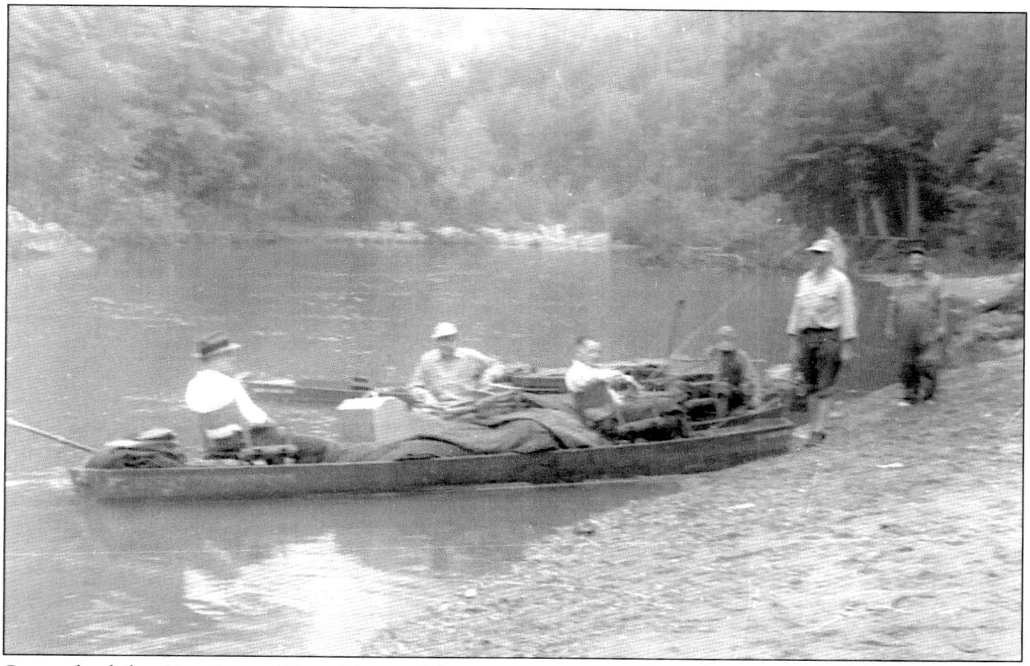

Several of the Jim Owen Boat Line guides prepare to travel on downstream along the Buffalo River in northern Arkansas, south of Branson. The two guides standing left to right are Randa Layton and "Little Horse" Jim Jennings.

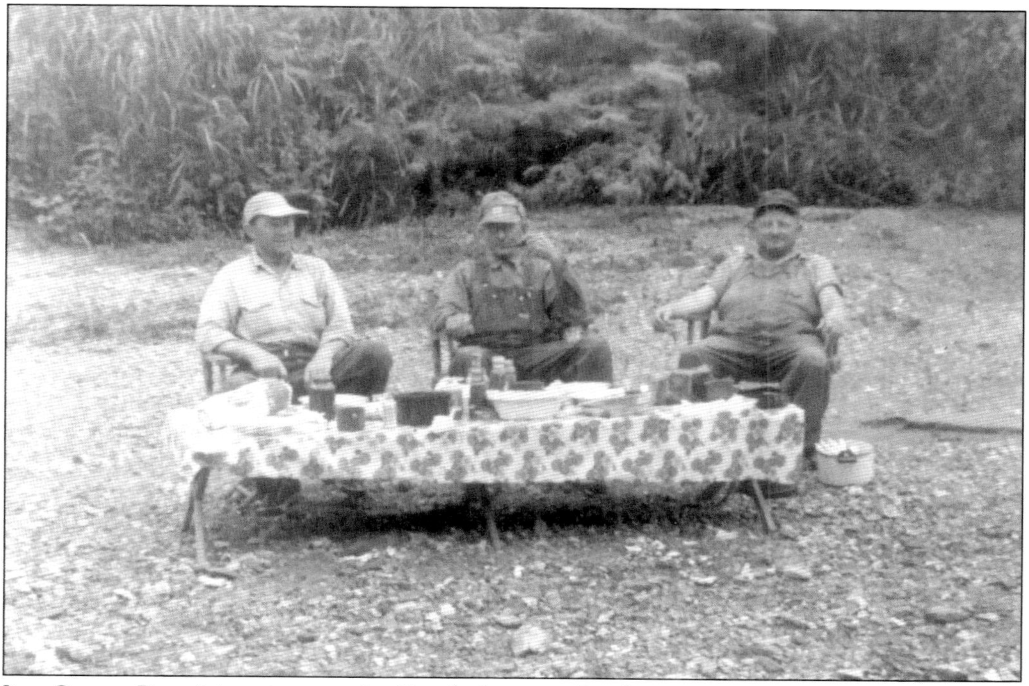

Jim Owens Boat Line river guides Randa Layton, Frank Persinger, and "Little Horse" Jim Jennings are pictured somewhere on the White River in the early 1950s.

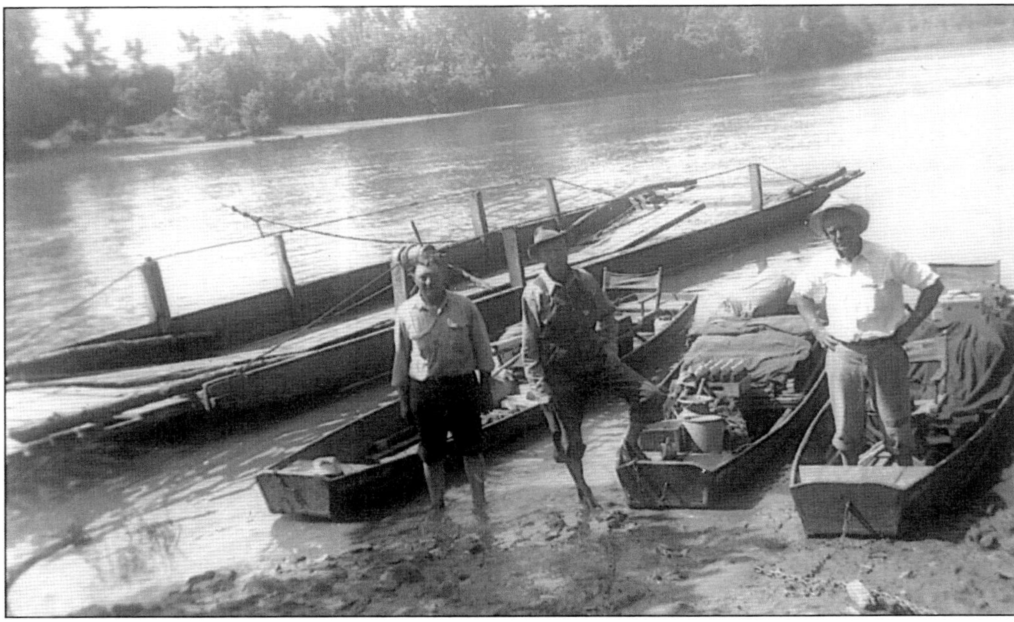

Moore's Ferry near Kirbyville is shown here around 1950. River guides are Randa Layton, Henry Gibson, and Ollie Biles. With the commissary boat full of provisions and camping gear, they stand by the jon boats measuring 20 feet in length as they await the float party to climb aboard these vessels—rarely seen in today's modern world of fishing.

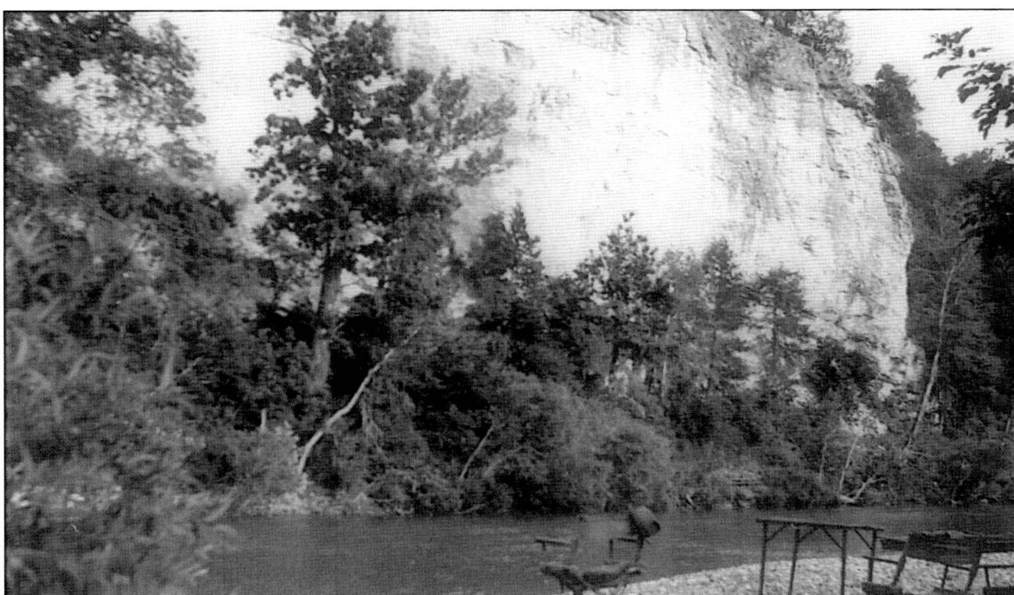

When Randa Layton guided for Jim Owens Boat Lines, he enjoyed the scenic photographs taken by members of the float party along their many river trips. They had stopped across from this bluff on the Buffalo River to fish and eat their lunch. Randa often told stories about the river guides down in Arkansas who guided for other outfitters and their attempts to seek revenge on Jim Owens guides by throwing rocks or dynamite from the bluff tops above the river.

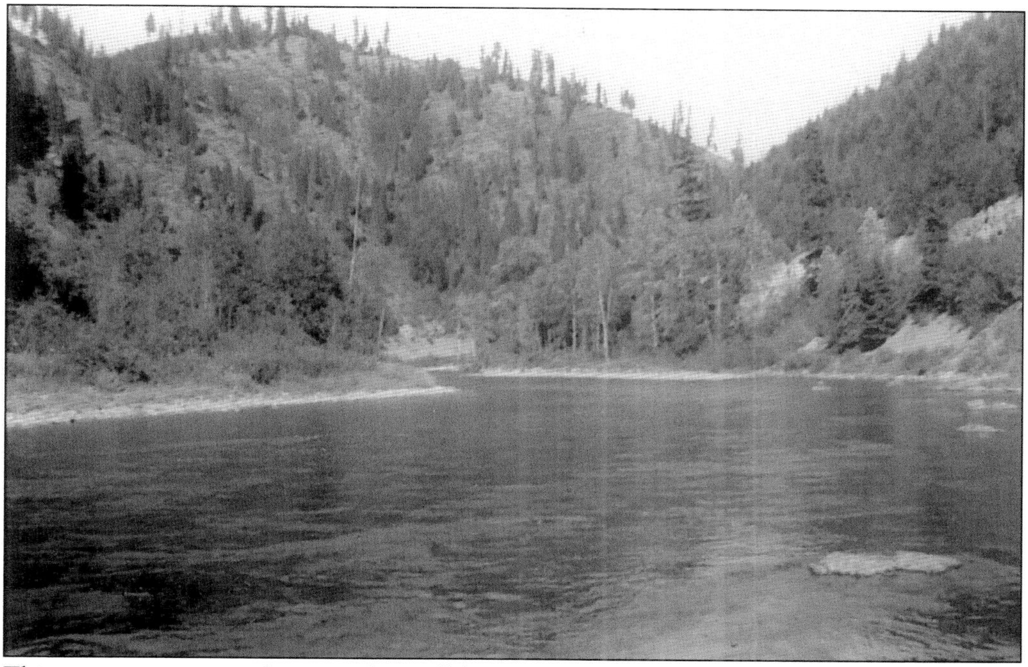

This river scene somewhere on the Buffalo River was taken by the man Randa Layton was guiding downstream.

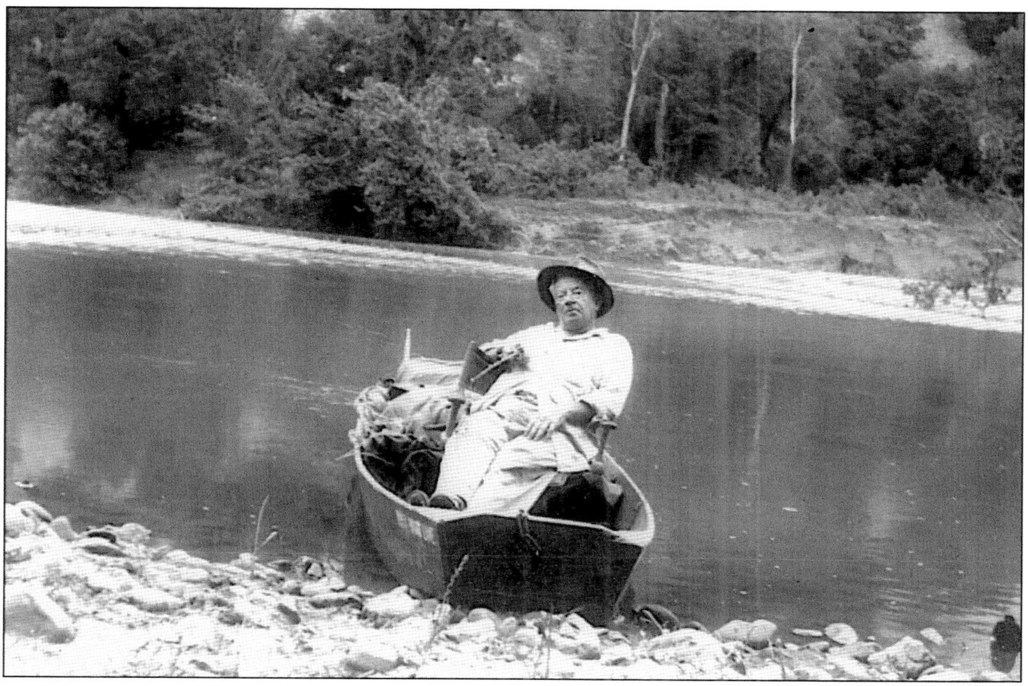

This photograph was taken on the Buffalo River, south of Branson in northwestern Arkansas. The German man seated in this relaxed pose told Randa Layton after the float trip was over, "when you're on the river, think of me."

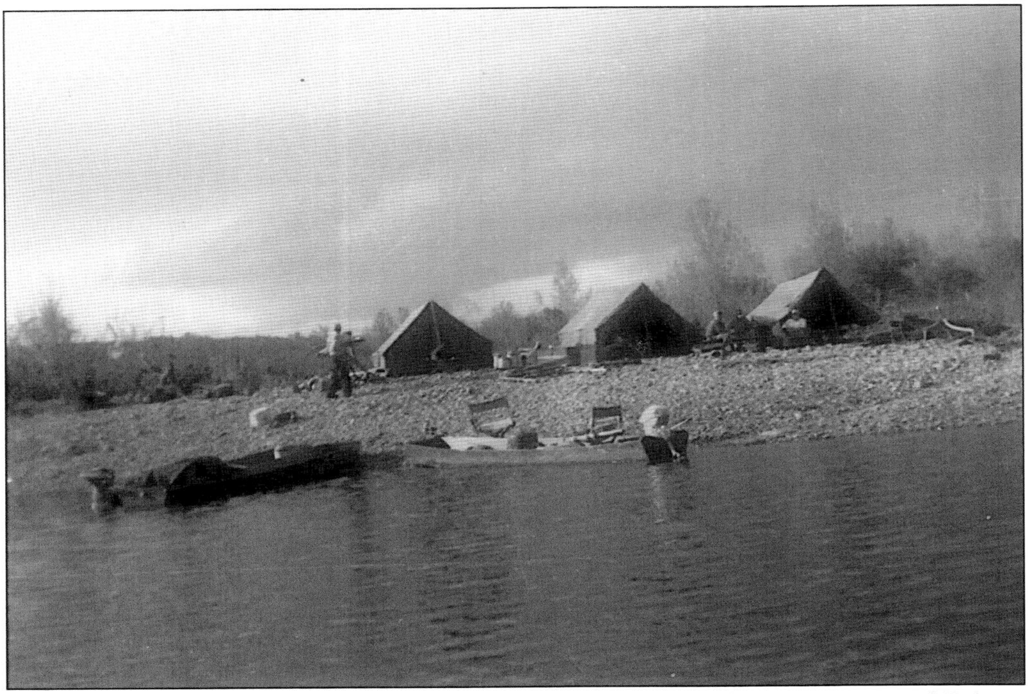

In March 1967, Randa Layton guided for Bill Rogers Motel and Float Service out of Galena, Missouri. This photograph shows their campsite and tents set up on the gravel bar somewhere on the White River near what was known as the "Buffalo Station" in northern Arkansas.

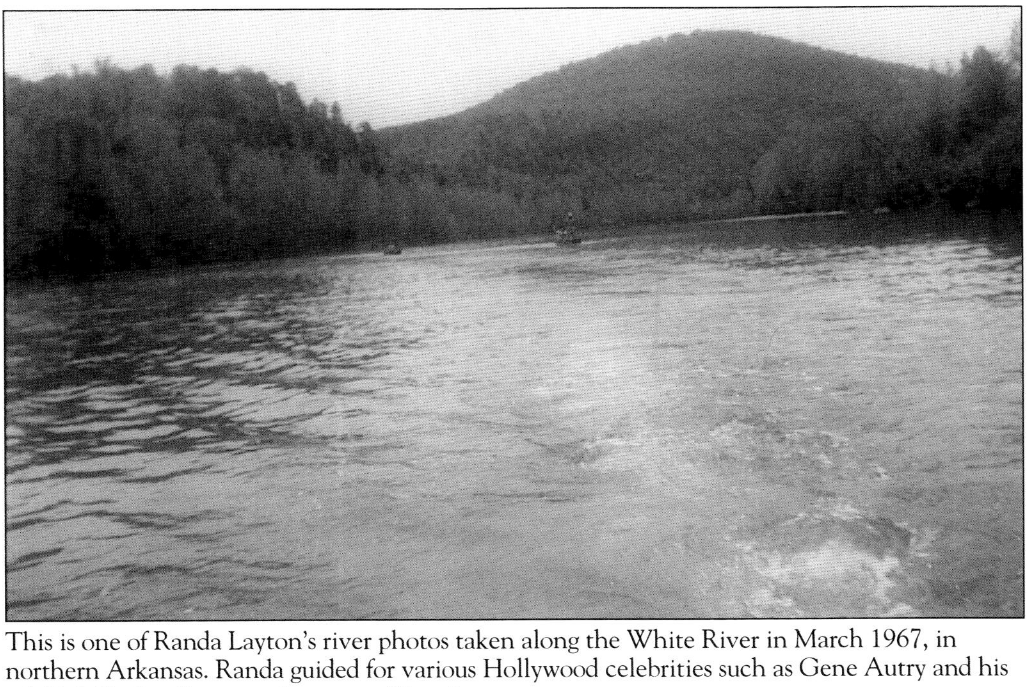

This is one of Randa Layton's river photos taken along the White River in March 1967, in northern Arkansas. Randa guided for various Hollywood celebrities such as Gene Autry and his sidekick Smiley Burnette, known as "Frog."

This view is on the White River in northern Arkansas, March 1967, on a float trip with Randa Layton as a guide.

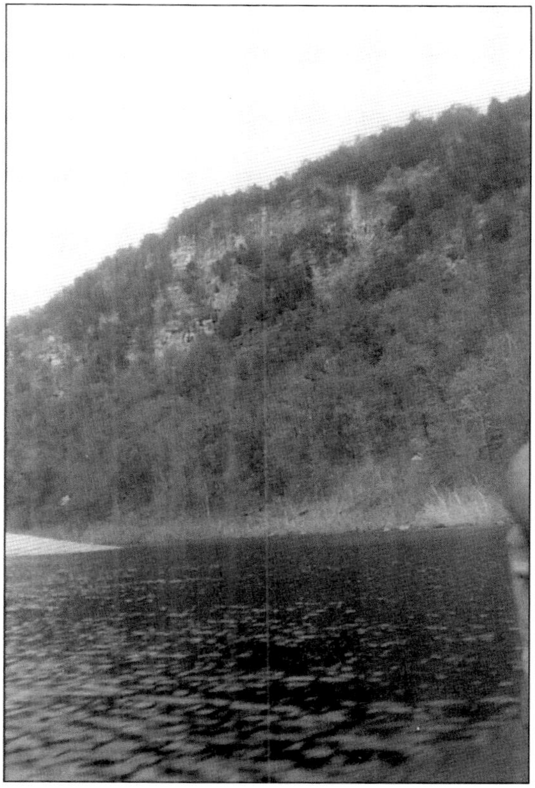

In the 1960s, Randa Layton guided for Bill Rogers out of Galena. They were on the Buffalo River near Woolim, Arkansas. The guides could run a boat back into the cave leading back into the side of this bluff.

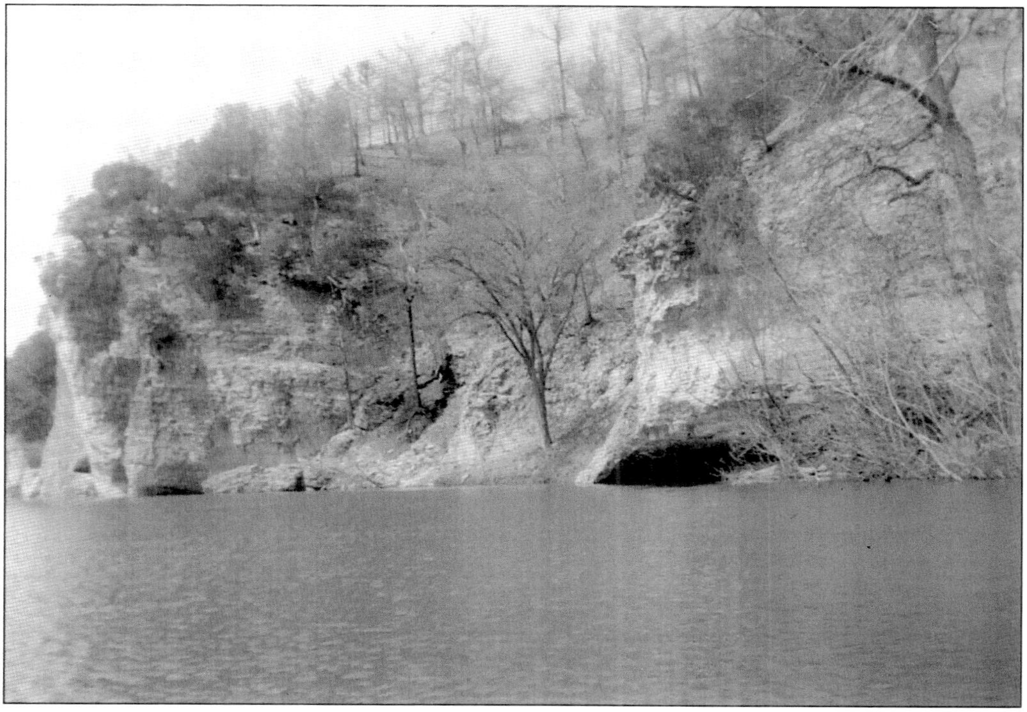

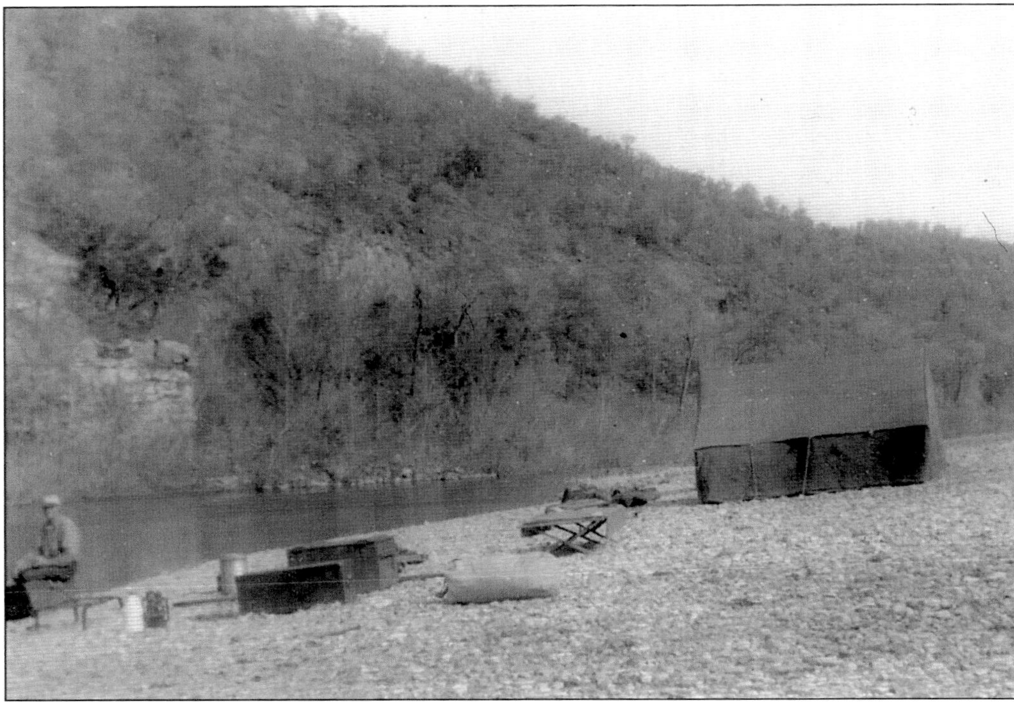

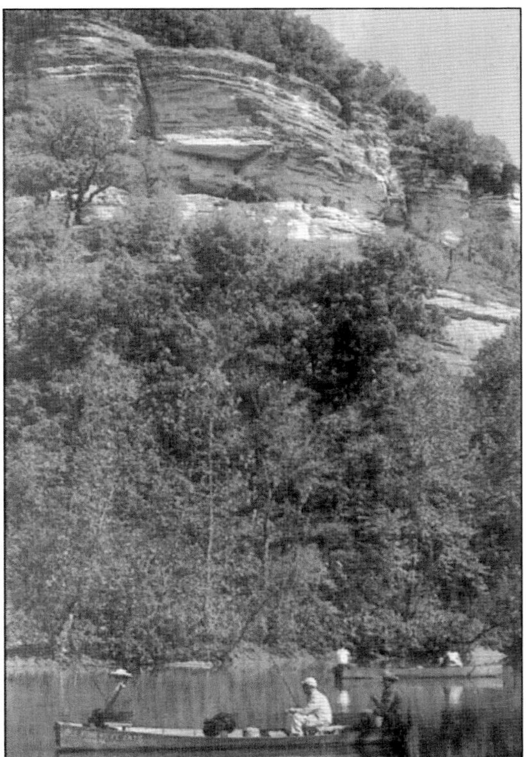

Randa Layton is pictured here at a campsite where the Buffalo River runs into the White River. Randa was often in charge of the commissary boat, which was used to transport the camp provisions. This was taken in the 1960s.

Bill Rogers of the Galena Boat Company and Float Fishing Services is pictured on the James River, north of Galena at the Horse Creek Access beneath Echo Bluff. River guide Randa Layton paddles the front boat.

Pictured at right is Elephant Head Rock on the Buffalo River near Rush, Arkansas. Randa Layton guided for Bill Rogers at this time.

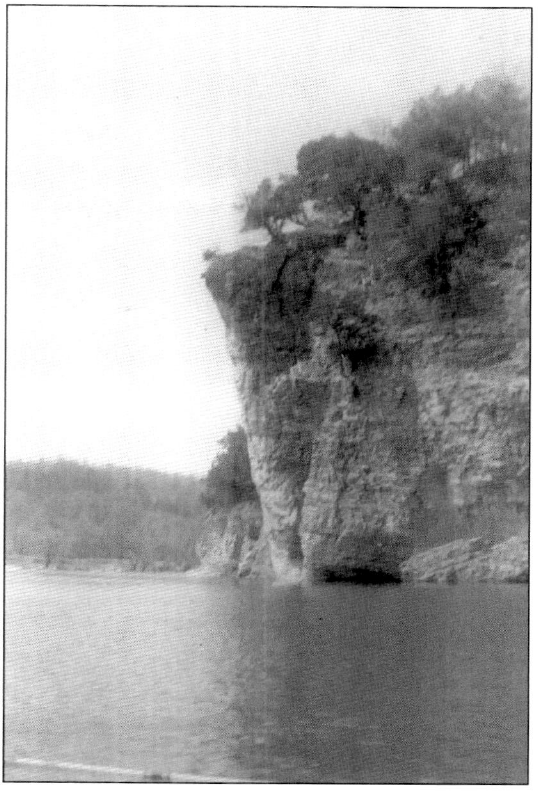

Standing in the front to the right is Randa Layton with a float party he was guiding. Their campsite is set up on the Buffalo River where it runs into the White River. This photograph was taken in the 1960s.

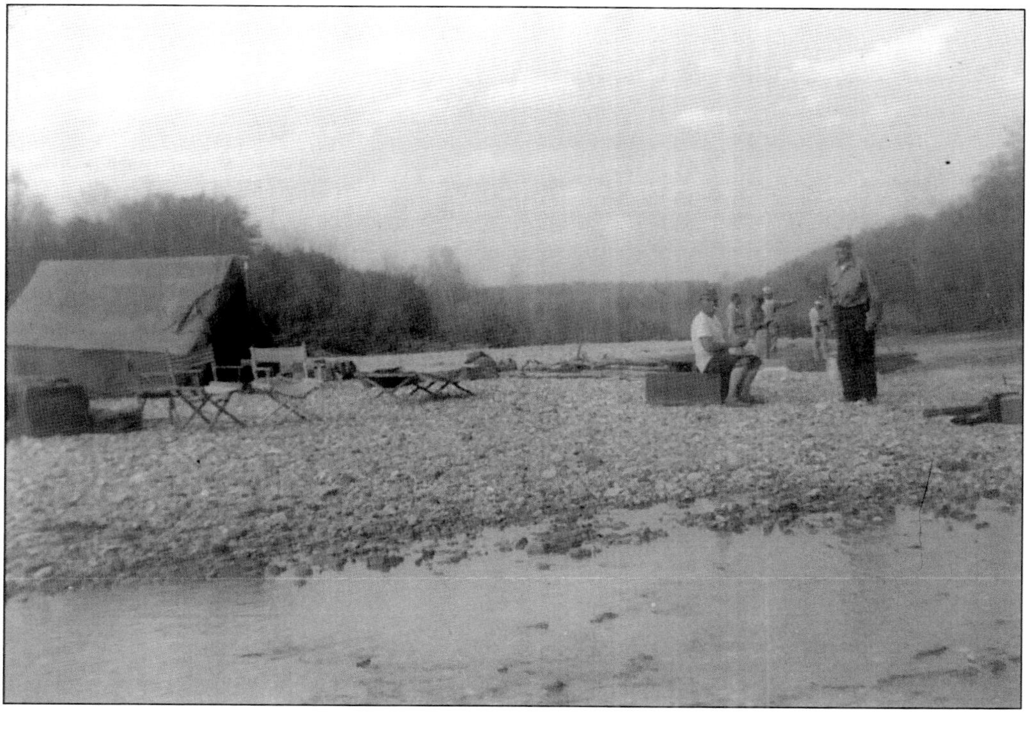

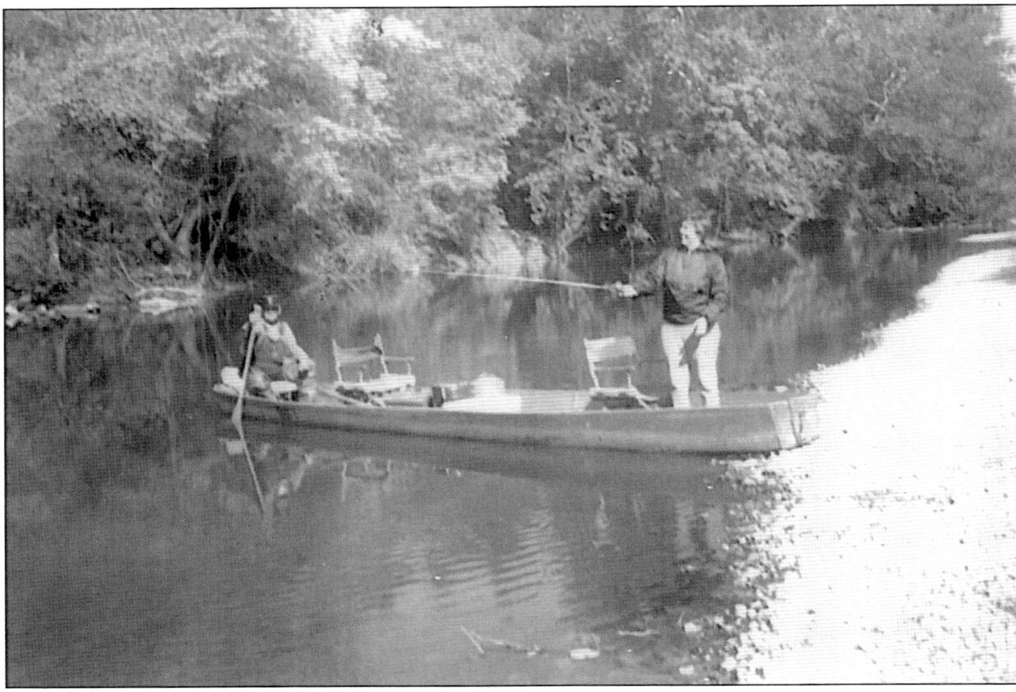

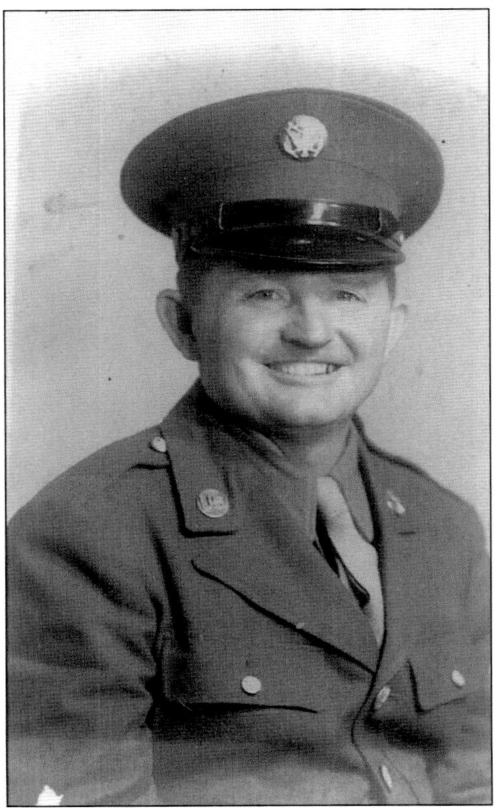

"Little Horse" Jim Jennings guides for this woman on the James River during the early 1960s.

Randa Layton spent many days and nights on the river with "Little Horse" Jim Jennings, pictured here as a young man in his Army uniform. During the author's childhood, she remembers the many times her daddy drove the family truck along the west side of the square in Galena, where she currently resides. There seated on one of the benches beneath the shade of a maple tree would be "Little Horse" Jim Jennings, waiting for his next call to take a float party out on the river.

Seven

Interesting Scenes no Longer Seen

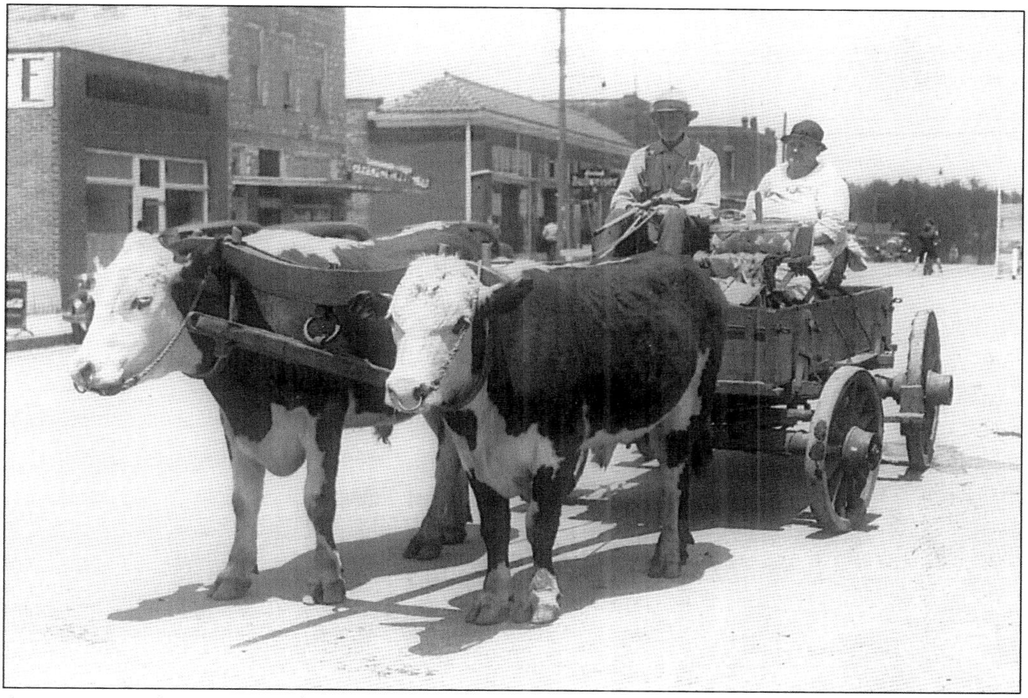

A common sight among early Taney County residents and tourists in the early 1900s was Uncle Jim (Gemes) Whorton and his wife, Almede, traveling in their ox-drawn wagon along Main Street in downtown Branson. To tourists, this was a rare sight to behold. The Whortons took cans of fresh cows' cream and as many as 97 dozen eggs into town at one time, to trade or sell to the general mercantile store for other necessities such as coffee, salt, sewing material, or whatever else was needed. This photograph was dated April 26, 1936.

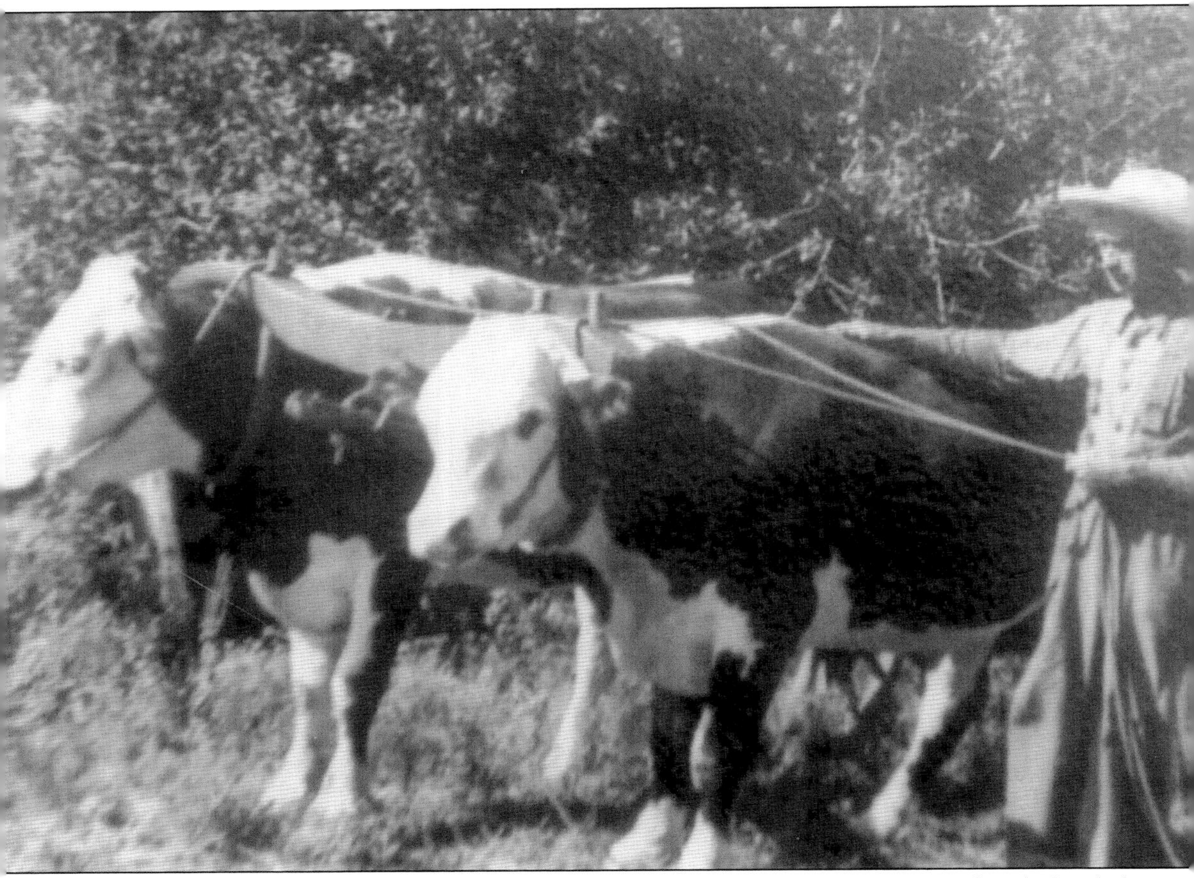

Jim Whorton stands alongside his oxen team, Duke and Line. Jim "Gemes" hand chiseled and carved the names, dates, and decorations on many of those buried in the Whorton family cemetery by Turkey Creek in Hollister. This photograph was contributed by Marietta Layton.

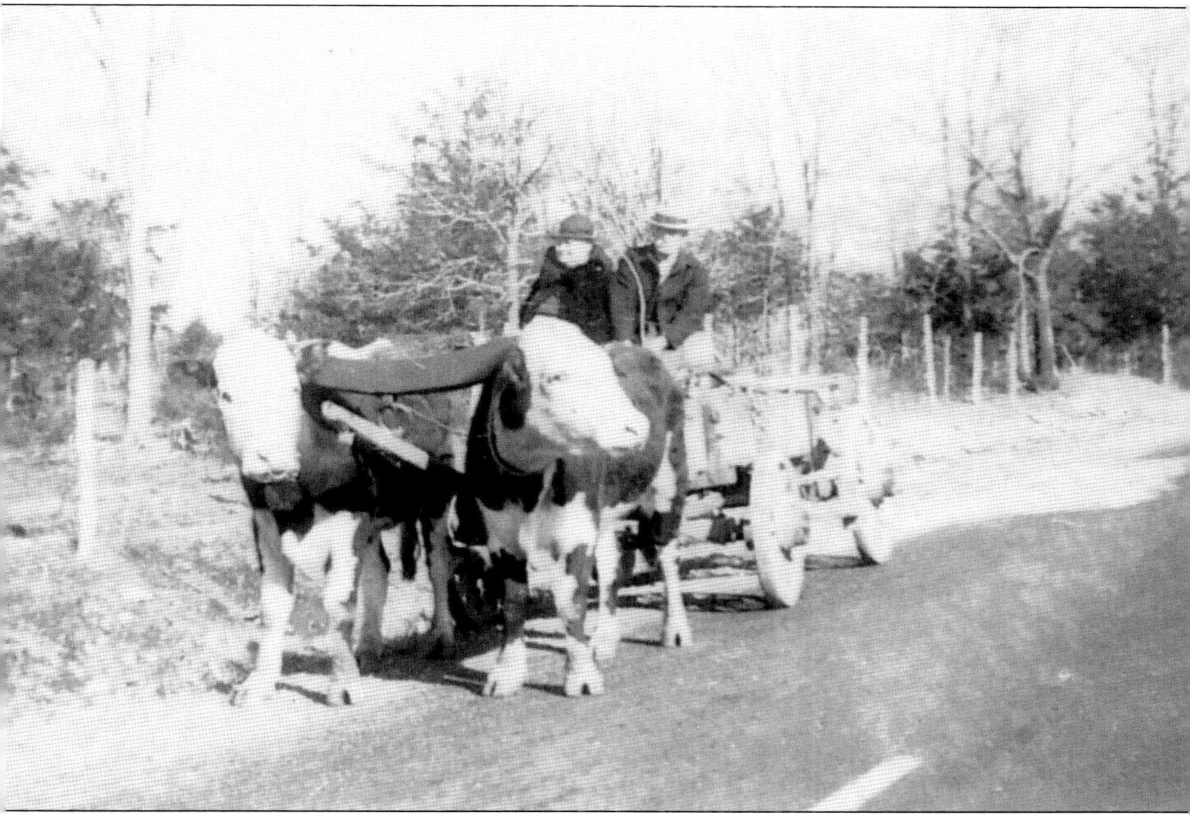

Jim and Almeda Whorton travel T Highway east of Branson, with their team of oxen. They had different oxen over the years, but they always named them after the original pair—Duke and Line. This was a sight rarely seen by motorists traveling then, and many stopped to photograph the rare scene.

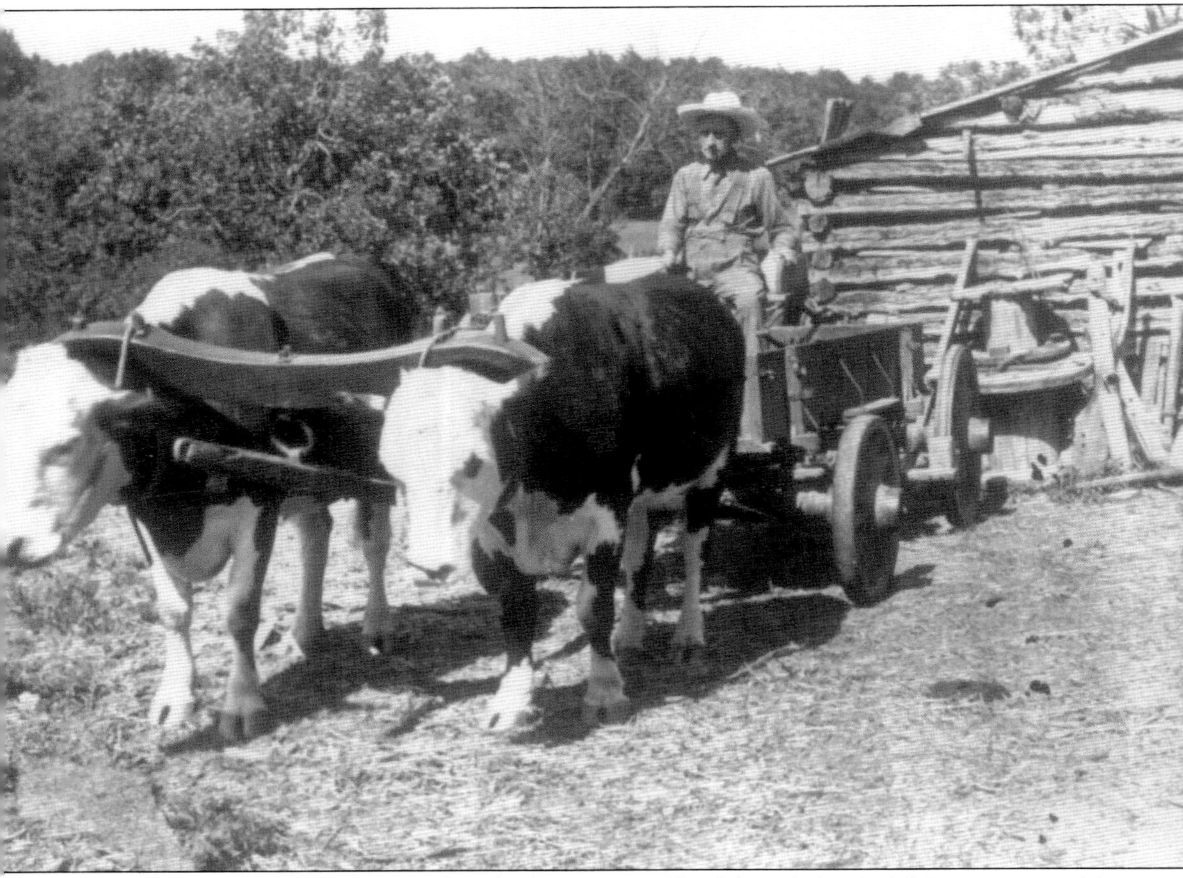

Uncle Jim Whorton is pictured in the later years of his life with his faithful oxen team. After Uncle Jim's death, the familiar sight of an ox-drawn wagon was forever gone from Taney County. Jim was born October 13, 1865, and died October 14, 1937.

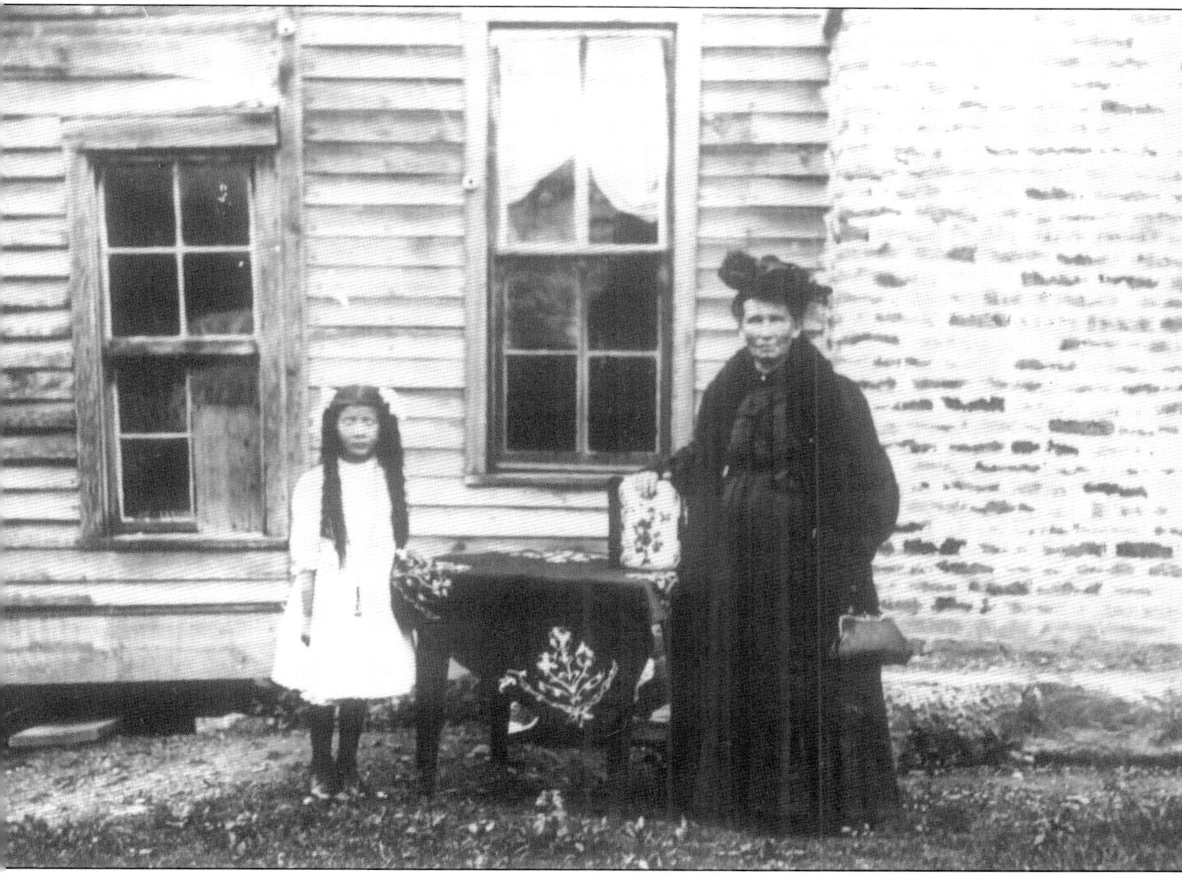

Mollie Johnson is pictured at her Rogersville home with her granddaughter, Opal. This photograph was taken in the late 1800s or very early 1900s. She was Jep Whorton's daughter.

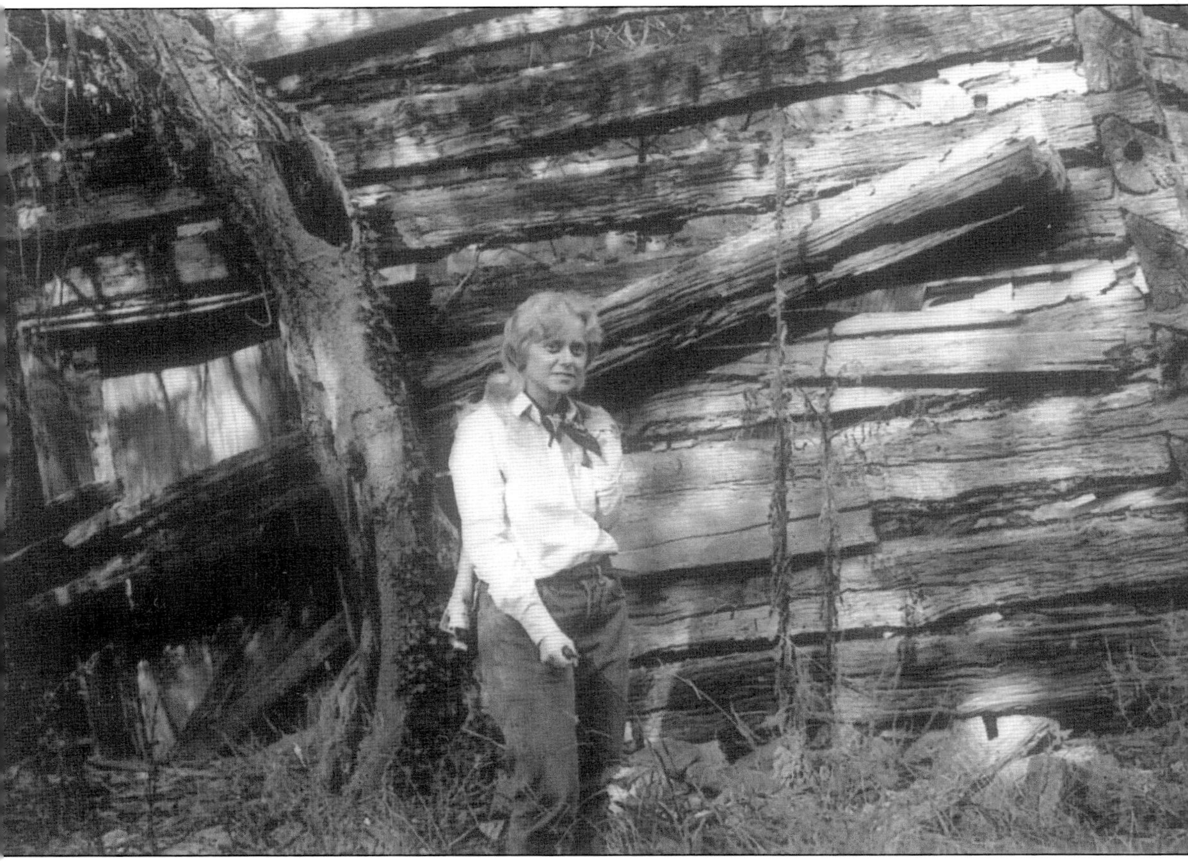

The author, Vickie Layton Cobb, stands beside the abandoned log cabin in Oak Grove, once home to her maternal great-grandmother, Safronea Whorton Layton. Even in the year 2001, part of the cabin still stands. Its logs deteriorated over the many years, as it has weathered nearly 150 years of existence, give or take a few. This photo was taken 1990.

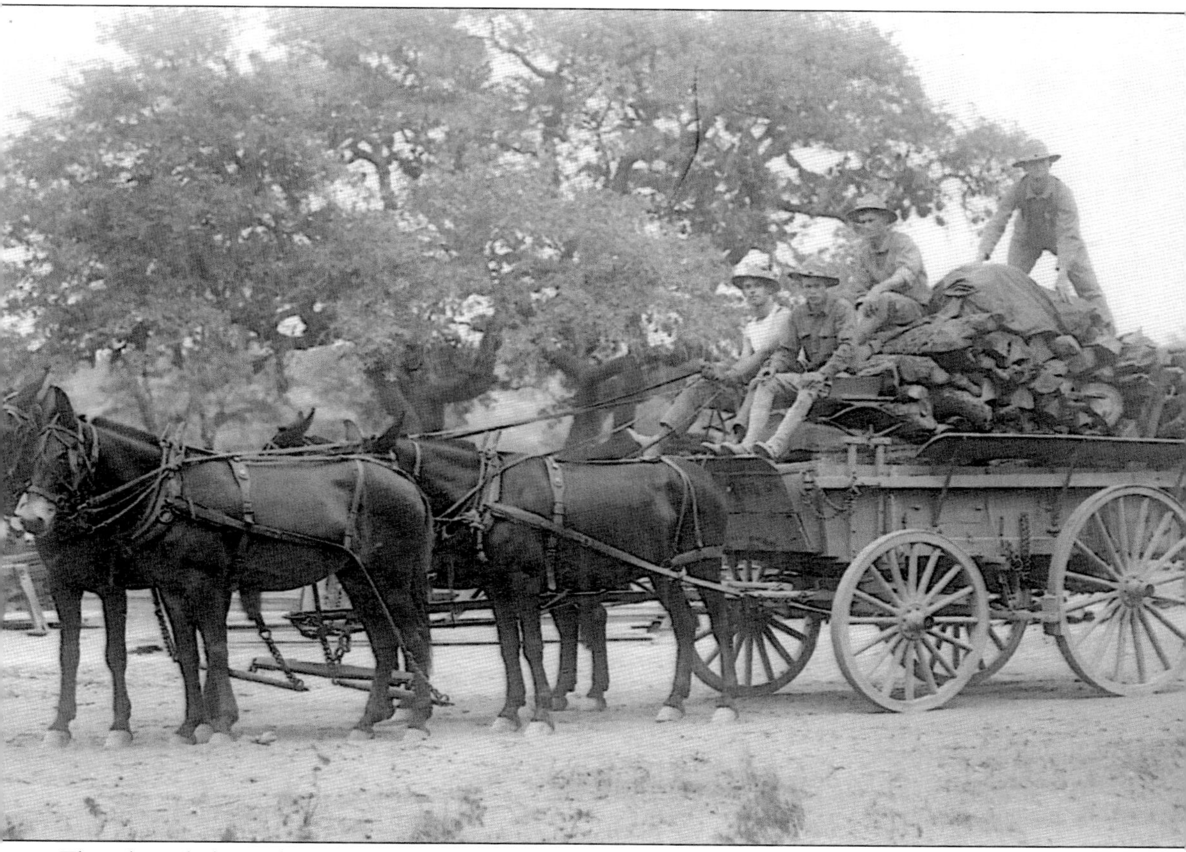

This photo belonged to Ira Rittenhouse. He is shown here on top of a lumber wagon drawn by two teams of mules. Detailed information about the photo is unavailable, except that it was taken about 1920.

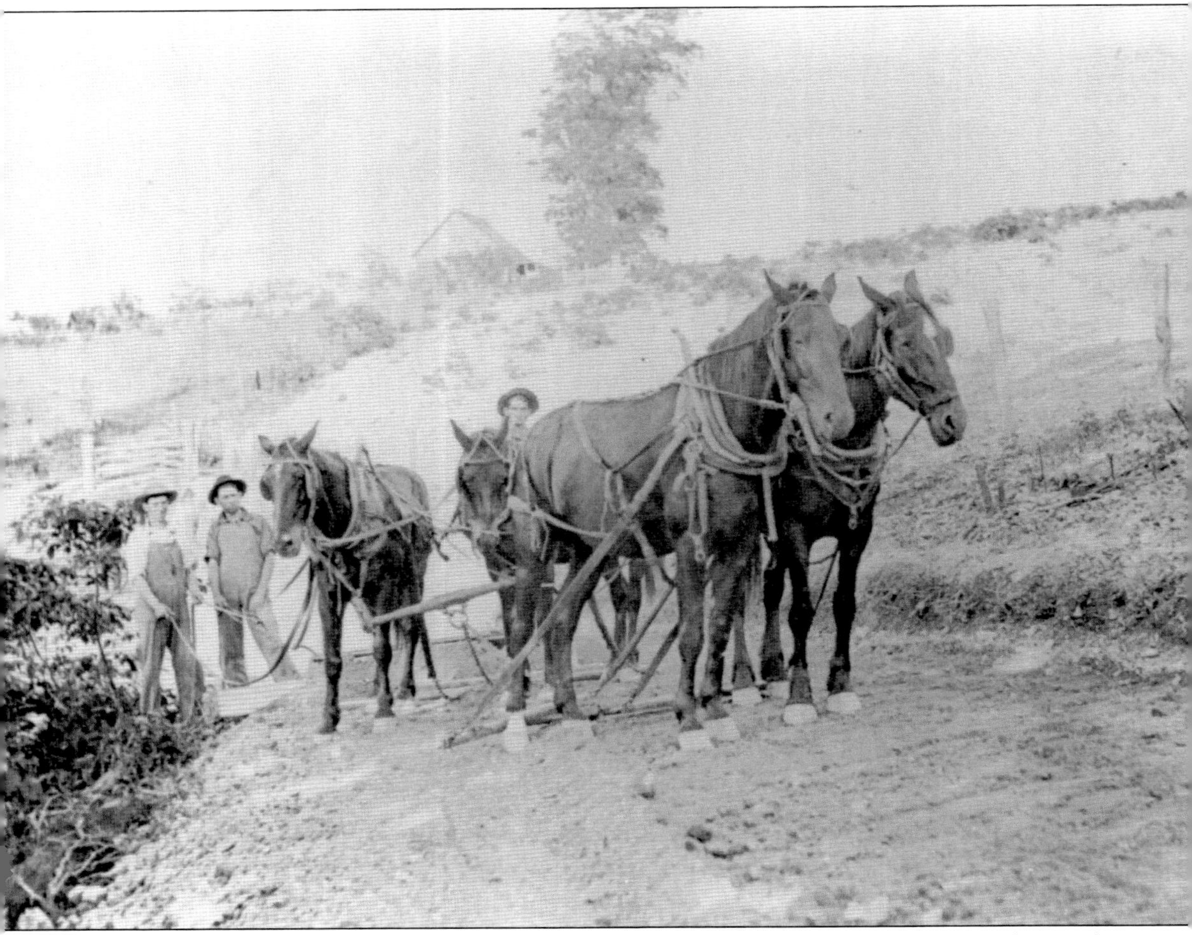

The author's great uncle Truman Smith is photographed with two teams of horses and two other local Kirbyville men working on a wagon road in the early 1900s.

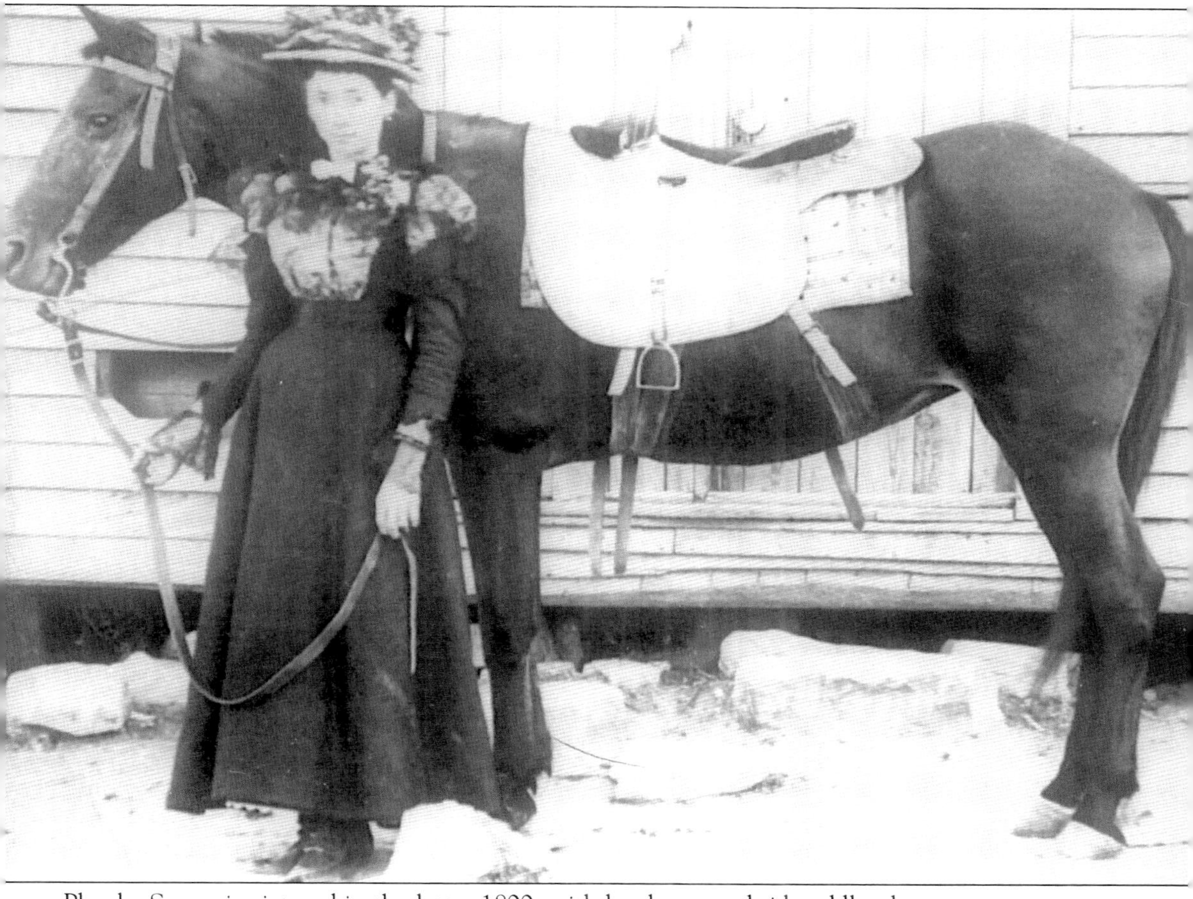

Phoebe Snapp is pictured in the latter 1800s with her horse and sidesaddle, the customary way women rode horses in those days. At that time in history, it was considered a disgrace and not becoming of a lady if she rode with one leg over each side. This was taken in Kirbyville.

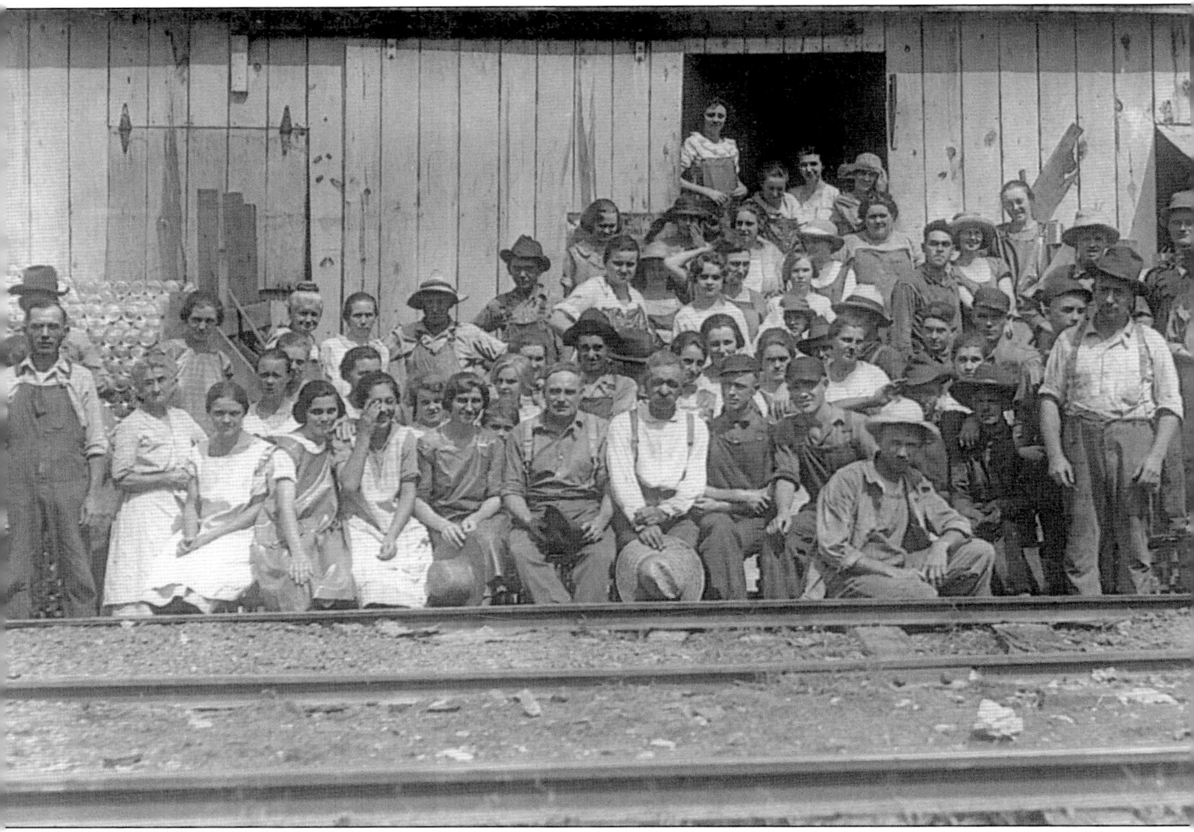

This photograph depicts the crew that worked on the railroad in the early 1900s in the Hollister and Branson area. No identification is available.

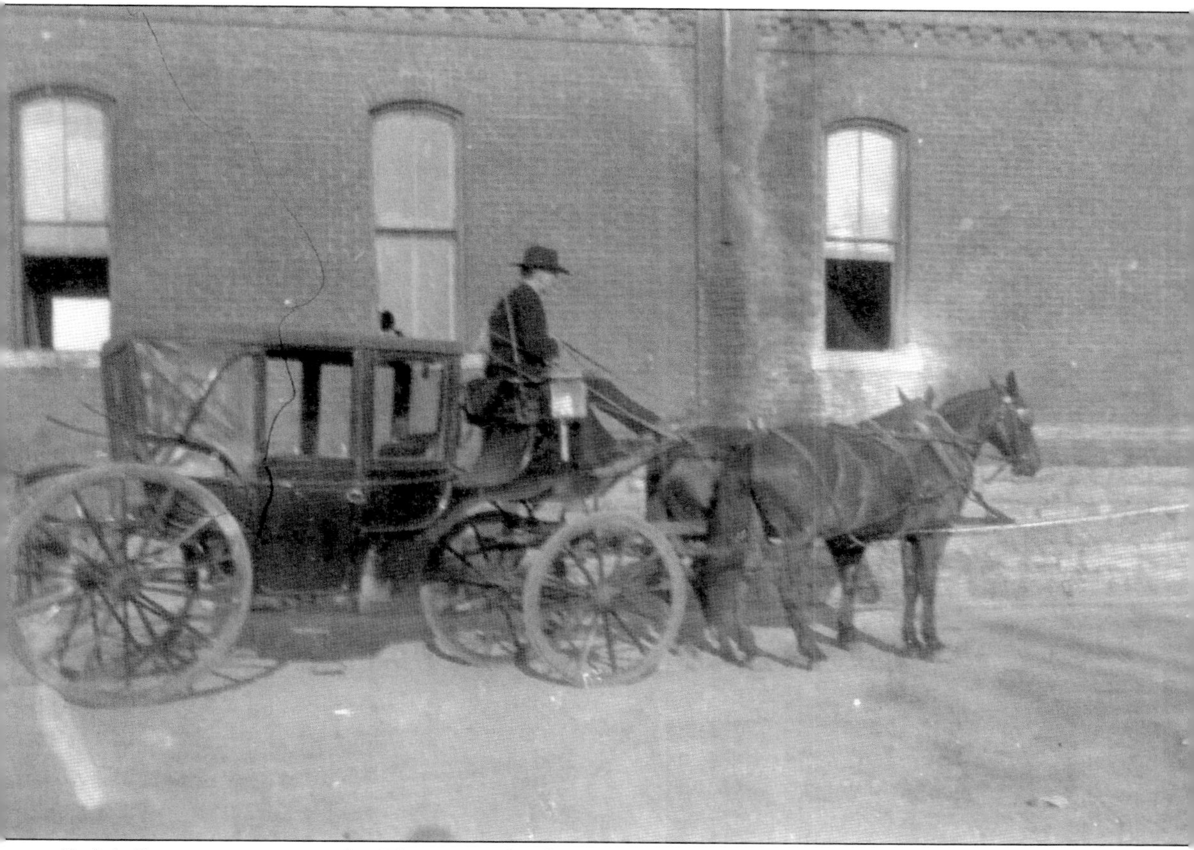

Ralph Reese, a cousin to the Thomas and Julia Layton family of Hollister, is shown driving an old-time "hearse" in Springfield during the very late 1800s.

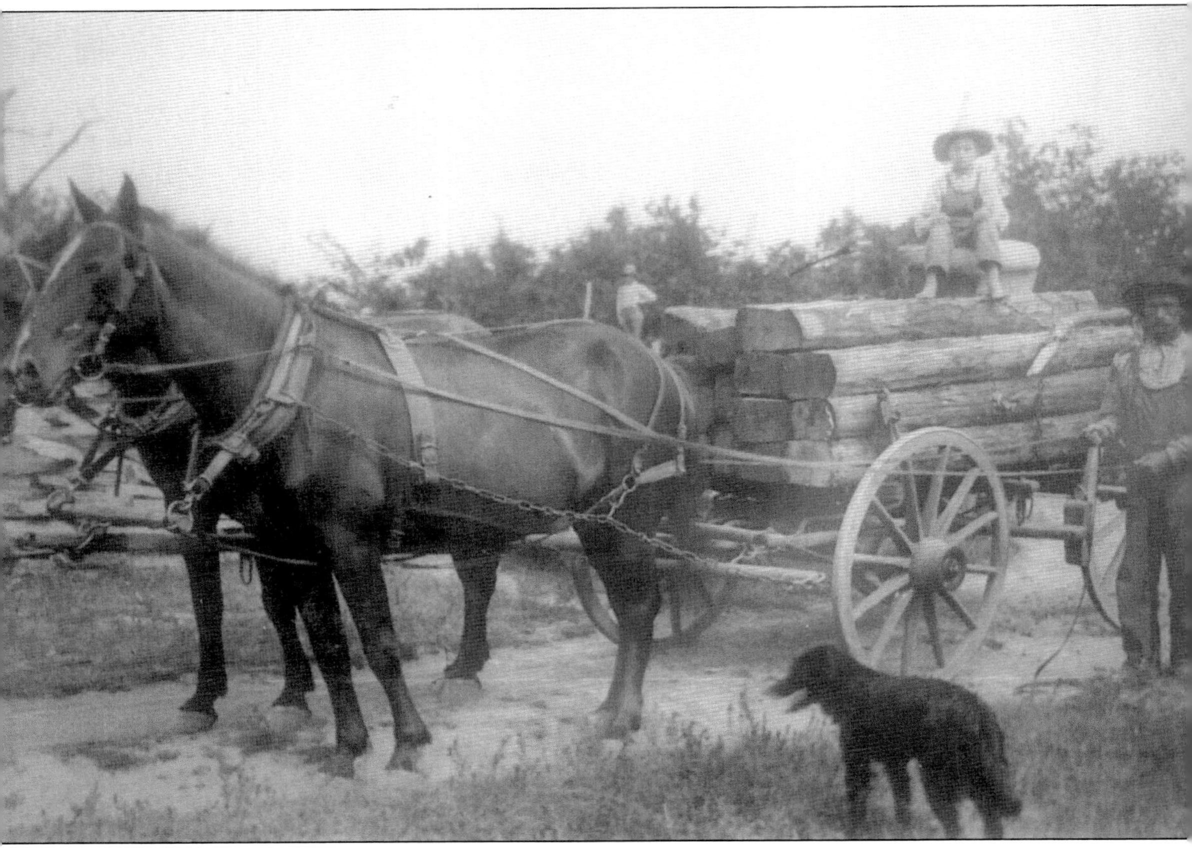

The author's great-great uncle Gemes "Jim" Whorton, with his son, Albert, and a wagonload of railroad ties. Ben Layton stands in the background. They were photographed in Oak Grove east of Branson during the early 1900s.

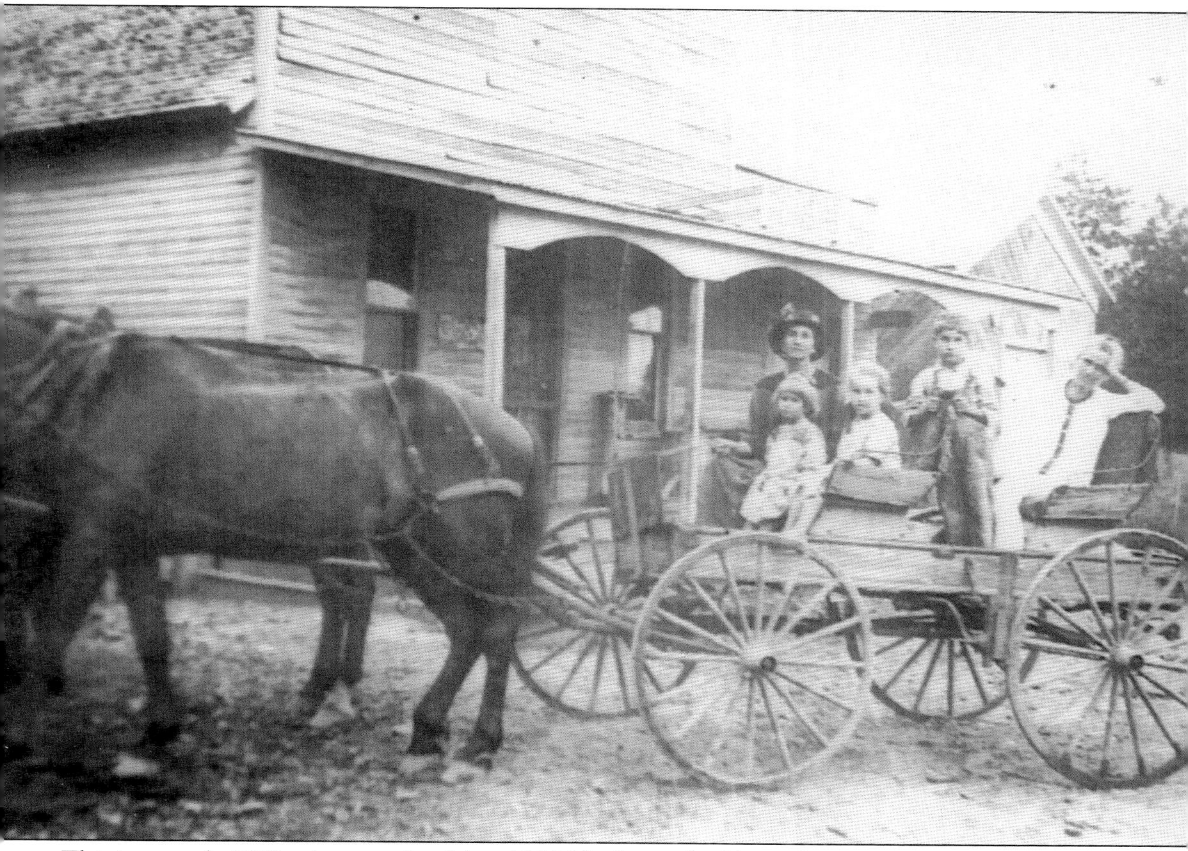

This is an early 1900s photograph of the old Mildred store building, the center of commerce for local residents. The wagon and its occupants were making their weekly trip for supplies. Their identities are unknown. This photograph was contributed by Marietta Layton.

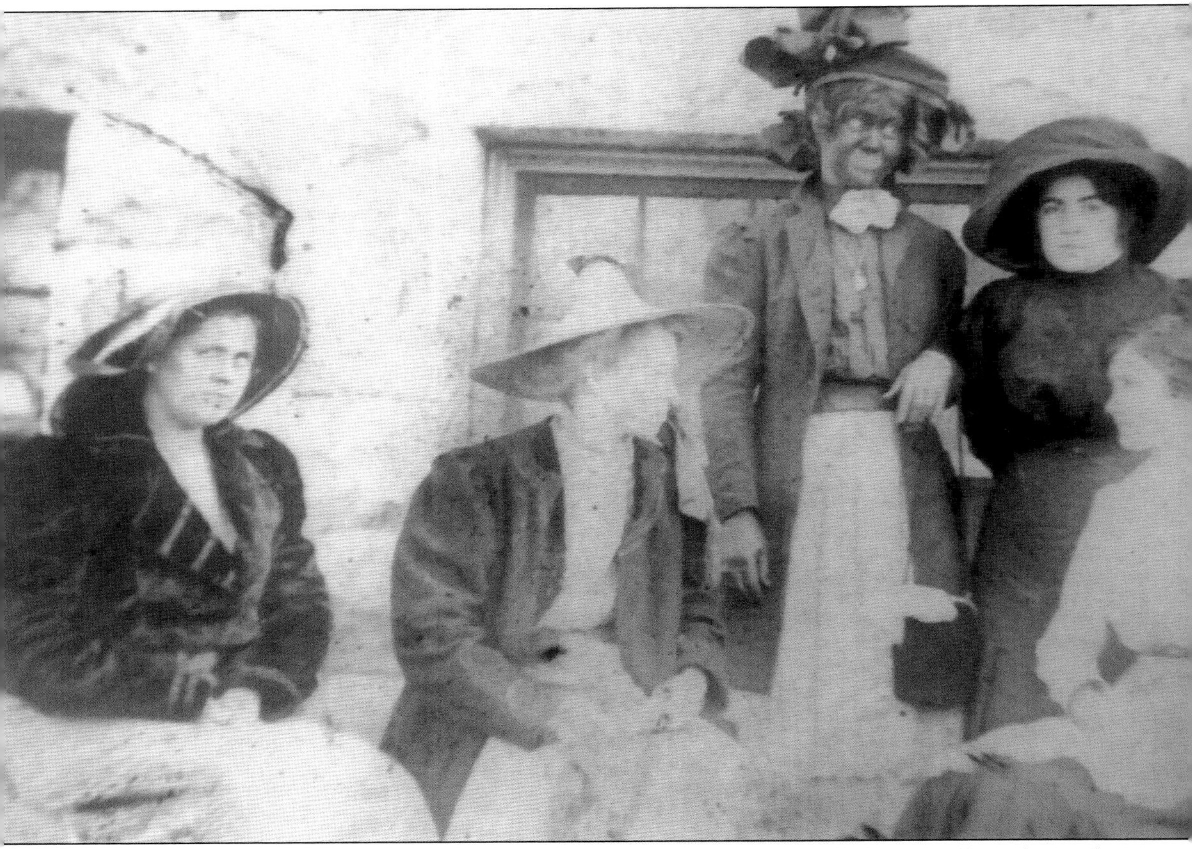

These ladies were actresses in a play performed at the School of the Ozarks College, located at Point Lookout near Hollister. The land where the college was built was purchased from John Layton, brother of Thomas Layton. John was among the first Laytons to homestead in Taney County during the 1850s. Rosa Victoria Kaneaster Layton is the second lady from the right with the dark dress and hat on. This photograph was contributed by Marietta Layton.

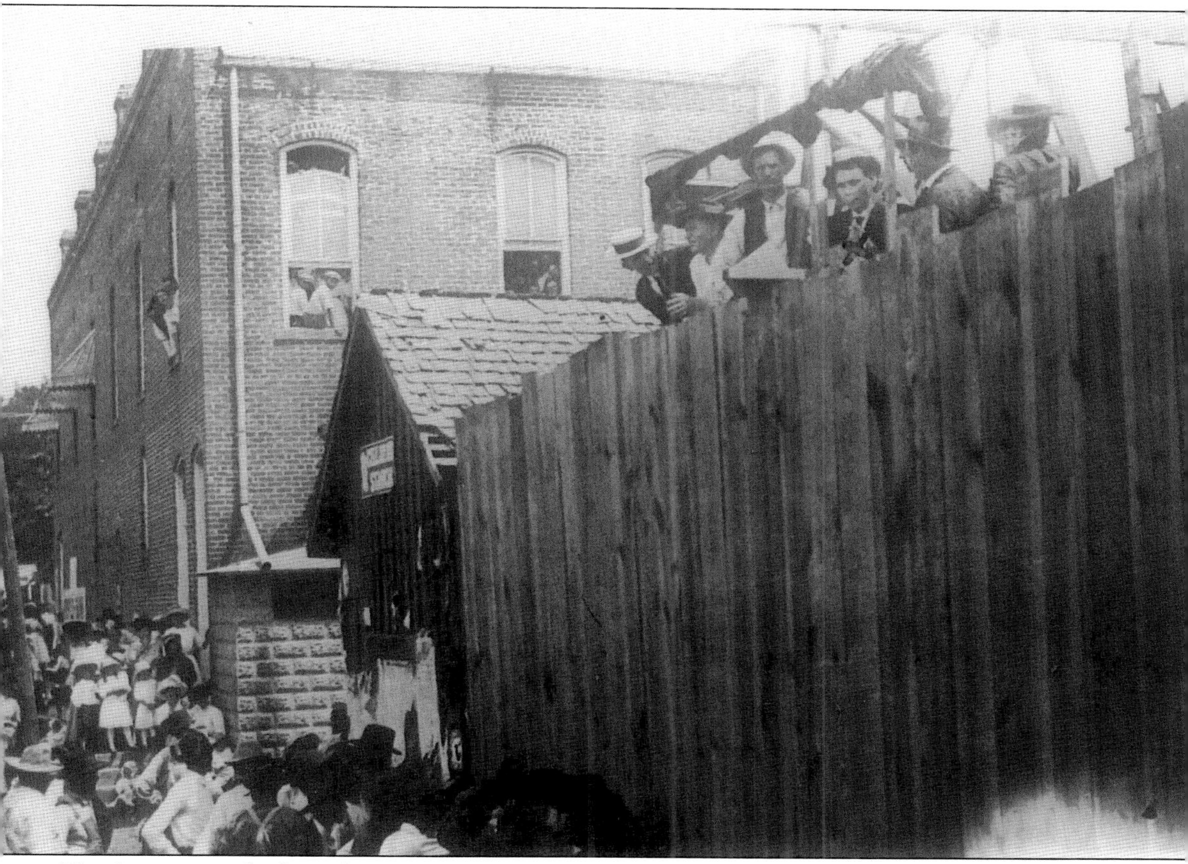

This hanging took place about 1900 in Harrison, Arkansas. Ernest Pruitt, who was a little boy at this time and whose family lived at Mincy, went to Harrison that day with his father David Pruitt. The prisoner is wearing a dark suit jacket and tie. He was found guilty for the murder of his girlfriend, whom he killed with a chopping ax. This photograph was contributed by Bobby Pruitt, Grants Pass, Oregon.

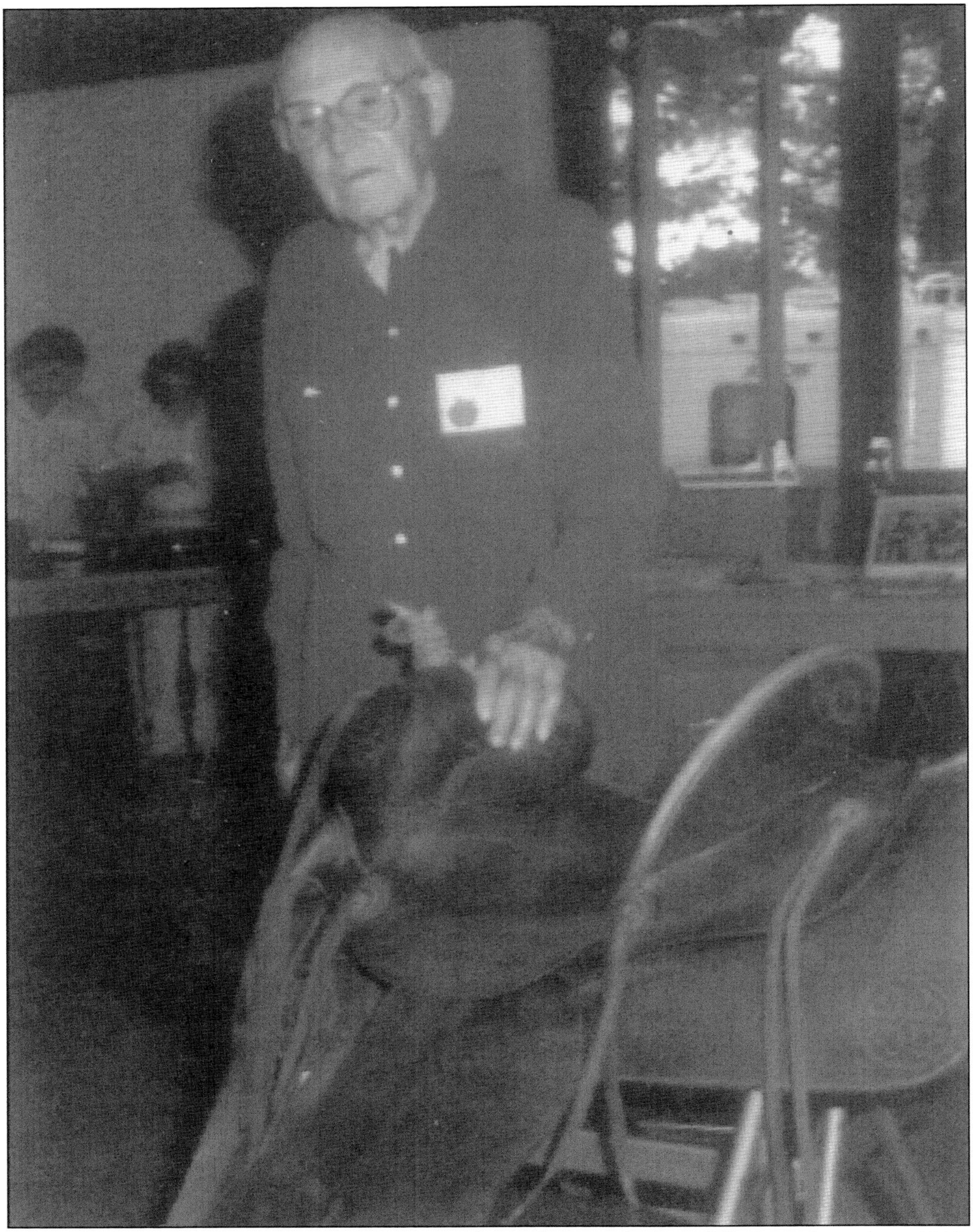

Ben Pruitt, at the age of 100 years in 1989, is shown here with the saddle he rode with in 1911, on a horse drive from Bonanza, Oregon, to Doyle, California. They then traveled by train from there onto Hollister, Missouri. The drive consisted of 115 head of wild mares. Ben, Ernest, and Commie (his brothers) Pruitt, along with Will Moore handled the herd of wild mares, while the Pruitt boys' father, David, along with a friend drove a four-horse team with a wagon. The entire trip lasted 13 days. While making the journey from California to Hollister, the men made their living quarters in the train's caboose. Ben died in 1993 at the age of 104.

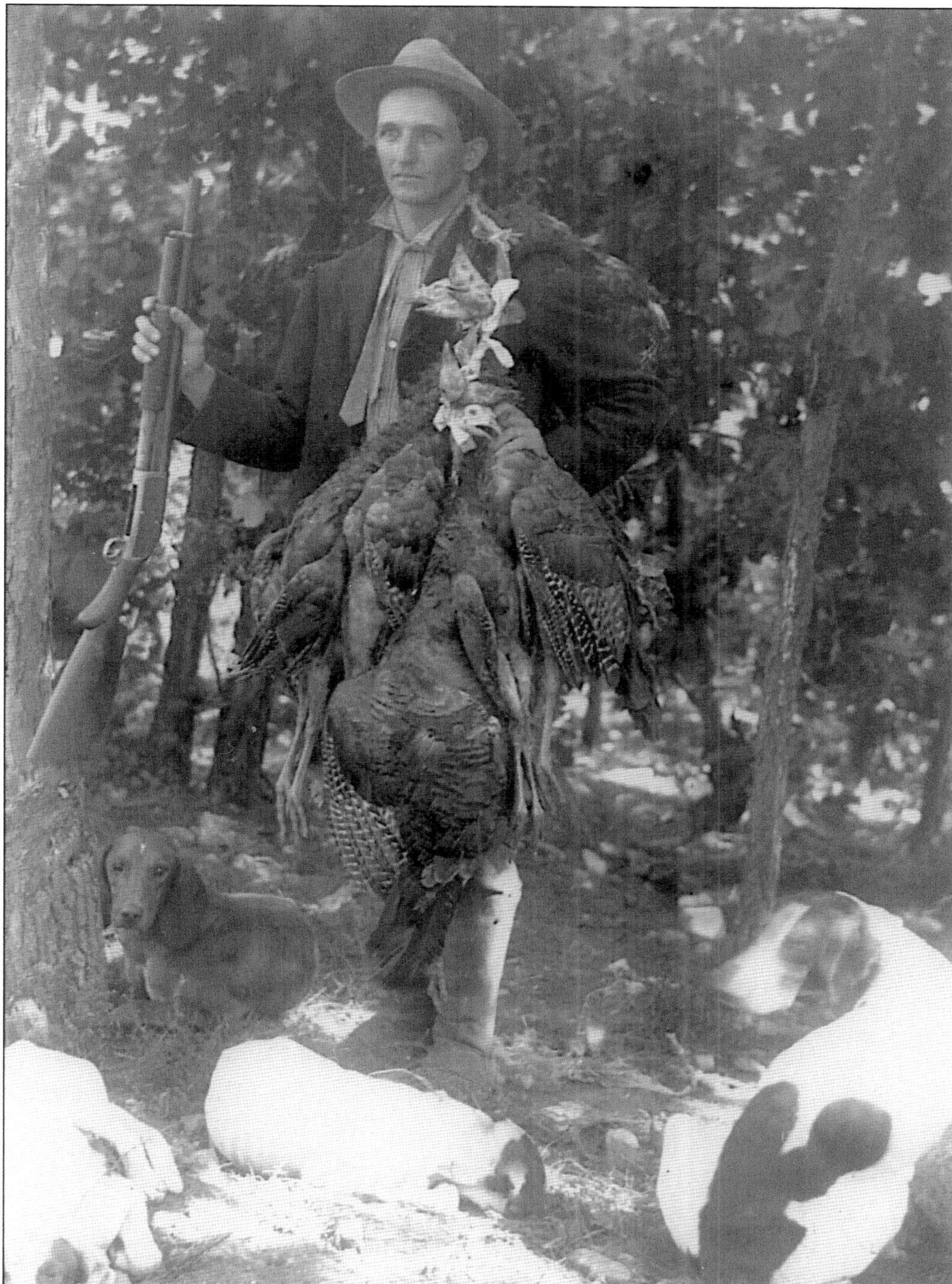

Robert Pruitt holds some turkeys he killed in the Pine Top area south of Mincy before 1920. He moved to Oregon shortly afterwards to live. Robert married Laura Inman from Lickbranch, Arkansas. They lived on the old Bracken place, located along the Springfield-Harrison Road south of Kirbyville. Robert was born in Kirbyville in 1883.

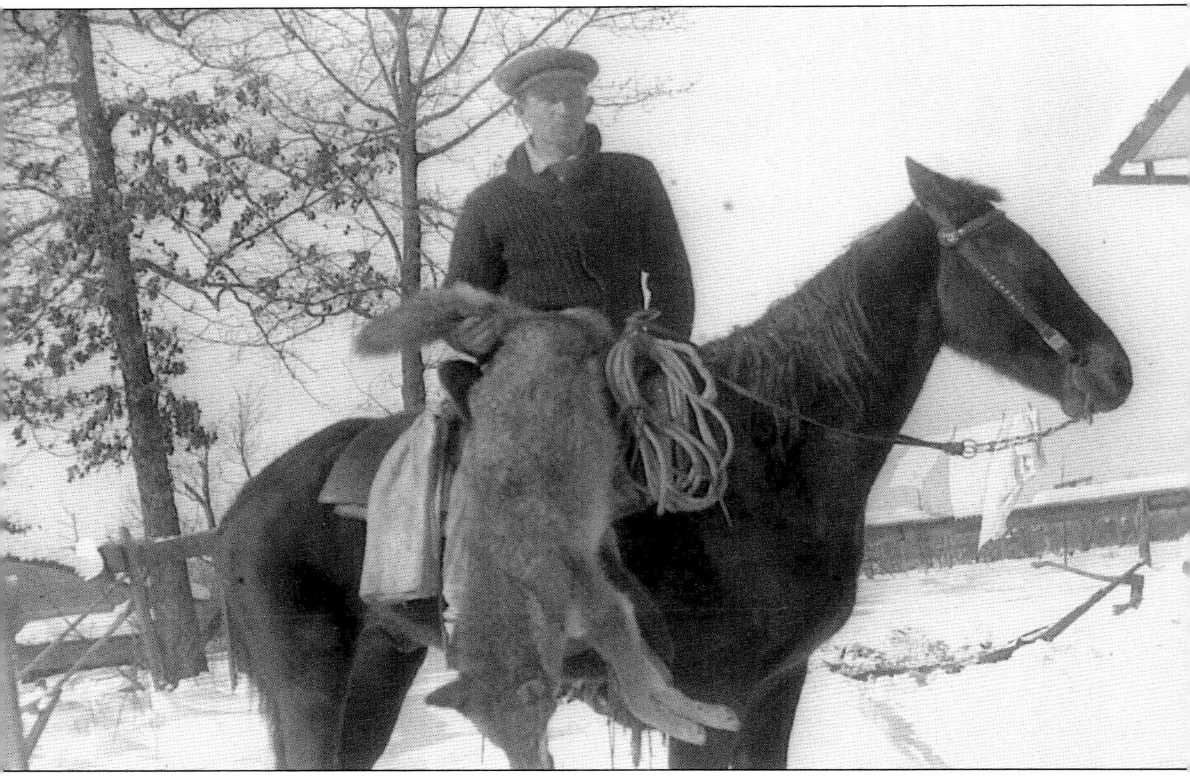

Robert's brother, Ernest Pruitt, holds one of the wolves he killed in the winter of 1917–18. Wolves threatened the livelihood of those who depended on livestock from which they not only made their living, but also kept their families fed. This was in the Mincy area, where many related families lived. Will Puterbaugh, husband of Lula Pruitt, built the house in the photo, and it was always known as the old Puterbaugh place. Will and Steven Bedford hauled Murana Layton Bedford's (Steven's mother) casket by wagon during a snowstorm from Burlington, Arkansas, to the Vanzandt Cemetery in Kirbyville by way of Springfield-Harrison Road, which ran through Mincy.

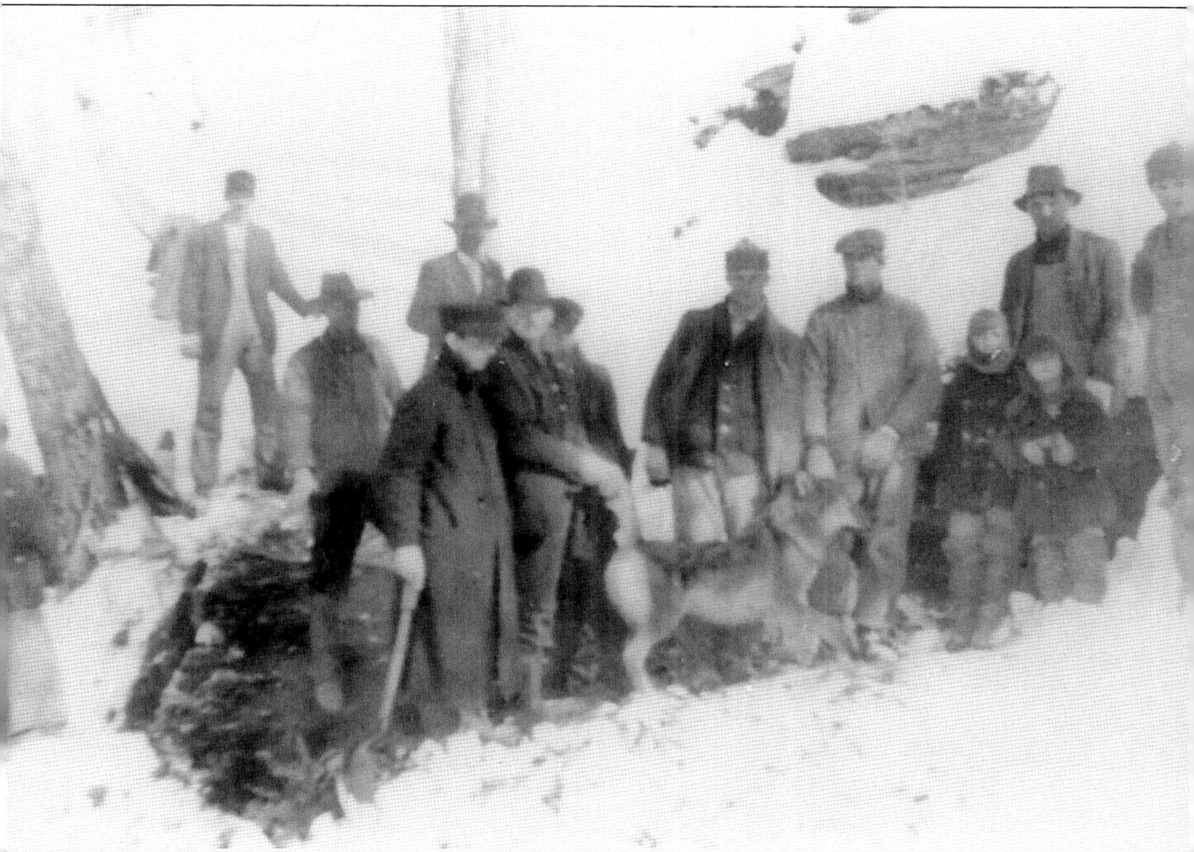

In the winter of 1917 and 1918, with a heavy snow and extremely cold temperatures, Robert Pruitt chased this wolf into a cave. Robert built a snowman at the cave's entrance and removed his clothing, except for his long john underwear and boots, in hopes that the snowman decoy would keep the wolf from escaping. Robert spent the night en route to his brother's for help. Arriving at daylight, Robert dressed, and along with his brothers Ernest and Ben, he returned to the cave. The wolf still inside, Ernest and Ben pinned him to the back wall with forked tree branches and tied his mouth shut with rope, then tied its legs. They spent half the day getting the wolf out, and by then others came to help. The Pruitt brothers caught two more wolves that winter in the same manner.

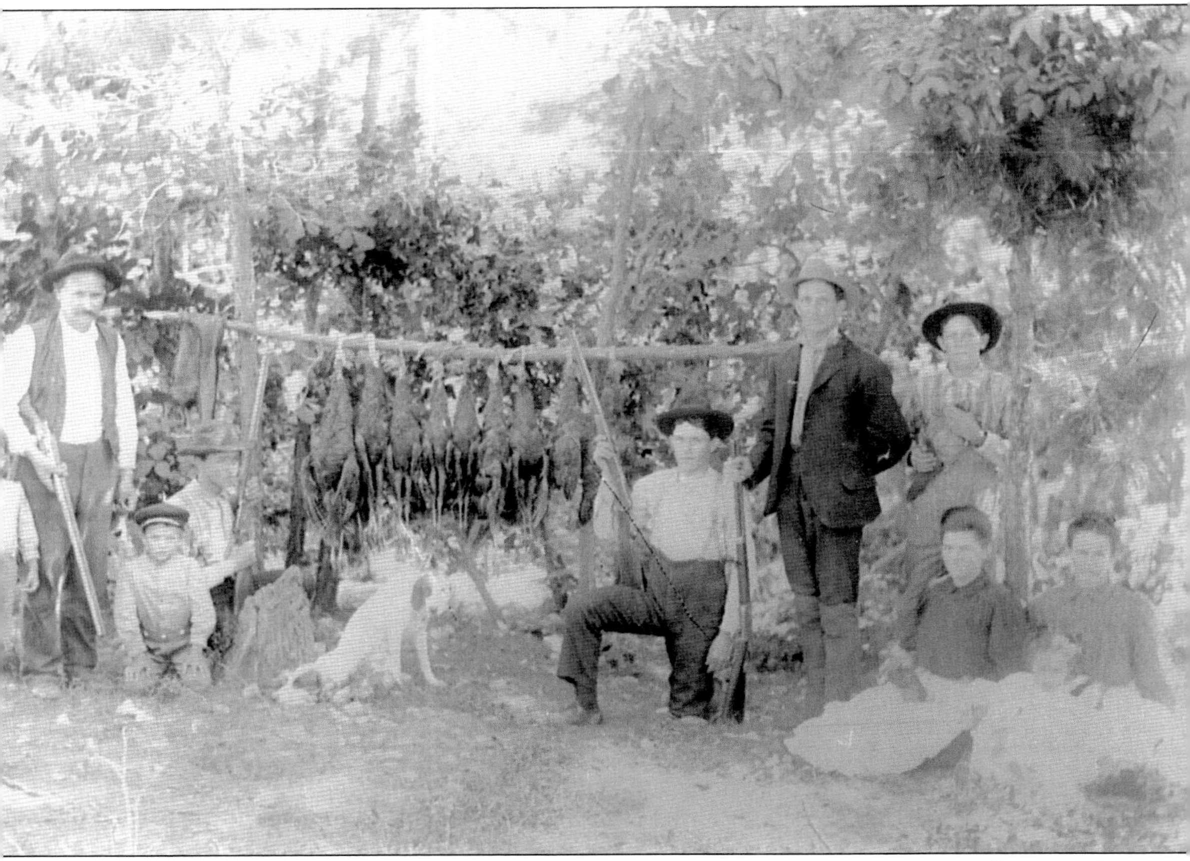

This was either at Pine Top, Missouri, or between Omaha and Burlington, Arkansas—the exact location is unknown. The year was 1907. The Pruitt men killed these turkeys between themselves, and they are photographed with family members. Pictured from left to right are: Blaine Byrd Pruitt (boy), David Leroy Pruitt is holding the gun, Roosevelt McKinley (Veltie) Pruitt (boy), Ernest William Pruitt is holding the gun, Benjamin Harrison Pruitt, Robert Howard Pruitt, Commie Andrew Pruitt, Laura Pruitt, Tabitha Pruitt, and Argil Pruitt (baby). David and Tabitha were the parents. The Pruitt family moved to Idaho that same year, but they returned in 1909. Robert and Laura's first child was born in Gooding, Idaho.

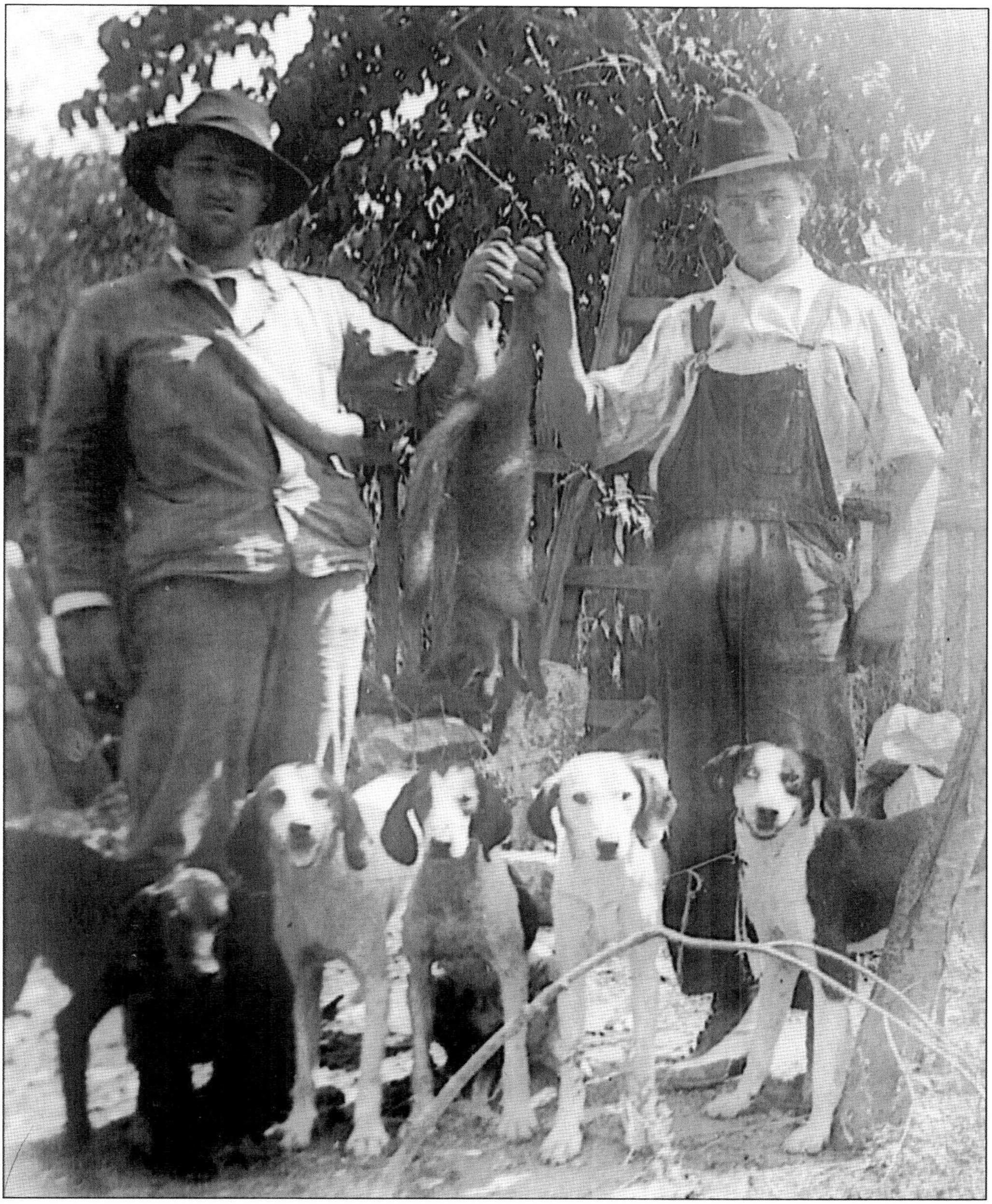

Ben Layton (on the left) and his younger brother Randa are pictured before the 1920s, in their mid to late teens with their hounds and a night's catch, a red fox. Chasing coons, foxes, or other varmints that roamed the hills provided food and an income from the hides. Randa Layton told fascinating stories about those early hunts. Sometimes they encountered panthers that roamed the hills preying on unsuspecting victims and livestock. Randa said that many times an old hound came running in and stood between his legs, trembling all over. A panther's voice sounded like a woman screaming when terrified. Ben never left Taney County, but he acquired a reputation all over the country as a dog trader. Ben was also the town marshal of Hollister at the age of 17.

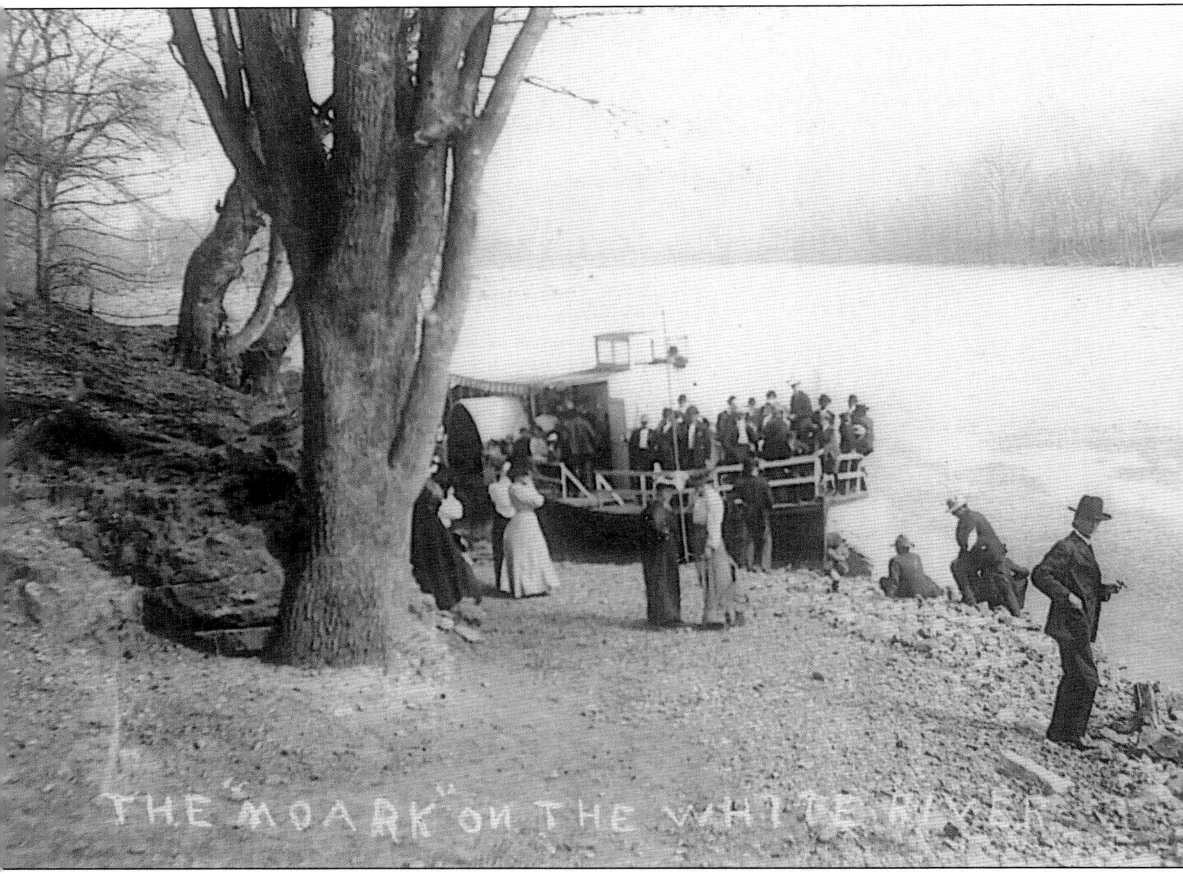

One of the many steamboats that traveled the upper White River was the *Moark*. According to Taney County historian and lawyer Douglas Mahnkey, this particular scene was at the mouth of Swan Creek, southeast of where Forsyth exists today. At the time, Old Forsyth was situated by Swan Creek and later moved up the hill to its new locale. This photograph, according to Mahnkey, was made after the Civil War. The *Moark*, along with the *Eureka*, was gasoline powered.

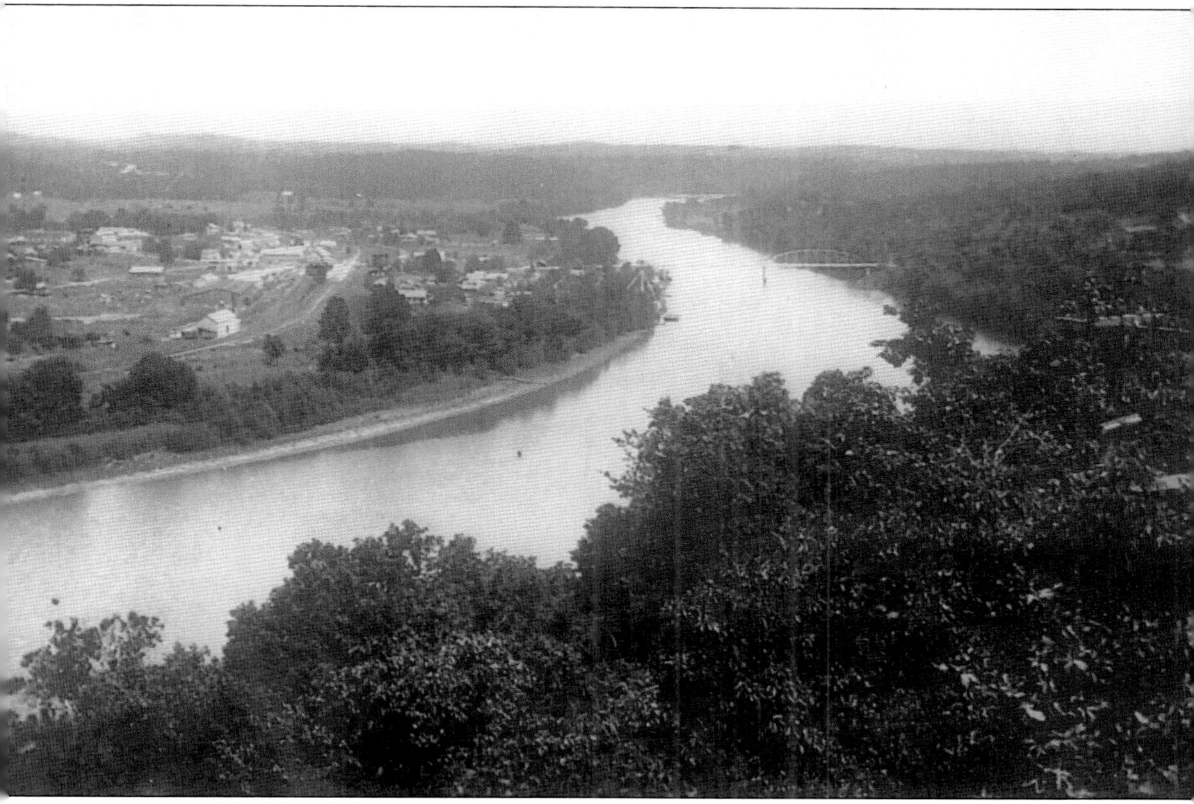

An early White River scene shows Branson in the early 1930s before Table Rock Dam was built and Lake Taney Como came into existence. The photographer stood on Presbyterian Hill on the east side of the river and took the picture while facing the northeast.

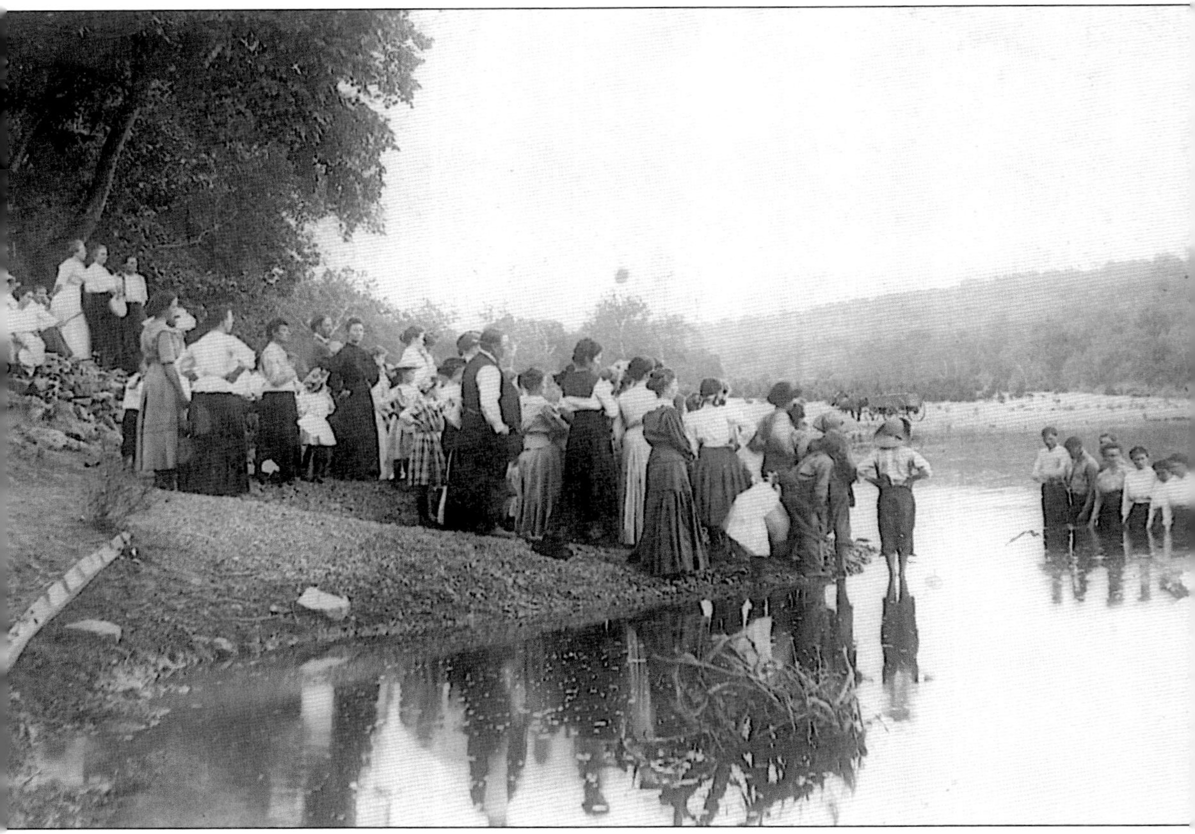

In the mid-1890s, along the banks of the White River, which flowed through all of Taney County before Table Rock Dam was built, it was a common sight to see country church baptismal services. The old-fashioned "fire and brimstone" preachers convinced many a sinner of the need for repentance and the requirement to follow the example of Jesus. So when the words to the old gospel song *Shall We Gather At The River* was sung, it took on a different meaning to new converts.

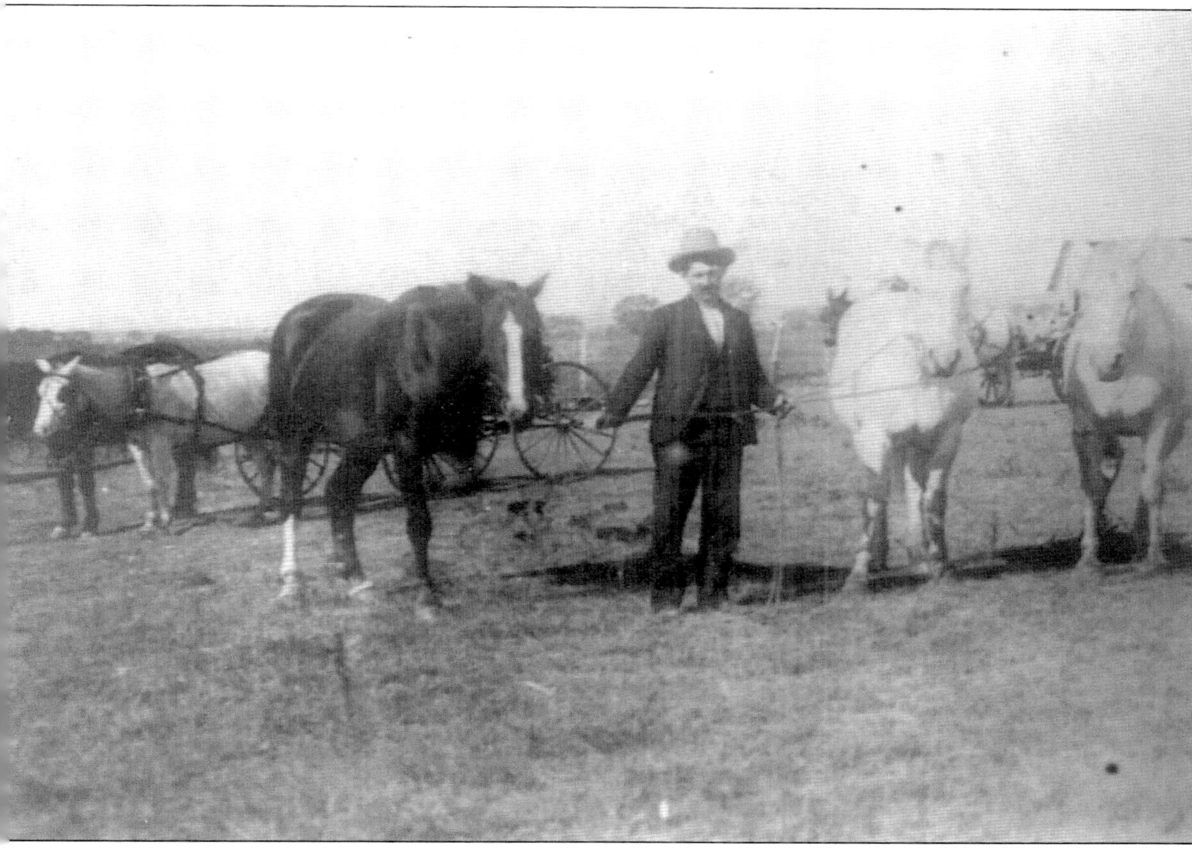

The author's great-great-maternal grandpa, John Layton, is pictured in Chickasaw, Oklahoma, before he moved his family to homestead in Taney County. He owned the land where the School of the Ozarks College began in the early 1900s, at Point Lookout near Hollister. During the Civil War, Layton was one of the Union Scouts and General Thomas W. Sweeney's principal guide. Layton was also a former sheriff and county collector of Taney County, prior to the outbreak of the war. John joined the Union forces while his brother Augustus (A.S.) Layton chose the cause of the South. So it was brother against brother in their case, as it was for so many Taney County families divided by the war. John was also an officer in the Christian County Home Guards during the war.

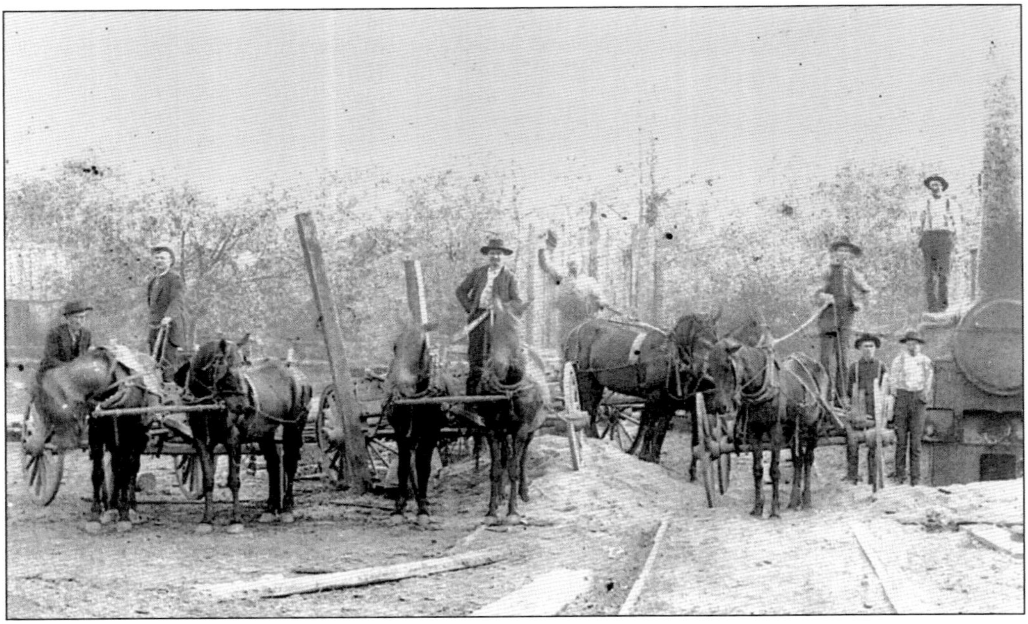

The Hall family was also among the early Taney County pioneers to homestead the area. Carl Hall's location in this photograph is unknown. He journeyed to Wisconsin in the 1880s or 1890s to work at this lumber mill for a period of time.

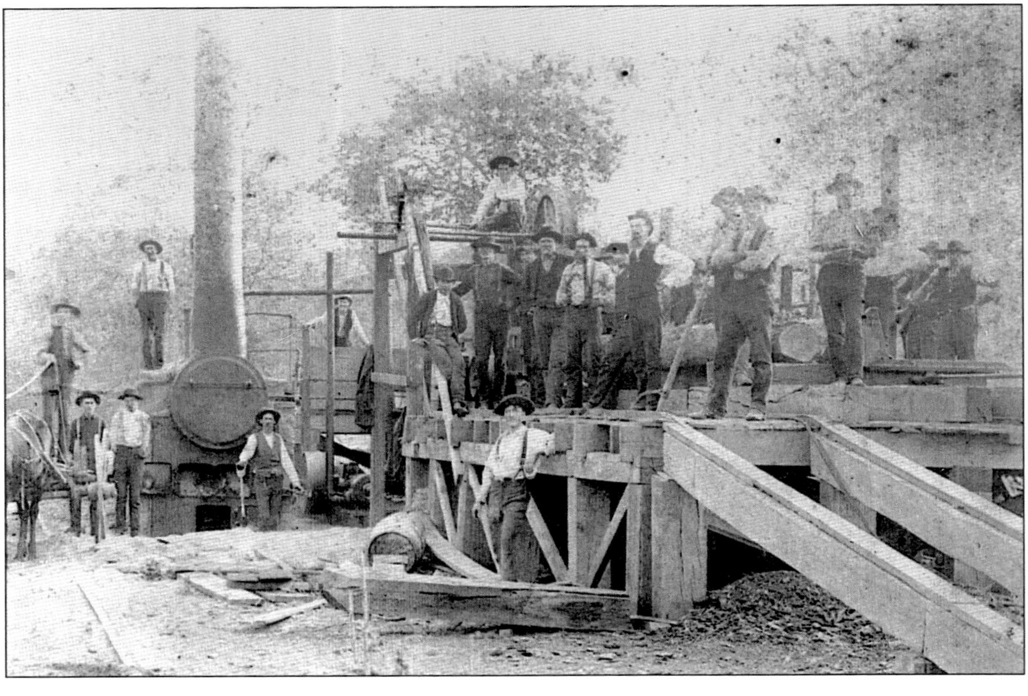

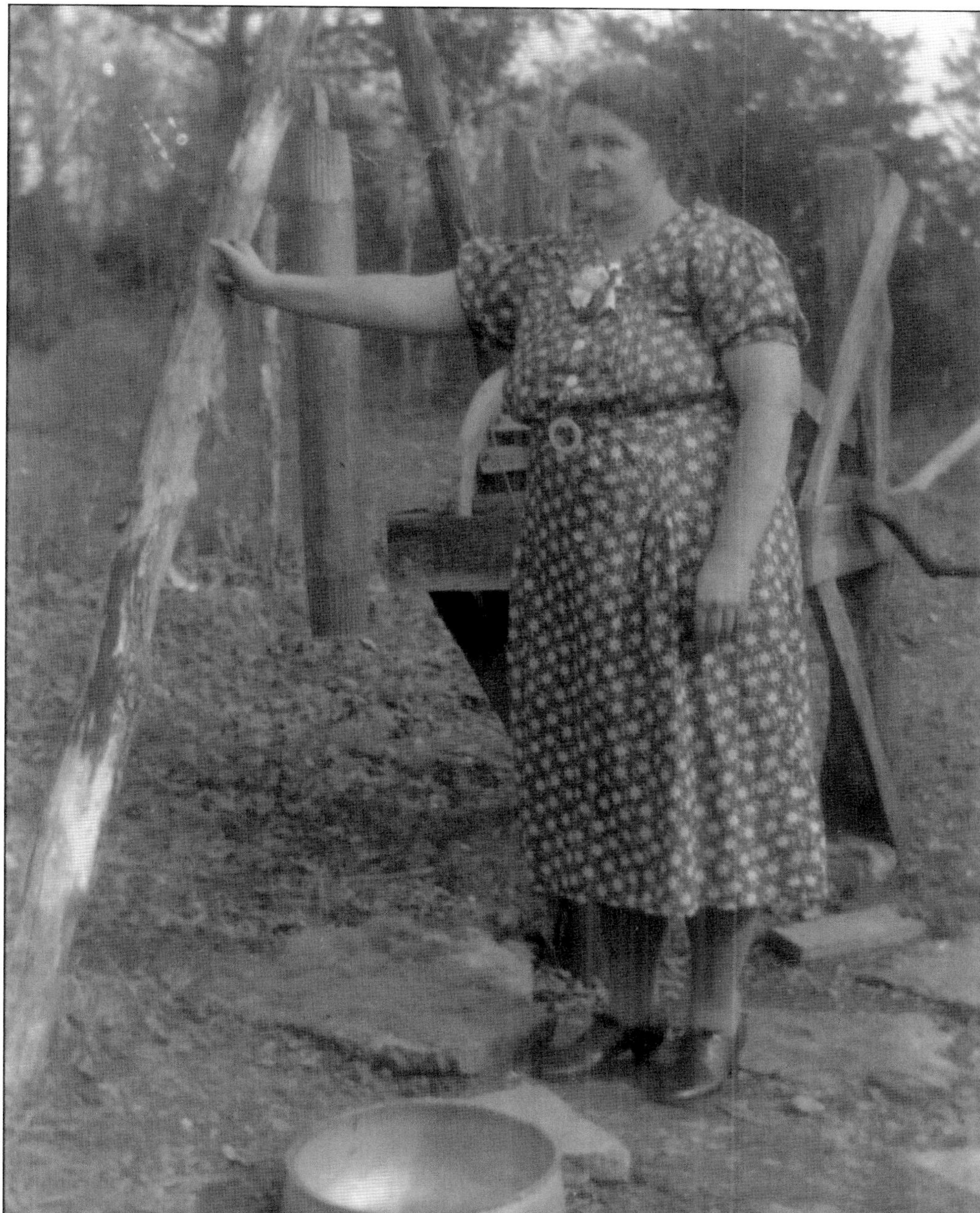

Ethel Smith Layton, Taney County pioneer family descendent of the Coggburn and Smith family, became part of the Layton pioneer family when she and Randa Layton married. Ethel stands here beside the old well on the Pleake place near Hollister, not far from Happy Holler and Turkey Creek about the year 1940. Water was pulled up from the well with the long water bucket rope on a handle windlass. Turning the windlass one way lowered the bucket into the well, and by turning it the opposite way, the water bucket was pulled up when full and emptied into water pails (buckets) to carry back to the house. The old pan near her feet was kept full of water for the dogs.

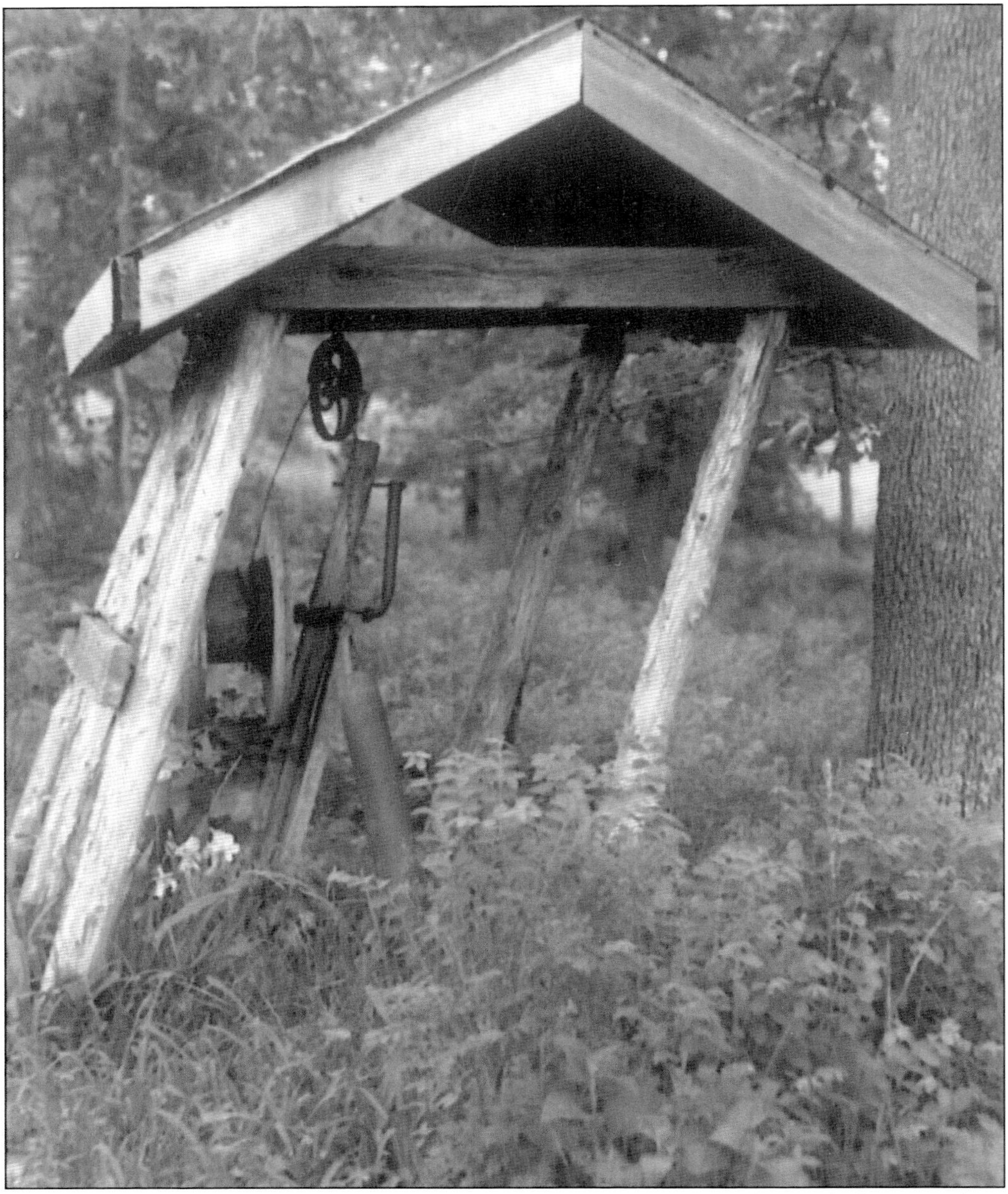

The old abandoned well still stood as of 1992 on the Pleake place, where Ethel Layton drew water from in 1940.

"In our hearts are many sorrows, here today and gone tomorrow; and as we sleep in the sod, I hope we live a life for God; and in the resurrection morn', we'll see that He will not forget you and me. As we leave the winter drift and pass to the spring, soon the birds will begin to sing and build their comfy nests, and cover their fledglings under their breasts, and then we shall stop and think and look and read God's Holy Book, that God is love, yes, God is love."

This was in Ethel Layton's scrapbook, a clipping she cut out and saved back many, many years ago entitled "In Memory," which is what this book is all about—memories.